DIALECTIC IN ACTION

An Examination of Plato's *Crito*

MICHAEL C. STOKES

The Classical Press of Wales

First published in 2005 by
The Classical Press of Wales
15 Rosehill Terrace, Swansea SA1 6JN
Tel: +44 (0)1792 458397
Fax: +44 (0)1792 464067
www.classicalpressofwales.co.uk

Distributor in the United States of America:
The David Brown Book Co.
PO Box 511, Oakville, CT 06779
Tel: +1 (860) 945–9329
Fax: +1 (860) 945–9468

ISBN 0–9543845–9-8

A catalogue record for this book is available from the British Library

Typeset by Ernest Buckley, Clunton, Shropshire
Printed and bound in the UK by Cambridge University Press

The Classical Press of Wales, an independent venture, was founded in 1993, initially to support the work of classicists and ancient historians in Wales and their collaborators from further afield. More recently it has published work initiated by scholars internationally. While retaining a special loyalty to Wales and the Celtic countries, the Press welcomes scholarly contributions from all parts of the world.

The symbol of the Press is the Red Kite. This bird, once widespread in Britain, was reduced by 1905 to some five individuals confined to a small area known as 'The Desert of Wales' – the upper Tywi valley. Geneticists report that the stock was saved from terminal inbreeding by the arrival of one stray female bird from Germany. After much careful protection, the Red Kite now thrives – in Wales and beyond.

To Joan,
without whose encouragement and loving help
(not least with sentence-length)
it would never have been finished

CONTENTS

PREFACE

This book amounts to a running exposition with commentary of Plato's *Crito.* My intention has been simple. It is to help those who read the dialogue, whether or not they read Greek, to understand what Plato and his character Socrates are up to. It has proved impossible to make the exposition altogether simple, since the dialogue's argument is complex. Despite every effort to secure clarity, I have relied in the end (like Plato) on my readers' intelligence and persistence.

The book has been too long in gestation, for reasons not all within my control. The result is a certain unevenness in bibliographical information, particularly for the present millennium. I hope I have missed nothing of high significance, but it is human to err.

I would have missed more, and the book would have been worse, without the help of colleagues too numerous to mention here. Two good friends I must mention with specially deep gratitude: Spiro Panagiotou and Gabriel Danzig. Each has read the whole or extensive parts in draft, and furnished me with the most helpful criticisms. Each has also over years of friendship talked or corresponded with me about all sorts of problems in the *Crito.* To their respective Universities, McMaster and Bar-Ilan, I owe opportunities to talk to them, and to John Glucker, face to face, with great profit to me. My mistakes will surely be found in places where I have ventured to go against their arguments and advice. I am indebted to Anton Powell for his careful and constructive editing of my typescript. One other debt of a more personal and less academic nature I have reserved for my dedication.

References to Plato are to the Oxford text. In the case of the *Crito* itself and other dialogues in the First Tetralogy I have tried to be constant in using the lineation of the new Oxford text vol. I, edited by E.A. Duke and others.

Michael C. Stokes

PROLOGUE

Methodology is not everyone's cup of tea. Readers with no taste for it, and wishing to proceed at once to the interpretation of the *Crito*, are welcome to pass over these prolegomena and turn immediately to the Introduction below. Those interested in the methodology of reading and interpreting Plato, with special reference to the 'early' dialogues, are invited to ponder the brief remarks on this subject which follow here. Interested readers deserve a warning that the principles underlying the present study of the *Crito* remain much the same as those developed and used in my *Plato's Socratic Conversations* of 1986. The principles, however, have not pleased everybody. It is therefore necessary to restate them in a form modified to take account of some criticisms, to add certain new features and to subtract some rash over-statements. The subtraction owes something to a judicious article by M. Frede which mentioned no other scholar than Frede himself; the re-statement and the subtraction owe their very existence to some pages of stimulating criticism from J. Beversluis;[1] the new policies on interpretation result pretty directly from some helpfully provocative comments, most kindly contributed by Dr Gabriel Danzig, on an earlier draft of this study.

The method deployed here is one of close analysis, step by step, of everything that the parties to the dialogue say. In this it is not distinctive.[2] It treats the 'early' Platonic dialogue as not only a slab of philosophy but also a work of literature, a drama, with a situation, plot and characters.[3] In this, too, it does not differ from many ways of reading Plato – and in particular the *Crito* – advocated or exemplified in recent years.[4] What distinguishes it most sharply from the great bulk of modern Platonic scholarly writing in English is its determination to treat the questions that Socrates asks as questions, and not as thinly disguised assertions. In rash moments I have suggested that the *only* aim of those questions was to discover and elicit the respondent's beliefs, and, by implication, that the respondent owes his refutation *only* to the inconsistency or to the absurd consequences of his own beliefs. That was too exclusive, ignoring as it did the Platonic Socrates' dialectical skills in phrasing and ordering his questions. But there remain reasons for holding that Plato saddles the respondent with almost all the responsibility for his defeat. There is a further nuance distinguishing the present approach from most others. The present approach assumes that where the course of the argument appears to leave the respondent a way out which he fails to take, the failure is not necessarily due to Plato's not having seen the need for an additional premiss, or to his portrayal of Socrates' bullying of his respondent. The respondent's failure may be due rather to the blockage of the escape-route by things Plato has had the respondent in character say previously, or by assumptions inherent in the respondent's professional or other main activity, or by the circumstances of the respondent's encounter with Socrates, or by character-traits of the respondent appearing in Plato's portrayal before or, less often, during the more obviously philosophical part(s) of the conversation. Nor is this merely a way in which Plato can browbeat his readers. No reader is compelled to identify himself with the character whom Socrates defeats; but the dialogues would be difficult to explain if there were not some readers who could identify themselves with, or at least recognize the humanity of, a given defeated or enlightened character.[5]

This means that the final upshot of a dialogue as a whole, so far as there is one, is in some measure hypothetical. What Plato says, so far as he could actually bring himself to say something, is this: *if* you resemble in relevant ways the respondent he has duly characterized, or *if* you accept certain views he has attributed to the respondent, then you have to follow out the argument to its conclusion. If you are not thus similar, or do not accept such views, then you are not compelled to accept the conclusion. This may seem a ridiculous mouse to spring from a mountain of argument. Plato, however, was a shrewd enough thinker to be fully aware that, if the person or kind of person one is arguing with does not accept the premisses of one's argument, then no amount of argumentation will convince them. He was also well aware that different premisses, or sets of premisses, appeal to different sorts of people.

Be that as it may, to dig out and fill such apparent gaps in the line of argument down which Socrates and his respondent travel, one must go step by step through the conversation. At each stage we should ask not only what the argument is, but also several other questions. We should inquire, in the more strictly argumentative parts of the dialogue, not only what admissions the respondent has made, but why he has made them.[6] We should ask what alternatives he had, and why he did not choose one of those alternatives. We ought to look for reasons of previous commitment, or of professional or other circumstance, or of recognizable personal character, to explain why the respondent chooses the responses he does. The upshot will not be to remove all taint or suspicion of fallacy or enthymeme from Plato's writings, or in the present case from the *Crito*; the set of tools and materials used here does not include whitewash. The technique will, however, reduce the number of dubious arguments or assertions in the *Crito* by showing that some apparently missing premisses or apparently faulty inferences or doubtfully acceptable statements are warranted by Crito's previous remarks, his circumstances at the dramatic time of the dialogue, or by his well-established character. It may also explain how and why genuine weaknesses arise in some arguments.

This manner of interpretation seems relatively little affected by the disturbing article of S.M. Cohen and D. Keyt on the principles of charity and parsimony.[7] In supplying a premiss, they ask, is one divining Plato's thought or extending it? In charity an interpreter supplies a suppressed premiss rather than charge a great philosopher with a *non sequitur*. There are broadly two alternative procedures: the first is to supply the most reasonable premiss, reasonable either supposedly for the philosophical author – which ultimately takes us to the second procedure, dealt with below – or in fact for the interpreter. Adequate interpretation on these lines will remove all *non sequiturs*. If the philosopher's conclusion is false, then at least one of the philosopher's explicit or implicit premisses must be false. If one interprets all the premisses and conclusions charitably, all the arguments end up being both valid and sound: valid and sound, that is, in the eyes of the interpreter. Cohen and Keyt offer as corollaries that all philosophers are contemporaries, all interpretation is anachronistic, all classical philosophers are infallible and omniscient, and major philosophers never disagree. This splendid jeu d'esprit has, obviously, serious consequences. These are not mitigated by the principle of parsimony or (if you like) simplicity. The simplest explanation *for* a text with a missing premiss is that the philosopher failed to notice that it was missing. Parsimony may, however, guide the interpreter to the simplest, most elegant supplement *of* the text. But that places no significant restraint on the above-mentioned paradoxes of interpretation.

A version of the second alternative procedure is adopted here; this, though not without pitfalls, carries less drastic risks. The present type of interpretation tries to 'extend the context', in Cohen and Keyt's phrase, of remarks made by Socrates or his interlocutor to a point where one can see why one or the other, especially the interlocutor, goes – or seems to go – astray. The procedure presupposes that in many cases, though not necessarily all, Plato did in a way write down the missing propositions: one may unearth them from what he wrote by studying the characters, circumstances, methods, and previous words of the Socrates and the interlocutor whom Plato as an author created. It would be idle to pretend that such study does not, as the saying goes, read between the lines of an argument under inspection. But it does so in the main by observing and applying what stands on other lines of the same work.

This whole method treats the Platonic dialogues as containing a substantial proportion of *ad hominem* argument, of a normally serious and not frivolous kind. It thus reads Plato's Socrates as pursuing dialectic in his questions and his reception of answers. It comes close, despite differences, to Cohen and Keyt's 'retrospective' model of interpreting a real enthymeme. On that model,

> [T]he interpreter supposes either that Plato consciously entertained the supposed premiss but, for one reason or another, did not write it down, or that there is a premiss he would have supplied if he had been queried about the gap in his argument.

But the present contention will be that Plato often not only entertained the apparently missing premiss but did in effect write it down, *and* that if queried Plato would have been able to point to it. The method contends also that in quite a strong sense such arguments are not Plato's. True, Plato constructed and wrote each argument which emerges from Socrates' talk with his respondent. Nevertheless, how much of the argument Plato endorsed, how many of the premisses or inferences he would in his own person have accepted, is a question not always answerable at all, and rarely, if ever, with certainty.

The principle of charity in interpretation, then, lays down that between any pair of interpretations one should if at all possible adopt the interpretation which attributes less obtuseness or factual inaccuracy to the philosopher being examined. This principle is one of the foundations of the present method; if there were no apparent call on one's charity in Plato's works then the method would scarcely be needed. The method does therefore lie open to some of the criticisms Cohen and Keyt level at charitable interpretation. It will, for example, be a partly subjective matter to determine which propositions or inferences one can supply or account for by the method sketched above. Which propositions or pre-suppositions is it 'reasonable' for the interpreter to *attribute* to the 'character concerned'?[8] Clearly they will sometimes be propositions it would seem reasonable for the author to hold, including on occasion those which the *interpreter* finds reasonable; sometimes, for reasons which need not stand to the character's discredit, they will not. In these circumstances what is reasonable to attribute to a character will be subject to differing views and attitudes in interpreters. However, in principle there seems to be no cause to doubt that in such matters, as in literary interpretation generally, though one can never be sure that one has the truth, the whole truth and nothing but the truth, it is in most cases possible to tell a good interpretation from a bad one, and one containing a measure of truth from one that contains none. The text itself is the measure of one's interpretative success; if the interpretation fits and explains the text, then it is at least tenable until someone finds an interpretation with wider explanatory power, or an overall more satisfying approach or type of interpretation. If other interpretations prove to work better than the present one, no-one would be more pleased than I. Meanwhile it is comforting to find that Cohen and Keyt's earthquake has its epicentre some distance away from the site where I am at work.

But there is another potential earthquake to be guarded against by building a structure strong enough to stand up to it. It has a name: the 'documentary fallacy'. The name, if not the concept, was apparently introduced to classical scholarship by A.J.A. Waldock in a brilliant little book entitled *Sophocles the Dramatist*, and it has been familiar for many years.[9] But the full measure of its applicability to the interpretation of Plato only became clear to me from friendly criticisms levelled by Gabriel Danzig at a draft of this book. He pointed out that if one read too much between Plato's lines, one began in effect to diagnose what, e.g., Socrates and Crito thought at each stage as if they were not literary constructions but real personages whose speeches had been taped for analysis. There are limits beyond which such diagnosis cannot go without leaving behind the concerns and perceptions of ordinary readers, for whom (at least among others) Plato presumably wrote the shorter and less technical dialogues. If no ordinary reader, even if intelligent, is likely to perceive the thoughts the critic attributes to the characters in a drama, then the critic is committing the documentary fallacy, treating the work not as a drama but as a documentary record of real events and conversations.

Does this mean the interpreter should give up reading between the lines? Not at all. But it does mean that interpreters should exercise care and discretion in 'extending the context' of an argument. The extension should not go beyond the abilities of all the readers Plato may have had in view. The relevant abilities include verbal memory, precision in understanding words, and logical penetration. The difficulty lies in the dual nature of the great dramatic dialogues: they are both literary masterpieces, widely accessible as such, and intellectual explorations of a subtlety and depth likely from the start to be fully accessible only to those prepared and equipped for detailed study. Those equipped for detailed analysis might find some of the more rhetorical arguments, or some of the fallacies in Socrates' apparent reasoning, beneath them; those reading for the vivid characters, for the comic or tragic brilliance, or for Plato's marvellous eloquence, might find stretches of verbal in-fighting tedious. The interpreter must, in reading on or between the lines, bear this nest of difficulties in mind.

One way – not necessarily the only way – of bearing it in mind is to suppose that, like other dramatists, Plato wrote for more than one audience simultaneously. Like Sophocles, in my view at least,[10] and Shakespeare in many critics' assessments, Plato will have written to be read or heard on more than one level. In the case of Shakespeare, some of the groundlings will have enjoyed the gore at the end of *Hamlet*, and the long-drawn-out suspense that precedes it, allowing the subtleties and beauties of the poetry to roll over them in a sonorous blur. More sophisticated theatregoers will have appreciated Shakespeare's gloriously mixed metaphors and the simpler beauty of lines such as 'But, look, where the morn in russet mantle clad Walks o'er the dew of yon high eastern hill.' In the case of Plato, some readers could be expected to follow the argument in some detail, spotting apparent fallacies and perhaps using what they read elsewhere in a dialogue to close the gaps in the argument; some could be expected to appreciate Plato's stylistic virtuosity; and some could be expected only to be moved or amused, as appropriate, while exposing themselves to a splendid sermon on, e.g., the importance of behaving justly or of recognizing the limits of their own knowledge. To descend for a moment to the autobiographical, I myself first read the *Crito* as a first-year undergraduate, appreciating something of its eloquence, being uplifted by Socrates' heroism, and feeling for the finally silenced Crito; analysis of how, and how legitimately, Socrates silences Crito came later. It is at least a plausible hypothesis, and one worth exploring, that Plato wrote, as it were, both for raw freshmen and for their teachers, both at once. On that hypothesis it becomes worthwhile to examine the effect the *Crito*, in each of its parts, may have had on different kinds of readers in Plato's own day.

To 'explain' the text: that is the object, and an interpretation must fulfil it. But the proof of the pudding is in the eating; a method can in the last resort be defended only if it works, that is to say if it provides an explanation which satisfies. Who, then, is the judge of what works, or what satisfies? H.W. Ausland wrote some years ago of something very like the present method, 'somehow unsatisfactory'.[11] In part this verdict rested on a review of Stokes (1986) in *Classical Philology*. The reviewer took me to task in effect for neglecting the sweep of argument developed by some of Socrates' interlocutors in favour of niggling minor points and questions. To this criticism the proper answer is to point to a very important precedent. The precedent is that of Socrates himself. Socrates in the *Protagoras*, after thinking for a while at the close of Protagoras' 'Great Speech', does not develop at once a critique of the sophist's main line of argument. Instead, he asks a single small question about what is, to all appearances at the time, a mere detail.

In any case other ways of reading Plato, much though I have learnt from them, do not satisfy me. In particular the 'doctrinal' way, reading Socrates' questions mostly as embodying and laying down Socratic and/or Platonic doctrines, does not. It is still unclear to me what, on such doctrinal ways of reading Socratic questions, is the point of the sometimes elaborate and always skilful characterization of Socrates' interlocutors. It is also unclear why Plato should not have expected, or at least hoped, that his contemporary readers would take Socrates' questions as, genuinely, questions – of whatever sort. True, Aristotle takes the early dialogues as in part reports of Socratic doctrine. But he may have been arranging history (or biography) to fit his own form of dialectic, and in any case his accounts do not go into the detail of the arguments in Plato's shorter dialogues.[12]

There is, moreover, in Plato's *Apology*, what may be a warning against taking the questions in Socratic argument as in effect assertions: at 23a Socrates explains his reputation for wisdom as due to those bystanders who took him as being 'wise' on the topics of his refutations – apparently, in Socrates' view, mistakenly. Socrates refers in the sequel, at 23b, to his habit of questioning people. In this passage Socrates declines to take to himself the authority to make pronouncements on the subjects he discusses. This implied refusal is fully in keeping with the Platonic Socrates' habitual reluctance, stressed by Thrasymachus at *Rep.* 337a, to answer questions – a reluctance, that is, to venture even firm opinions, let alone a claim to knowledge. Indeed, if Socrates' normal stance in argument were not genuinely interrogatory, it would be hard to explain why he so seldom allows himself to be questioned.

Other passages sing the same tune. When in the *Gorgias* (462b ff.) Polus is allowed to take on the role of questioner, it is clear that the questions are genuine – if feeble – attempts to find out what Socrates thinks before refuting it, and that Socrates is trying to strengthen them as such. This passage suggests that there is something more than merely formal about Socrates' use of questions in 'early' Plato. The same suggestion arises from the slave-passage in the *Meno* (82a–85e), where, as I have previously argued, if Socrates is teaching Meno, or us as Plato's readers, anything, it is that he does not teach by his questions.[13] The slave *recollects* under the stimulus of Socrates' interrogation; he does not learn from Socrates, whether the interrogation results in the slave's possessing opinion or knowledge. The *Theaetetus* gives us several remarks in the same vein. At 157c Theaetetus himself says, 'I don't know, Socrates; for I can't make out about you either, whether you are saying things you think are right, or whether you are testing me.' Here the victim himself shows uncertainty, corresponding to modern scholarly uncertainty, whether Socrates believes the propositions he puts to his respondent or is merely exploring the respondent's own views. Socrates replies, 'Do you not recall, my friend, that I neither know nor claim any such [opinion] as my own, but rather am unable to give birth to them, and act as midwife to you...until I help to bring your opinion into the world... Answer as you think on the topics of all my questions.' Plato here acknowledges that there does, or could, arise a question or doubt whether or not Socrates is pushing views onto his interlocutor; he has his Socrates politely but firmly slap down the suggestion that he is doing that. Plato's Socrates produces very little he wishes to call his own. Again in the *Theaetetus*, at 161a6, Theodorus says to Socrates, 'By the gods, say how it nevertheless is not so.' And Socrates says in the course of his reply, '...you think I am a bag of arguments and that I am going easily to take one out and say how, nevertheless, it is not so. You don't see what is going on, that none of the arguments comes from me, but always they come from the person conversing with me, and [that] I know no greater knowledge except for a little one, as much as to be able to extract an argument from someone else [who is] wise and receive it appropriately. So now I am going to try [to extract] this from [Theaetetus] here, not to say anything myself.' Socrates vigorously repels the suggestion that he *says*, or even tries to say, anything; he is simply drawing an argument, a theory, a λόγος, from a respondent. A further revealing remark at 167d–e includes the idea that Socrates demonstrates to his partner in conversation only such mistakes as the partner has been pushed into by himself and by his previous discussions. The Socratic dialectic does indeed confute a man out of his own nature and out of his preceding remarks. Socrates clearly, though not quite explicitly, disclaims responsibility. The same distinction emerges also from a brief passage of the *Crito*: at 49e5 Crito says, 'Say on!', and Socrates answers, 'Then I say the next item – or rather ask it.' Even though Crito's request is natural after Socrates says 'Listen to this!', the correction of the request is pointed: Socrates is not about to *assert* anything, only to ask questions.

Admittedly passages such as these have been dismissed by some as mere Socratic irony, or even as farce; there is an unfortunate tendency among scholars to take Plato's Socrates' words seriously only as long as it suits them to do so. Hopefully this book will avoid that tendency. In this whole context, *prima facie* one can readily accept that not all grammatical questions straightforwardly require information from the respondent, without supposing that one could transpose Socrates' questions into assertoric form without discernible effect on the argument. The present work aims to provide an interpretation of the *Crito* which will enable readers to understand Socrates' questions as questions, while distributing the responsibility for the course of the argument fairly between Socrates and Crito. It will implicitly explain the necessity for Crito to be in the dialogue the kind of person he is.

Some of Socrates' questions, at least, must be exploratory of the respondent's views: if he asks 'What is courage?' or any similar question, he is obviously transmitting nothing, only probing his interlocutor. So where is one to draw the line between exploratory and didactic, or otherwise virtually assertoric, questions? Socrates sometimes distinguishes the respondent's views from his own, with expressions, normally used after the event, such as 'as you say', or 'on your view' (ὡς σὺ φῄς or κατὰ τὸν σὸν λόγον). But that is a long way from proving that only answers so tagged after the event are answers with which Socrates would not agree. There is no immediate formal feature that reliably distinguishes between views Socrates shares with the assenting respondent and those he does not share. This is a state of affairs consistent with the suggestion that the point of Socrates' questioning in what are commonly called the early dialogues is normally to lead to a confutation of the respondent. What Socrates needs is to elicit responses which suffice for confutation. It should be clear that for purposes of refuting the respondent out of his own mouth it need not matter at all whether Socrates would give the same response as the interlocutor, or whether Socrates in some measure agrees with the response he obtains, or not.

It is none the less true that Socrates does obtain the respondent's assent to some propositions with which Socrates would in all probability have agreed if pressed. This is in spite of Socrates' well-known love of paradox. Indeed, as scholars have noted, Socrates does not put the paradoxes direct to an interlocutor until or unless he has prepared the interlocutor, and built up an argument for them. It would be curious if Socrates did not agree with *some* of the wide range of non-paradoxical propositions he puts questioningly to his respondents. But that does not imply that he palms off on those respondents any proposition he wishes; nor does it mean that he forces propositions upon them because he agrees with the propositions himself. It would be surprising if there were no common ground at all between Socrates and any of his interlocutors. J. Beversluis is right, nevertheless, to argue that the interlocutors do not always give their sincere prior beliefs, and that Socrates by no means always asks them to.[14] Plato perhaps intends his Socrates even when he is not explicit to be seeking such beliefs. Many of Socrates' questions, however, concern topics on which it would not be normal to have a sincere prior belief; the questions come at the respondent out of the blue. Plato perhaps overestimated the capacity of ordinary folk to summon up a sincere prior belief when arguing on their feet under close questioning conducted usually with a veto on long explanations, evasions, and the like. What Socrates undoubtedly does require as a minimum, though he does not say so in so many words, is that the respondent should shoulder the responsibility for his responses, at least until the conclusion of the argument. At the conclusion he sometimes relents and offers the respondent the chance to withdraw or modify his previous answers, but pending that offer the responsibility rests with the respondent.

To take such responsibility means to take on a commitment. It is essential to decide what sort of commitment Socrates requires. No doubt some interlocutors for some of the time give answers to which they have a firm, if not a lifelong commitment. One imagines that Nicias at least, in the *Laches*, must think he is giving answers of that sort; otherwise his remarks at 187e–188c about Socrates' turning his respondents' lives inside out would be beside the point. But one cannot expect all interlocutors to offer such commitment all the time. What sort of commitment, then, can they offer? Here one must distinguish two different sorts of commitment. The distinction is not one of degree but of kind. One can call them internal and external commitment respectively. One is internally committed to a proposition if one sincerely believes it and has no expectation of abandoning it. One is externally committed to a proposition if one gives voice to it in a context where one will, or will be afraid to, lose face, be accused of instability or weakness or incompetence, or the like, if one were openly to abandon it.[15] Full internal commitment, when answering questions on the spur of the moment, is more than Plato's Socrates, or anyone else, has any right to expect. Socrates behaves as if he expects at least external commitment from the victims of his chains of questions. He would no doubt like, and no doubt sometimes obtains, internal commitment. But he ought not to feel entitled to it more than is possible in the circumstances; even the external commitment of the respondent he allows on occasion, in friendly mode, to be provisional. Naturally different sorts of confutation correspond to different sorts of commitment. Nicias in the *Laches*, again, has clearly in the past had deeply-held views apparently refuted by Socrates and has felt his life altered as a consequence. Other characters sometimes make admissions on their feet which on reflection or under pressure they wish to withdraw: one thinks of Callicles' turnaround at *Gorgias* 499b4 ff.

Without some such commitment on the part of the respondent, the conversation would be entirely frivolous, not to say irresponsible. There is, however, no corresponding reason why Socrates should be responsible for any of the propositions he puts to his interlocutor. *For the purposes of confutation*, it does not matter whether Socrates takes on any commitments or not. The victim suffers confutation in Socrates' eyes, as his contretemps with Polus in the *Gorgias* makes clear, if and only if two conditions are fulfilled. First, the victim must take on some commitment to the propositions put to him. Secondly, he must accept that at the conclusion of the argument *he* has indeed been reduced to absurdity or contradiction. When Plato chooses to have Socrates make specially clear that he does *not* wish to take on a commitment even temporarily, the reason is likely to be *either* because to risk that particular commitment would be to imperil the remarkably consistent intellectual and moral characterization of Socrates throughout the early dialogues, *or* because the particular commitment concerned would endanger Socrates' position in the particular dialogue.

One thing in all this is clear: Socrates does not need to share beliefs, or commitments, with his interlocutors as a condition of his conducting a meaningful discussion with them. This results from the simple truth that Socratic conversations in the 'early' dialogues, once the scene-setting and the characterization are tolerably complete, are not 'discussions' at all, in the sense in which we should use the word. A free and unfettered exchange of views these dialogues certainly do not present. Socrates very rarely puts forward a proposition as explicitly his own view; and he very rarely indeed submits to questioning about such a proposition. One can think of one passage which might be construed as saying that shared beliefs are indispensable for Socratic dialogue, but that would be a mistaken construal. The passage is *Crito* 49c–e. There (not to anticipate too fully the discussion below) Socrates says to Crito that he should take care not to answer contrary to his opinion, since the proposition concerned is one which few will share, and those who share it can have no meaningful joint *deliberation* with those who do not. It is clear that Socrates does himself subscribe to the proposition in question, and it becomes equally clear that if Crito did not subscribe, or were not prepared to subscribe for the duration of the conversation, Socrates could not launch his deliberative argument at all. Nor would it be possible for subscribers and non-subscribers to deliberate together about any single serious joint moral choice. For this kind of deliberation common ground is necessary, because the argument must end in action, and the action must – or they are not 'deliberating together' in any helpful sense – be acceptable to both parties in the light of their respective ultimate goals. The same is not true of Socratic confutation in general, which has nothing directly to do with such deliberation.

But why all this talk of 'commitment'? Why is it important for the student of Plato's 'early' dialogues? It is important to the present discussion for a particular but significant reason. In criticizing my previous stance on

Socratic questions, with its emphasis on the illegitimacy of interpreting them as disguised transmissions of doctrine, Beversluis said, rightly, that a question can serve different purposes and have different functions in different contexts. Socrates' questions do not have to be all of one sort, the sort which requires simply information from the respondent about his or her views. But one thing is common to most of these types of question; not 'all', but 'most'. By asking a question the speaker, however internally committed to the proposition at the core of the question, usually avoids – whether deliberately or not – at least the external responsibility for the proposition's truth. If one says, to take an example from Beversluis, 'There is a faculty meeting this afternoon, isn't there?',[16] then one is shifting the responsibility for the truth of the proposition that there is a faculty meeting this afternoon to one's respondent or interlocutor. One may make it very clear, e.g. by tone of voice, that one regards the proposition as certainly true; but it is always open to the respondent to say 'No. As a matter of fact, there isn't; it's next week', or something of the kind. If the respondent says nothing or assents, then he or she is responsible for the truth of the proposition, and subject to possible fault-finding by the questioner if the proposition turns out to be false. There has to be some reason why Socrates does not normally take the answerer's role in a question-and-answer bout. A very likely reason is that that role, unlike that of the questioner, would saddle him with the responsibility for propositions contained in the questions, or their contradictories if he answers 'No'. He might be willing to take the responsibility for some answers – he declares at least his belief in some. But there are also some questions for whose answer, knowing nothing worthwhile, 'nothing fine and good', as he says in Plato's *Apology*, he would not wish to be held responsible, not even as far as the end of his current conversation.

Here, then, is my answer to Beversluis' criticism that I do not allow for the many different types of question. It gives also the reason why Beversluis, in criticizing my more extreme previous pronouncements, has not even touched the points made with greater circumspection by M. Frede and others.[17] One cannot land Socrates with the whole responsibility for the course of the argument. The choice of questions, yes, that is Socrates' responsibility, as I.G.Kidd pointed out in 1992.[18] Some of Socrates' questions one could regard as leading, perhaps on occasion unfairly or too strongly leading. Socrates evidently bears a large part of the responsibility for the shape of the argument. The more cleverly and artfully he tailors his questions to the responses he can expect from this particular respondent as characterized by Plato, the more evident and the greater his share of the responsibility becomes. But that does not make him responsible for the answers the respondent gives, for the propositions the respondent accepts. Plato as author has of course the ultimate responsibility; within Plato's fiction the respondent has to accept the burden of responsibility for his answers.

It is this abdication of responsibility by Socrates and transfer of responsibility to the respondent that lends significance to the inquiry which the present study pursues. One needs to know, in order to understand what is going on, why the respondent at any given point shoulders the burden. One needs to know what alternatives were rationally open to him; one needs to know, when a proposition he accepts seems at first glance arbitrary, or seems not to follow, or seems in any way *prima facie* unacceptable, why – irrational propaganda apart – Plato should have made him concede it. An assumption of the argument is, of course, that Plato is not writing mere irrational propaganda. Another assumption is closely akin to that, viz. that Plato is writing with a reasonable degree of realism. We ought to find, on these two assumptions, that these are the answers that such a respondent as Plato has given Socrates, on such an occasion, in such circumstances, would offer. If other responses would have turned out better for the respondent's case, then we must seek good reasons why those more convenient responses – more convenient for the respondent – did not find their way into the respondent's mouth. But this programme necessitates the step-by-step examination of the conversation announced at the opening of this prologue. To that examination we may now turn.[19]

1
INTRODUCTION

The *Crito* has aroused in our time deep, on occasion passionate interest, for two main reasons. What has generated passionate interest is that it has seemed to be arguing about civil disobedience. Civil disobedience has played a significant role in more than one great popular movement within living memory. Lovers of Plato in particular have found a less popular but also less time-bound reason for deep interest. The *Crito* portrays Socrates, for the first and last time in the pages of Plato, deliberating jointly with his interlocutor whether or not to perform a particular specific single action. That the choice lies, in Socrates' view within the dialogue, between death and injustice heightens the moral tension.

Hence scholars and general readers alike know the plot of the *Crito* as well in outline as that of any of what are commonly called the 'early' Platonic dialogues.[20] Socrates lies in prison awaiting execution, after being condemned to death for alleged impiety. His old friend Crito comes to see him with the news that his execution, delayed for reasons of state religion, is now imminent. Socrates remains imperturbable; Crito strongly, even vehemently, urges Socrates to escape, and suggests ways and means. Since people know – and knew in Plato's day – that Socrates was indeed executed, it comes as no surprise to us or to Plato's original readers, that Crito's arguments fail to persuade Socrates. Since people know – and some perhaps knew – that Socrates, at least in Plato, exhibits considerable argumentative skill, the end of the dialogue, leaving Crito with nothing to say, and his arguments apparently routed, strikes no-one as abnormal. What is more, simply on the level of plot, the dialogue as a whole makes a most moving drama. There is for most readers a great tragedy, reminiscent for some of certain plays of Sophocles, in Socrates' heroic refusal to sacrifice his principles for his life, in face of his friend's urgent appeals and vigorous arguments, and in his friend's final reduction to silence. What one may call the externals of the work present no difficulties.

But once readers dive beneath this transparent surface, they encounter the murkiest of perplexities. The meaning of the dialogue, the purpose of its inner structure, the nature and even the number of its arguments,[21] to say nothing of the precise sense of significant individual sentences, have puzzled both ordinary and professional readers for generations. This is not the place to rehearse the many different, often finely nuanced views expressed in the scholarly controversy that has surrounded the *Crito*. But a reminder is in order that competent scholarly interpreters have maintained that the dialogue allows, and that it disallows, disobedience to a properly constituted state issuing orders deemed morally wrong.[22] They have taken the arguments Socrates puts into the mouth of the personified Laws of Athens, in the passage leading up to Crito's acknowledgment of defeat, as expressing, and as not expressing, as contradicting, and as not contradicting, the views Socrates expresses elsewhere, whether within or outside this dialogue.[23] They have believed Socrates genuinely to refute Crito's points, and they have believed that Crito gives in far too easily.[24] Though working Platonists assume with normal interpretative charity that the dialogue presents a coherent structure, the questions what that structure is, and even what constitutes in this case a coherent structure, have formed the subject of lively debate. A significant sub-question asks whether, and if so in what sense, Socrates in the dialogue is committed to, or even endorses at all, the remarks he himself puts into the mouth of the personified Laws. On this sub-question hangs another: how continuous, and how self-consistent, is Socrates' overall reply to Crito's initial arguments in favour of escape?[25]

The present study seeks to establish, or rather re-establish, a degree of co-existing continuity and consistency in the *Crito* greater than some recent scholarship (particularly in English) would countenance. In the first half of the dialogue Crito himself will seem in this version less incoherent, less unintelligent and/or less suggestible than he does in some respectable scholarly accounts. Socrates, on the other hand, we shall find guilty of some dialectical sleights of hand. In other words, his arguments are in various ways, not all of them in modern eyes creditable, *ad hominem*. In the dialogue's second part, the closing argument of the personified Laws of Athens will here take shape as a piece of 'dialectical rhetoric' – the expression is R.E. Allen's.[26] The dialectical rhetoric is designed, together with the previous questions and answers, to overcome Crito's particular considerations in favour of Socrates' escape, and to leave Crito as an individual with nothing to say at the end of the dialogue. The term 'dialectical' as used here, though not as used by Allen, excludes the importation into the argument of premisses derived from other Socratic arguments. Crito's long-standing friendship with Socrates does not guarantee that he has fully understood or properly absorbed such arguments. It ought not to compel him to adopt in the context of this dialogue any view of Socrates' expressed elsewhere; if Crito does accept such a view the interpreter must offer a reason why, in context, he should. Socrates' substantive dialectic, it will be argued below, takes the form of a single continuous and consistent argument, employing only such premisses and inferences as one could sensibly expect someone like Crito to accept in the context in which he hears them.

Readers will need some advance warning of the type of continuity and the type of consistency attributed to the *Crito* in this study. The intention is not to argue that every premiss, every inference, every conclusion and every intermediate step in the Laws' argument at the dialogue's close is consistent with what Socrates says elsewhere. The continuity and consistency here argued for are essentially those of method. The Laws, though clothing their argument in rhetorically styled and composed sentences and paragraphs, as indeed Plato's Socrates sometimes does, deploy in essence the method Socrates uses in many dialogues. They make use of propositions, whether in interrogative or rhetorically assertoric form, which their puppetmaster Socrates has reason to suppose or to suspect Crito will accept. Their employment of these tactics leaves us not knowing whether they or Socrates would, if questioned, fully endorse the propositions so used. We know in truth little about what the Socrates of Plato's refutatory or confutational dialogues would endorse, since this Socrates regularly uses his opponents' premisses without committing himself to them. We have accordingly no right to be surprised if we find the Laws in the *Crito* using premisses certain or likely to be Crito's without committing themselves – let alone Socrates – to them. This may give the following analysis of the *Crito* an isolated position in the modern discussion of the dialogue: it would make the Laws collectively a 'Socratic' figure, without necessarily committing the Platonic Socrates to any proposition forming part of their argument. The Laws, we shall find, continue and complete Socrates' confutation of Crito. In doing so, however, they do not have to parrot, or indeed pay more than a passing attention to, views or arguments which Plato's Socrates could himself have accepted. This leaves us in ignorance of the premisses and inferences by which Plato would have envisaged his Socrates defending under interrogation his decision not to evade the death penalty by escape. I have argued elsewhere, and do not repent of arguing, that in many of Socrates' conversations as Plato depicts them we are similarly ignorant of how Socrates would himself have arrived at certain conclusions.[27] On this view, the Laws in the *Crito*, 'Socratic' in method but not necessarily in all their *apparent* doctrine, present just one more instance of Plato's technique in the more obviously interrogatory dialogues.

One thing in particular Plato's readers and mine ought to check, as some recent attempts to give the *Crito* a unity do not. This is that Crito's stance in the argument is reasonably defensible or understandable at each and every step in the developing conversation. If not, then Plato either failed to observe the gaps in the chain of statement and inference or deliberately set Crito up as a straw man. Either of these alternatives devalues the dialogue. The former raises the question why – dramatic pathos apart – we should continue to read a thinker *ex hypothesi* so slipshod. The latter raises the question why – political or moral propaganda apart – Plato should have composed an argument which would convince only people of straw. Those initially disposed, as I am, to doubt that Plato was either a pure dramatist or a slightly naïve propagandist, or indeed a dramatizer of naïve propaganda, must therefore examine Crito's arguments, his admissions, and his other utterances with the utmost care. It is necessary to extract from the text everything we legitimately can about Crito's character, feelings and abilities, in order to see whether the positions he takes up match them. In doing this one must be clear that Plato cannot give Crito character, feelings or abilities that are too inadequate to the occasion or too far beneath those of normal people without, again, turning him into a straw man. There is a limit to the excuses we can allow Plato by way of Crito's stupidity, confusion, suggestibility, illogicality, emotional distraction and so forth without removing all sensible reasons Plato might have had for 'arguing' or making his Socrates 'argue' with such a person.

Another matter calling for vigilance from my readers, and from Plato's, is the internal consistency of Crito's personal character in the dialogue. The defensibility or human intelligibility of Crito's stance at any given stage should not, since he is admittedly unphilosophical, rest too obviously or exclusively on a subtle philosophical distinction or a complex argument.[28] Nor ought Socrates' questioning to rely too much on Crito's having a developed philosophical understanding of precisely what nuance he has previously agreed to. Unphilosophical but intelligent readers ought, if Plato is writing in the way I think he does, to feel at one with Crito from start to finish. They ought to be able to read the dialogue and follow its general train of thought to its conclusion without being compelled to take on board subtleties too deep for their lack of experience. But that does not mean that the dialogue cannot reach such depths; they may be there, and indeed are there, for those who are able and willing to dig down to them, and still more for those prepared to *study* the dialogue. To interpret thus is to walk a slippery tightrope with no visible safety net. There are, however, few gains to be had without risk.

Reading Plato by these lights is one way of taking the dialogue form seriously. It is not the only way, and the interpretation that follows is by no means the first to attempt to read the *Crito* as a genuine dialogue.[29] One could of course hold it against such dialogic readings that practitioners of dialogic method in interpreting Plato do not agree among themselves. But Plato is an elusive writer, and that argument would rule out virtually any approach to the dialogues. One thing which differentiates the present monograph from other works seeking to make sense of the *Crito* as a dialogue is, hopefully, the step-by-step analysis of Crito's position as the argument develops. For 'ordinary' readers among Plato's contemporaries the analysis should not normally need to use hindsight; that would be available only to those prepared to pore over the dialogue. Another differentiation lies in the attempt to explain the *Crito* out of itself rather than out of other dialogues: we shall be asking always what sense Crito's position makes in the context of his own dialogue. A possible, but potentially controversial, exception could be to take account of the reactions of readers who knew the *Apology*, to which the closing pages of the *Crito* may openly allude.

Despite this possible exception, it still seems to me right to interpret each Platonic dialogue *in the first instance* as on the whole a distinct and separate work. This is not because it is obvious *a priori* that interpretations of one dialogue with continuous reference to others are mistaken from the start, though such comprehensive intertextuality within the oeuvre of a single writer is very rare in classical antiquity.[30] It is rather because an argument with premisses and inferences aimed *ad hominem* at one individual in one dialogue cannot without risk of serious distortion be used simply and straightforwardly as an aid to the understanding of another argument aimed at another individual in another conversational or rhetorical context. The utmost caution is necessary in such comparisons. The *ad hominem* nature of the 'early' dialogues' arguments has gained recognition over the years from many scholars. Recognition in practice has not always accompanied recognition in principle, but has become commoner in recent years. The results it produces for the *Crito* seem worth airing.

They are not any the less worth airing because not only Socrates' arguments are (at least in detail) fictitious, but also Crito's views. It is a legitimate question why one should pay any attention to an *ad hominem* argument which is not aimed at a real person who is present to answer for himself but addresses rather a character of whom the author of the whole can make within limits what he wishes. The answer has to be that the character so addressed must be one with whom some of Plato's readers could identify, or with whose reactions they could in some measure sympathize, or whose stance in the conversation they could at least understand. The portrayal of Socrates refuting some quirky or stupid or otherwise atypical individual would carry little or no weight. The interlocutors whom Plato provides for Socrates have to be both convincing individuals and recognizable types. In particular we shall find Crito to be perhaps unusually well off, but at the same time in most respects a typical Athenian gentleman, with the instinctive or socially inculcated reactions and judgments of the type. The results of analysing the *Crito* as an interrogation by Socrates of someone like Crito cannot be ignored simply on the grounds that Plato was not writing only for Crito.

To say this is not to decry other approaches, still less other scholars. Specifically it will be useful, here as elsewhere, to take advantage of some of the best work done on the basis of the 'doctrinal' approach, which tends to treat Socrates' questions as offering Platonic/Socratic doctrine or argument. Somewhat less notice needs to be taken of a recent major attempt to read some of the early dialogues as a pre-planned series.[31] The attempt does not convince me, for other reasons and because Plato had little or no control over the order in which people read his works, and therefore could not sensibly have written them to be read in a certain order. But in any case the attempt does not specially link the *Crito* with any particular other work apart from the *Apology*. So, though much is to be learnt from this too, we may concentrate on the *Crito*. This is in full awareness that we are all trying to sharpen and deepen our understanding of the argument and of the drama bound up with it – a delicate task approachable in more than one way.

The phrase appeared above 'someone like Crito', and not just 'Crito', because evidently the dialogue is not likely to have been written only for Crito himself, even if he was alive when the dialogue came out, which is not specially probable. If Crito is not a recognizable type, with recognizable views, values and prejudices, then Plato was wasting his and his readers' time in displaying Socrates as confuting him. But to settle what 'someone like Crito' might accept, we must begin with Crito himself and ask in detail, what is he like? My readers are invited to take down their texts or translations of the *Crito* and very occasionally, where unavoidable, of other Platonic dialogues, to follow both the portrayal of character and discussion in Plato's text and the following analysis of them.

The analysis will begin with Plato's portrayal of Crito's character in this dialogue and, so far as is necessary, in other dialogues. We shall examine next the actual arguments that Crito produces in order to persuade Socrates to escape from prison. The arguments themselves both help to develop the portrayal of his character and spring from that character as already portrayed. An account follows of Socrates' immediate response to these arguments. We shall see how this response takes advantage of Crito's inexperience in dialectic in persuading him to argue seriously rather than take his opinions ready-made from other people. Once Socrates has convinced Crito of the need for serious argument he can probe seriously the moral beliefs on which Crito bases his advocacy of escape. Crito has said that Socrates would be doing injustice, wrong, to certain parties if he did not escape but stayed to die. Socrates extracts from Crito accordingly an agreement that it is *never* right to commit injustice. Crito accepts the consequence that it is wrong to do injustice even to those who have done you injustice. It will appear that this consequence is fraught with ambiguity. After puzzling Crito with a couple of very surprising questions, Socrates personifies and brings on stage, as it were, the Laws and City of Athens. In their section of the dialogue Socrates through the personified Laws explains the surprising questions and bears down on the ambiguities of Crito's accepted consequence. He gets Crito to rule out one possible meaning. He then gives the argument of the Laws a cleverly devised strategy. By confuting Crito even if he holds the weakest possible remaining version of the 'ambiguous consequence', the Laws effectively confute Crito whichever meaning he holds to. Socrates would, they argue, be doing the Laws and City an injustice if he escaped, even though they have done him an injustice by condemning him to death. Crito is silenced. For explanations of points necessarily made briefly in this summary readers are requested to wait for the relevant sections of the analysis. We shall see that the Laws' argument fits Crito's views, situation and character like a well-made glove. The analysis seeks throughout to exhibit the *Crito* as a genuine *dialogue*, portraying two minds at work, not just one, and to show how Plato carefully characterized each of them.

2

CRITO'S PERSONAL CHARACTER

(a) General

The best way of introducing the character of Crito is to follow, with explanation where necessary and with discussion of controversial points to follow, Plato's own introduction to the *Crito.* This is a minor masterpiece combining remarkable dramatic economy with the most natural-sounding conversation. Natural questions from Socrates and natural answers from Crito set the scene with elegant clarity. Roughly, it goes like this:

> SOC. Why have you come at this hour, Crito? Isn't it still early?
> CR. Yes.
> SOC. About what time?
> CR. Early dawn.
> SOC. I'm surprised the gaoler answered your knock.

Already here we know that Socrates is in prison, and we surmise that Crito has come so early on an urgent errand. Socrates was in prison only once in his life, and that was between the sentence of death and his execution.

> CR. He knows me well by now, Socrates, from my frequent visits, and moreover I've done him a good turn.

Socrates must have been in prison for some time before the gaoler knew Crito well.

> SOC. Have you only just come, or have you been here a long time?
> CR. Quite a long time.

Crito's errand must have been urgent indeed. Socrates must have been asleep when he came.

> SOC. Then why didn't you wake me up, instead of sitting silently beside me?
> CR. Socrates, I wish I were not so wakeful and distressed myself. I've been marvelling for a long time at your sleeping so sweetly. I refrained on purpose from waking you up, to let you pass the time as agreeably as possible. Often before over your whole life I've thought you blessed with your character, but most of all in your present trouble, which you bear so easily and gently.

This exhibits Crito as a lifelong friend of Socrates. Crito's wakeful grief contrasts strongly here with Socrates' calm sleep. The calm is evidently typical.

> SOC. Crito, that's because it would strike a false note for me at my time of life to be disturbed at having now to die.

Crito has not mentioned death. Socrates helps him out by showing awareness that Crito must have come to tell him his execution is now imminent.

> CR. Other old men are caught up in similar troubles. Their age doesn't stop them from being disturbed by what is happening to them.
> SOC. True. But why have you come so early?

Socrates perhaps doesn't see what is so urgent about telling him he's to die soon.

> CR. I've come with sad news, Socrates, not sad for you, I think, but sad and grievous for me and for all your friends. I think I'm the one who would take it hardest.
> SOC. What news? Has the ship arrived from Delos on whose arrival I have to die?

Socrates helps Crito out again.

> CR. It hasn't, but it will come today, to judge from the report some people have brought from Sunium, where the ship was when they left. So, Socrates, your life will necessarily end tomorrow.
> SOC. Well, Crito, good luck! If that's the way the gods like it, so be it. However, I think it will not arrive today.
> CR. What do you base that on?

This seemingly simple, but in truth artful introduction reveals the general situation in which the ensuing conversation takes place. Some modern readers have believed also that it reveals aspects of Crito's character and feelings that make him a less than worthy sparring-partner for Socrates. Certainly the contrast between Crito's depth of feeling and Socrates' calm will prove significant later. But attempts to read more into the text seem to fail.

(b) Lawlessness?

Scholars have, for example, occasionally supposed that the same Crito who will propose Socrates' illegal escape is characterized as a lawless person from the start. It is, however, genuinely open to serious doubt whether Plato prepares the reader for Crito's illegal proposal by painting him from the beginning as a man careless of the law. Crito says (43a7–8) that he has done a good turn to the gaoler who let him in early. That need not, however, be interpreted as a bribe designed to procure his disobedience to the law.[32] There is no evidence that the gaoler's early opening of the prison doors was against the rules or regulations, let alone against the law. In our ignorance of prison regulations in classical Athens, we do not know that early opening to visitors was a matter of law as opposed to a matter of the time when a gaoler could reasonably be expected to be out of bed,[33] or the other prisoners (if any) awake.[34] To visit prisoners appears to have been easy in Athens, but there were obviously some normal practical limitations. Socrates could well be surprised, as he is at 43a5–6, at the gaoler having got up before dawn to let Crito in. We can hardly be sure that a gaoler would not normally have said, 'No, you can't come in; we're all still in bed', rather than 'No, you can't come in; it's against the rules.' Crito's service to the gaoler was most probably of a worldly or material nature in essence. But that does not make it, in this context, any more of a bribe than any other help from Athenian A to Athenian B offered in the hope that B would sometime do A a service. That was how Athenian society largely worked.[35] What the passage shows is not so much Crito's lawlessness as his eagerness to gain Socrates' ear as early as humanly possible on what he later paints as an urgent errand. The evidence for a *generally* lawless Crito is slight indeed. It gains no weight from Crito's 'easy familiarity' with the uses and prices of sycophants.[36] Is to be a victim of sycophants, and to have paid their price, a sign of 'a certain moral laxity'?[37] Surely not, any more than to offer a highwayman one's money rather than one's life. Crito may or may not live up to Socrates' high standards, but is not, so far as the text reveals, more than normally casual about obeying the law.

This seemingly trivial point does have some wider significance. For the rest of the dialogue, in my view, Crito's character and assumptions are those, not negligible to Plato's readers at any level, of a normal law-abiding Athenian gentleman who happens to be distinguished by his friendship with Socrates and, as we shall see, by his worldly success. To make of him at the outset a rogue prepared to disobey the law any time it happened to suit him to do so would not only drastically cheapen his willingness to risk breaking the law in order to help Socrates to escape. It would mean also that, in view of the normal close association in Athenian eyes of the 'just' and the 'lawful', Crito's arguments from the injustice he supposes Socrates to be committing by staying to die would smack of insincerity: they would be purely *ad hoc*, and *ad hominem.* But normal Athenian gentlemen paid much attention to justice, and to make Crito fail to do this would seriously infringe his normality as an Athenian gentleman. Crito's friendship with the Platonic Socrates, too, would become harder to account for, either as fact or as fiction. Socrates' lifelong friendship with a knave who paid only lip-service to justice and legality would seem hard to explain – much harder than his friendship with a true gentleman who did not understand his arguments or find himself able on many occasions to accept their often paradoxical conclusions.

The end of the dialogue has offered a foothold for the attempt to damn Crito;[38] the attempt is no more successful there than earlier. The personified Laws of Athens speak at 53d of Socrates hypothetically going to Crito's friends in Thessaly and arriving at a place where there is very much disorder and license. The relevant passage comes too late to affect first-time readers' judgment of Crito's moral *bona fides* as they read his arguments. One might, however, on studying the dialogue, find Crito guilty by association with such people: according to Xenophon,[39] Critias, the notorious member of the Thirty Tyrants, stayed in Thessaly with men practising more lawlessness than justice. That, however, shows at most that there were such men in Thessaly, as in most places, and that *Critias* fell into or sought out bad company. In the *Crito,* we hear of Thessalian flesh-pots, yes, at 53e, but it is against no law to have a good dinner, even though Socrates might disapprove. We hear in the same context of ἀταξία and ἀκολασία – but these, disorder and license, are as likely to refer to immorality as to illegality. Further, the Laws say to Crito, some people there, if Socrates should displease them, will speak slightingly of his having 'transgressed the greatest laws', which is not a thing to which a habitual lawbreaker would pay much attention. True, the personified Laws may at 53b–d intend a contrast between the sound constitutions of Megara and Thebes (53b4–5) and the 'disorder' (ἀταξία) of Thessaly; but if that 'disorder' is political rather than moral it is a fault of Thessalian society rather than of Crito's friends in particular. It is not a crime, and need not even be a sin, to have friends who inhabit a disturbed society, but the personified Laws have to find *some* way to damn Thessaly as a refuge, and its alleged disturbance is an obvious one. We shall see that Crito's values are not Socrates', but that was true of the vast majority of Athenians, law-abiding or otherwise. As an item in the indictment of Crito for lawlessness this passage has no weight at all. As an indication of his values it adds nothing to what we knew before. And if the question be raised why Thessaly should receive a mention at all, the reason may be the reference earlier in the dialogue to the Thessalian district of Phthia, on which see below.[40]

More relevant to lawlessness, though less relevant to the *Crito,* is a passage in the *Phaedo* (115d). There we are told that in some sense Crito pledged to the jury that Socrates would not go away. It is by no means clear that Plato wrote the *Phaedo* before the *Crito*; most scholars, if they ventured an opinion, would hold the reverse.[41] Nor is it certain that the episode mentioned in the *Phaedo* is historical: our sources for Athenian law offer, so far as I have discovered, no parallel for it. In fact, as C.J. Rowe remarks,[42] we have no evidence for it outside the *Phaedo*. The imperfect tense of 'pledged' suggests in Greek (ἠγγυᾶτο) that the attempt to pledge that Socrates would stay may have been unsuccessful, i.e. that the jury may have rejected, or even declined to hear, the request. In that case Burnet ad loc. was probably right to suppose that Crito promised or wanted to promise that if Socrates were allowed to await death out of prison he would not run away. What Crito might or might not have done if his request had been granted is not a profitable question.[43] On the present hypothesis his honour was not put to the test. One cannot use what Crito might have done as evidence either way. If, on the other hand, the jury did accept such a pledge, and did trust Crito not to help Socrates get away in the enforced interval between sentence and execution, it is astonishing that Socrates in the *Crito* does not mention a fact so obviously relevant to his and Crito's disagreement. Indeed, a particularly pointed question here is why Plato should have suppressed all mention of such an episode in the *Crito*. The most obvious answer, if and only if one assumes the episode of Crito's request to be historical, and assumes also doubtfully and for the sake of the argument that it stood to Crito's discredit before the law, is that Plato did not want in the *Crito* to mention anything that stood to Crito's discredit before the law. That is to say, he deliberately suppressed anything that might suggest any prior *tendency* in Crito to illegal action, and was thus concerned *not* to present him as a habitual lawbreaker. On different assumptions, it is easy to believe that Plato thought the matter irrelevant to the *Crito*.

(c) Emotional distraction?

Somewhat similarly, some of the moderns have supposed that Crito's emotional state, as opposed to Socrates' placid demeanour, indicates that Crito is too distraught to think straight.[44] This is at least a genuine question: is Crito really too upset in his grief to think coherently? True, he is sleepless and grieving: see 43b, and readers observe the contrast between the grieving Crito and the peacefully sleeping Socrates. But almost the first thing we learn about Crito in the dialogue (43a9–b2) is that he has been waiting in silence for some unspecified time while Socrates sleeps himself out. This is not, one would have thought, the behaviour of a man too distraught to think, but rather of one who has himself well in hand. It was a kindly act, too, to let Socrates sleep while he could. Simply as human behaviour, though one doubts if the *Crito*'s first readers knew the *Protagoras*, it is instructive to compare Crito's restraint here with the youthfully excited irruption of Hippocrates at the opening of the *Protagoras.* When Crito comes to describe his grief, he does so in measured and even rhetorical Greek (43c); the emphasis he lays upon it, and on its exceeding that of any other friend of Socrates', even joined to Crito's admiration for Socrates' calm in contrast with his own grief, fails to show that Crito is distraught. He displays strength of feeling, but not distraction.

Nor, so far as I can see, does anything in his language indicate incoherence; the syntactical or, occasionally, logical roughnesses one finds in his part of the dialogue are not greater than can be put down to normal conversation or to normal textual wear and tear. That is a matter partly of personal judgment. But the most recent English contribution to this topic, C. Emlyn-Jones' commentary, adduces only a small number of passages, which certainly do not constitute overwhelming evidence. Two of his passages present no necessary incoherence at all. At 43b3 it makes very good sense to take Crito as answering Socrates' question 'Why didn't you wake me up instead of sitting beside me in silence?' by saying (in paraphrase), 'Socrates, I wouldn't have wanted to be awake myself in these circumstances.' Taking the negative Οὐ as anticipating and reinforcing the subsequent further negative οὐδ' gives both normal Greek syntax[45] and logical coherence, and it is hard to see why editors persistently render otherwise. At best this is a dubious example of Crito's 'emotional' syntax. Again, at 45b3 Emlyn-Jones supposes 'these strangers' (ξένοι οὗτοι) to be spoken by Crito in an excited state, as if the foreigners concerned are present beside him. One does not, however, have to be particularly excited to use the demonstrative pronoun thus, as is shown by Adam's parallel from Pl. *Symp.* 175a, and in any case ξένοι οὗτοι could just as well mean 'the strangers you know about'.[46] One passage presents irregular but in no way unclear syntax: the break-off at 45a6 after the first leg of a 'neither...nor...' construction, inserting reasons for the first leg before resuming. This results in no unclarity whatever; if *interrupted* syntax is a sign of anxiety or any other emotional state, is Socrates at e.g. Plato *Apology* 21a4–6 in an emotional state? One supposes not. Then 43d2–5 presents a degree of repetition and mild illogicality which are as likely to be the result of conversational as of emotional syntax, and may in any case be due in part to scribal interpolation.[47] Rhetorical or persuasive zeal may also be partly responsible. That would not be the same thing as emotional distraction.

Two passages, however, do present rather difficult syntax. What Emlyn-Jones calls the 'convoluted syntax' of Crito's sentence at 44b3–9 consists in effect of an inexact grammatical correspondence between the two halves of a μέν and δέ ('on the one hand...on the other hand...') contrast; for other instances of irregular μέν and δέ see Denniston *Greek Particles.*[48] Again some have emended: Schanz's excision of δέ remains possible, and won support from Denniston: short particles are peculiarly liable to textual corruption. Further, at 45e6–46a1 Emlyn-Jones ad loc. argues, 'Crito in his vehemence loses his way in the syntax of the long straggling sentence…' and indeed there may be a surplus infinitive δοκεῖν (to be thought) in mid-sentence. But what, and how much, do these two passages prove? Vehemence need not be a sign of emotional distraction as opposed to an urgent need to persuade. It is not as if Plato's ordinary conversational Greek were free of syntactic difficulties; when the Laws later produce supposedly awkward syntax this is ascribed not to their emotional distraction but to their making a 'formal and legal pronouncement'.[49]

Emlyn-Jones offers indeed a variety of explanations of syntactic awkwardness: anxiety, vehemence, eagerness to convince Socrates, excitement, 'exasperation verging on real anger', are all attributed to Crito at different points.[50] This very variety seems suspicious. What the passages do not suggest on this interpretation – or on any other that I can see – is a Crito driven to incoherence by a single over-mastering grief or any other single emotion. It is doubtful whether even the argument that the text presents a rather large number of phenomena requiring explanation would exert much force: the number seriously requiring explanation is not large – say two or three? And these, as we shall see, have to stand against the overall coherence and force of the argument that Crito develops, to say nothing of the polished rhetorical skill with which, as Emlyn-Jones himself shows, he develops it.[51]

(d) Stupidity?

A related question, which is perhaps best tackled at this point, is whether Crito is a fool, a stupid man who lacks the intelligence to see what Socrates is driving at. On this point Roslyn Weiss has recently argued afresh, following Marvin Fox,[52] for the description of Crito as 'unphilosophical'. The description fits the Crito of other dialogues besides this, provided that it is not taken to mean 'stupid'. We should not pay exaggerated attention to other dialogues which had probably not been read by the *Crito*'s original readers. But in the *Phaedo*, for instance, at 115c2–3 Crito ignores by implication the effect of the dialectical discussion, and that in a way which, according to Socrates at 115e4–7, affects not only the way one speaks but the soul itself. His remarks at 116e, ignoring the dialectical argument, do not suggest that he shares many of the Platonic Socrates' apparently cherished beliefs. The *Phaedo* portrays him as having passed through a lifetime of friendship with Socrates without being convinced by Socrates' arguments; but then Plato's Socrates notoriously convinced rather few people whether philosophically gifted or not. Crito's assumptions in practice remain, so far as the *Phaedo* is concerned, those of an Athenian gentleman, a shrewd businessman, and, by his lights, a good friend. His lack of attention to philosophy does not in itself make him unintelligent, or incapable of mounting a practical argument and sticking to a point of view.

In perusing Crito's part in the *Euthydemus* also, one should remember that the unintellectual are not all fools. True, though he enjoys listening to the reported conversation, Crito's values there again are not those of Socrates. Weiss well reminds us that at 304c3–4, in Socrates' ironic recommendation of Euthydemus and Dionysodorus, 'the factor he cites as being "for your benefit especially" ... is that their brand of wisdom "did not in any way hinder a man from making money."'[53] This suggests strongly that Crito valued money more highly than Socrates did. But then Protagoras and Gorgias in their dialogues – to say nothing of Callicles – also hold values different from Socrates', and most readers suppose that that does not indicate Plato's low view of their verbal skills and intelligence. But Crito likes to listen, and is glad to learn. As Weiss recognizes, he has the common sense not to want to refute people in the manner of Euthydemus and Dionysodorus, which suggests his ability to detect mere nonsense. Furthermore, what he knows as φιλοσοφία, 'philosophy', has for him (304e6–7) a certain charm or attractiveness. The value of this is reduced by the fact that Crito does not, when he says this, know what Socrates and the two sophists have been talking about, because he has been out of earshot. But what happens here is that Crito hears someone criticizing Socrates' talk and leaps loyally to his defence by speaking on behalf of philosophy. He simply assumes that Socrates will have been talking about philosophy – whatever he (Crito) understands by that term. This assumption shows in context that 'philosophy' for Crito at least includes the things Socrates normally talks about. The critic suggests that Socrates will do himself no good by talking with men who 'don't care at all what they say' (305a3–4); he says that Euthydemus and Dionysodorus are the best of their kind but their kind is feeble and laughable. He does not give their talk the name of philosophy, but calls it 'the activity itself' (τὸ πρᾶγμα αὐτό).[54] Crito assumes the critic to mean 'philosophy', and says to Socrates that the critic was wrong to blame philosophy. But he joins at 305b in the critic's rebuke to Socrates for conversing with such people – he means 'such contemptible people' – in public. The upshot of this passage is, among other things, to establish that Crito associates Socrates with 'philosophy'.

So what are we to make of *Euthydemus* 306d6 ff.? There, still talking to Socrates, Crito thinks he ought not to have neglected his elder son's education (παιδεία).[55] This is what he believes when Socrates is there;

but (306e) when he sees those who claim to educate (παιδεύειν), he finds them 'very strange, to tell you the truth'. So how is he to turn his young man to philosophy? Some[56] suppose the answer to this question to be so obvious that Crito is a fool not to see it: send the boy to Socrates! Crito has just implied that Socrates will have been talking about philosophy; and that makes all the more foolish Crito's failure to envisage the boy's learning about philosophy from Socrates. Crito, however, is not necessarily displaying simple folly. In the context, he distinguishes Socrates from 'those who claim to educate'. So Crito must be aware that Plato's Socrates makes no such claim; hence Crito cannot suggest *to Socrates*, almost in the same breath, that he (Socrates) should educate the boy; it is obvious that Socrates would demur. The nearest Plato can come here to having Crito's elder son sent to Socrates is for Socrates to advise Crito to evaluate philosophy for himself, and (307c) if he approves to pursue and practise it 'himself and his children'. Plato expects readers of the *Euthydemus* to be aware that Socrates makes no claim to educate in the proper moral sense: that is clearly implicit also earlier in that dialogue, at 274b1–2 (taken in context). Crito in that dialogue does not need a deep knowledge of or insight into Socratic-Platonic philosophy to be aware that 'Socrates' disavows any ability to instruct. But *some* readers will have read previously, say, the *Apology*. They might then have recalled the fact, which R. Weiss does not even mention, that Critobulus appears there in the list at 33d–34a of young men whom people might suspect Socrates of corrupting. So in Plato's pages Crito does take the obvious step of sending the boy to Socrates, even if he cannot mention such a possible step to Socrates in the terms of the discussion in the *Euthydemus*.

Crito may be unphilosophical, to the point of vagueness about what philosophy is; yet neither in the *Euthydemus* nor elsewhere does Plato represent him as a fool. In the *Apology* Socrates indicates that those he refuted did not necessarily believe that they themselves were at fault: people's characteristic reaction (*Ap.* 22e–23a, and 21c–d) was to dislike Socrates, and, when refuted by the young, to blame him for his bad influence, not to blame themselves. Were they all unintelligent? Plato and his Socrates do not say so. Crito clearly does not dislike or blame Socrates; nevertheless, he is apparently one of the many people this Socrates has failed to convince that they are as ignorant as he made them out to be or that they ought to espouse his more paradoxical conclusions.

But in any case the ultimate relevance of considerations drawn from other dialogues is dubious. One ought in the first instance to interpret the characters of a given dialogue out of that dialogue. Only in the case of a serious conflict between dialogues as to a particular person's characteristics, which does not arise in Crito's case, would a close comparison be necessary. In his own dialogue, then, Crito at least appears to share one principle which Plato's Socrates seems elsewhere to support: the principle of the paramountcy of justice in moral decision-making. But this is by no means purely Socratic; others besides Crito and Socrates were prepared, whatever their conduct in real life, to pay at least lip-service to justice. Approval of justice in behaviour was normal and respectable.[57] The *Crito* draws attention with emphasis to the possibility that Socrates' words and perhaps also his example strengthened Crito's own approval. But there is no reason for any reader to assume that consistency with his agreements on previous occasions is Crito's only motive for approving just behaviour now, or furnishes Socrates' only reason for asking him to confirm his approval on this occasion. For those who can see just a little below the surface, another reason is that it is helpful to Crito's argument, in his attempt to persuade Socrates to escape on grounds of justice, to allow no exceptions to the paramountcy of justice. Crito thus has a strong motive within the argument itself for adopting on this particular occasion this facet of Socratic-Platonic philosophy. In these circumstances it need not surprise anybody that Crito should, in answer to a question, affirm that one ought never to commit injustice. There is no need to account for such an answer by supposing, e.g., that he is too suggestible, too unphilosophical, or simply too stupid to make a worthy opponent for Socrates here. These points, here stated rather baldly, will be amplified below. So also will some arguments to show that Crito does not, in answering questions from Socrates, contradict himself quite so readily as, e.g., the dialogue's most recent editor in English supposes. We note meanwhile that 'un-Socratic' and 'intelligent', even in Plato's eyes, need not be mutually contradictory epithets.

(e) Weakness?

So, then, is Crito in sheer fact, for whatever reason, absurdly easy to shift from one position to another whenever Socrates wishes?[58] One might wonder in that case why Plato should bother to have Socrates *argue* with him at all. Specifically, however, in the early pages of the dialogue there occurs an episode offering a kind of opportunity, which scholars have not missed, to claim that Crito is too weak and meek, or to doubt whether he is fully capable of attending to and taking in what Socrates says to him. The episode is that of the dream Socrates describes at 44a10–b4. He brings it as evidence that he will not, as Crito has announced, be executed the next day, but rather in two days' time. The woman who appeared to Socrates was dressed in white – in itself more likely to be a good omen than a bad one.[59] In his dream she told him 'On the third day you would arrive in fertile Phthia.' This, as commentators say, adapts Achilles' threat at *Iliad* 9.363 to sail home on the morrow, and arrive the day after in his home town of Phthia, located in what later geographers called Thessaly. Crito's first and immediate reaction is that this is a strange (ἄτοπον) dream. Socrates replies that, on the contrary, it is clear ('Εναργές). Crito at once modifies his response with a possibly reluctant: 'Yes, too [clear], it seems.'[60] Since this might look like a meek or stupid reaction to Socrates' disagreement, it will be well to examine it further.

There are at least two reasons why Socrates might think this particular dream a clear reference to his death in two days' time. The first and less difficult for a casual and uninitiated reader in Plato's day is that 'Phthia' begins with 'phthi' (φθι) which is the root of the Greek verb φθίνω (*phthinō*) meaning (though not commonly in classical prose) 'die'.[61] The second is that Plato's Socrates might have thought of death as a return home for his soul, like Achilles' threatened return home. Crito seems not to see either of these points when he remarks that the dream is 'strange' or even 'absurd' (ἄτοπον). It is not hard to imagine an intelligent first-time reader of the *Crito*, without benefit of a modern commentary, having the same instant reaction. But Socrates presses the dream's clarity on Crito, and the latter, thus prodded, has to be supposed by readers either to see at least one of these possible readings of the dream, or to perceive that the dream must somehow speak to Socrates of his impending death. Again, a casual reader might react by noticing the etymological point, or the necessity of the dream referring somehow to Socrates' death, and pass on undisturbed. Those readers, and only those, who were steeped in Plato before reading the *Crito* will have seen the point about homecoming. This passage is certainly readable on at least two levels.

Crito's further response has a certain practicality about it; and indeed practicality is characteristic of him both in his own and in other dialogues. His purpose is to persuade Socrates to escape at once. If Phthia simply represents 'death', the dream may 'reduce the urgency of Crito's entreaty'.[62] If the dream means to Socrates, as to some readers, that death is a homecoming, this may further damage the efficacy of Crito's plea, by lending additional strength to Socrates' already visible calmness. In either case Crito's best policy is not directly to dispute the dream's meaning, since dispute on such a matter could be endless, and he clearly believes he has no time to lose. He should rather press on with his plea, and hope that an alternative view of the dream will prove at least possible.

On this passage E. Weinrib's verdict, though not wholly just, is not untypical of recent work:[63] 'A single sentence by Socrates is enough completely to transform [Crito's] view, although not enough fully to penetrate his consciousness.' Weinrib here alludes to Crito's remark later, at 46a6, that the whole thing must be done and finished by the following night, i.e. by the night of the day that is just dawning as he speaks. In this remark Crito might indeed seem to be ignoring the dream's apparent postponement of Socrates' death, and hence to have failed to take in Socrates' perfectly lucid remarks about what the dream means to him. But – and it is a large 'but' – in the meantime Crito has, without directly disputing Socrates' view of the dream, offered implicitly the alternative interpretation desiderated above. At 45c2–5, whether casually or not, he mentions Thessaly, where Phthia was located, as a possible refuge for Socrates. Thessaly was a good two days' journey from Athens. If his arrival there is what his dream foretells, Socrates had better, in Crito's view, make up his mind at once; he cannot, after all, count on a day's respite before his execution.[64] Why does Plato not have his Crito argue the point? Because, again, as a reader could see who had got as far as asking this question, the argument would be long and necessarily inconclusive. Neither man has any claim to expertise in the interpretation of dreams; Plato had no good reason for involving either characters or readers in a technical discussion. It is thus wholly unnecessary to suppose that Crito appears here as a person 'easily influenced by others and ready to follow their lead', or that 'Plato has economically and unobtrusively sketched a person who would both require and accept the [later] arguments of the Laws.' There are other possibilities, which we should not ignore, such as a degree of shrewd argumentative tact and understanding on Crito's part.[65]

In Plato's mind as author there was perhaps another reason, besides the depiction of such shrewdness, for avoiding any settlement of the dream's meaning. In the absence of any settled interpretation of the dream, the question whether Socrates will actually go to Thessaly remains open, not of course for the dialogue's readers but for Crito as a character in the dialogue. Thus Socrates does not, by insisting on his own interpretation, foreclose the debate. Plato's and his Socrates' tact matches his Crito's. There is no necessity whatsoever to suppose with Weinrib that Plato means to depict a Crito 'too distressed by the immediate catastrophe...to explore the implications of the dream'.

This present exploration of possibilities may perhaps be accused of reading a good deal into the text. But then denigrators of Crito's intelligence and independence of mind do not so much cleave to the letter of the text as read into it different and (which is a point of greater significance) more dangerous things. Weinrib, for one, for all his fine interpretation of the dream and of Crito's response, assumes apparently that Crito has not noticed that the dream could refer to a flight to Thessaly. Indeed, he goes so far as to add, after saying, 'A single sentence by Socrates is enough completely to transform his view,' the phrase 'although not enough to penetrate his awareness.' The danger of this kind of statement, it cannot be said too often, is that it reduces Crito to a straw man, and the *Crito* to a straw dialogue. It may seem an easy step from portraying Crito as 'not a philosopher, but a decent and ordinary person' to making him a fool; nevertheless it is neither a necessary step nor a safe one.

One should, moreover, guard against over-elaboration of the psychology of Crito's distress. J.B. White, for instance, supposes that Crito, as a friend of Socrates, needs in his distress to be with him.[66] Regrettably or not, the text lacks even the slightest hint of this. The text itself offers a straightforward and sufficient motivation for Crito's visit. It emerges very quickly that Crito is there in the prison to tell Socrates about the approach of his execution, and to try to spring Socrates from gaol. We need no further motivation, and no psychologizing. What we need is a step-by-step analysis of Crito's position and apparent thinking rather than sweeping generalizations about his emotional needs or states.

(f) Practicality

Crito has not appeared – so far at least – as a weakling. Nor is he too distraught to argue sensibly, even if his calmness does not match Socrates'. We have seen also that there is no reason to look on him as a lawless rogue, rather than a worthy if unphilosophical friend for Socrates. Readers embarking on the *Crito* should regard him at least provisionally as a characteristic Athenian gentleman. One might expect him as such to be a practical man.

Crito's response to the dream is indeed highly practical. He must in common sense realize that, if the dream represents Socrates' attitude to death, it is a setback to his purposes; if the question is one merely of the timing of Socrates' execution, it is an unwelcome postponement of them. Accordingly, regardless of the dream's meaning, he sets about overcoming the setback or postponement. In pursuit of his practical aims, Crito launches at once into his case for Socrates' escape. His case falls into two sets of considerations, one more worldly, the other more overtly moral. We start, as Crito does, with the more worldly set.

3

CRITO'S MORE WORLDLY CASE

Crito opens his remarks at 44b6 with two effects of Socrates' threatened death. Each of these he represents as a disaster (συμφορά) to himself:

(i) Socrates' death will inflict on Crito the loss of a unique intimate companion (ἐπιτήδειος).

(ii) Socrates' failure to escape (see 44b9 ff.) will give Crito a bad name, among many people unacquainted with them both, for apparently putting money before friends – this because by spending money Crito could have arranged the escape.[67]

It is easy to label each of these arguments as egoistic.[68] But Crito's self-appointed task is to persuade Socrates to escape. If contemporary readers had read the *Apology* of Plato they would not need much reminder that material or generally external considerations *on Socrates' own account* are unlikely to persuade him.[69] If not, Crito's words at 43b3–8 would suggest to an alert reader – one capable of noticing the egoism – that Socrates' calm and measured response to approaching death is no new reaction to apparent personal disaster, but a habit. But these egoistic and even worldly arguments do have moral overtones. To do a friend an injury would doubtless appear unjust both to Crito and to Socrates, and indeed to the general reader. The arguments seem to demand an answer.

Nevertheless, though (i) above is a very natural point for Crito to make, it receives no direct answer in the *Crito*.[70] Certainly Plato as an author could not, however much he may have wanted to, allow Socrates to agree that he is a unique companion in a Platonic sense without having him desert his usual irony, whether at this stage already made public by Plato or only planned by him. Moreover, it would be impossible to refute a Crito who maintained that Socrates was unique as a personal friend to him in a normal sense, however little he appreciated Socrates' philosophy or understood his detailed arguments.

Any philosophically uninitiated or merely casual reader could easily forget at the end of the dialogue, when Crito has nothing to say, that this argument has received no explicit answer. If Crito's argument or plea does stay in a reader's mind, Socrates offers through the personified Laws at least one relevant consideration. They point out (54a5–7) that Socrates will be no more use to his sons from his proposed Thessalian exile than he would be from the world of the dead. It is no long step from that argument to a similar one in which Crito is substituted for the sons. Furthermore, that argument about the sons occurs in a passage tying up loose ends from earlier in the dialogue and headed by a rhetorical question asking what good Socrates' escape will do to himself or to his intimate companions (ἐπιτηδείους). The Greek word quoted here was the word Crito used for 'intimate companion' at 44b8 when complaining of his deprivation by Socrates' death. Just two occurrences of a single not uncommon word might not by themselves jog a casual reader's memory. But the cluster of instances of the word on Crito's lips at 43c6, 44b8, 44e2 and 45e1 matches another on the Laws' imagined lips, at 53a9, 53b1, 54a7 and 54b1. It would take only a fairly observant reader to notice in the second cluster that Crito's earlier arguments were being alluded and attended to. Indeed, the Laws evidently in a kind of way respond at 53a–b to Crito's plea for Socrates to ignore the risks to his friends inherent in the escape. The same only fairly observant reader ought not to have to think very hard to notice the parallel between the Laws' actual reply to Crito on the sons and a possible reply to Crito on his own loss of a unique friend.[71]

If anyone, searching the dialogue for problems, were to think that Crito could have made a more impassioned appeal than he does on the grounds of his own prospective loss, and to wonder why Plato did not allow him to make more of this, the question is good. But perhaps – I do not say certainly, or even probably – Plato had an answer ready for such rebellious readers: Crito's and Socrates' respective ages. There is no need here to rely on the statement of Socrates in the *Apology* (38c1) that the jury have condemned him to death οὐ πολλοῦ γ' ἕνεκα χρόνου, 'not for the sake of a long time'. The *Crito* itself contains references to Socrates' and Crito's age. Socrates' age appears at 43b–c; both are old men at 49a9–b1 (with or without γέροντες ['old men'] actually in the text); Socrates is seventy years old at 52e, and at 53d he has in any case only, in all likelihood, a short time left to live. Crito, and an intelligent reader, could perhaps deduce this answer from Socrates' words at 43b10f. to the effect that it would πλημμελὲς εἴη, 'strike a false note', at Socrates' age to be disturbed at the prospect of imminent death. If that is 'a false note', then so, clearly, is Crito's disturbance at the prospect of losing his old friend.

The argument labelled (ii) above is a very different matter. To this Socrates retorts with a question, asking why they should pay attention to 'many people'. Those best qualified to speak or 'most reasonable' (ἐπιεικέστατοι), that is, presumably, those who share enough of Socrates' values, and perhaps therefore are at least acquainted wih Socrates and his old friend, will hold true opinions of the whole matter. That Crito has a ready comeback to this suggests that he is not wholly incapable of argument in ordinary terms, but is quite able to stand up for himself. The comeback presents an argument the common man as he reads might well have some sympathy with, especially if he recognizes that he is a common man. The many, Crito says, can do the greatest harm (by which he obviously means that they can kill), so that one must pay attention to them. At the same time, this reply shows, for those who come to the *Crito* from the Socrates of other Platonic dialogues, in particular the *Apology*, that Crito has himself no profound understanding of Socrates. Though the reply is, to normal people, in the circumstances, plain common sense, it is not calculated to convince Plato's Socrates, who says in the *Apology* (especially 29a5–c1) that he does not know whether death is a good thing or a bad. But Socrates does not make that point here. Plato does not need to have his Socrates enter, or re-enter, that controversy. His Socrates as well as his Crito may be presumed to see that their attitudes to death differ.

Socrates here says rather that since the 'many' (now those who convicted and condemned him) cannot make a man wise or foolish, they cannot do the greatest harm or the greatest good. Crito might or might not be persuadable of the equivocal value of death. A commonsensical sort of man would be likely to resist it. It is highly unlikely that such a man would either suppose the vulgar herd capable of transforming a man's intellect or wish in the present emergency to try and out-argue Socrates on what is clearly his own rather strange ground of the central value of wisdom. Sensible readers, whether practised or not, would doubtless adjust their expectations, if any. Socrates is choosing his argumentative weapons well already, and Crito lets the point pass, in an expression suggesting his no doubt reluctant acceptance of it.[72] Meanwhile it is significant, as we shall see later, that Socrates does not here deny that death is a harmful thing; his words imply no more than that death is not the greatest harm.

Thus far a number of Greek heroes would agree with Socrates.[73] So far even Crito himself might find a use for such heroic values, which he and Plato's readers presumably knew from, among other sources, a number of Attic tragedies. Indeed, as B.M.W. Knox showed long ago,[74] most extant Sophoclean tragedies, not to mention the pseudo-Aeschylean *Prometheus Bound*, and even the *Iliad* itself, show a stubborn hero(ine) rejecting the attempts of other characters to persuade him or her to soften or abandon a stubborn adherence to a heroic stance; the *Crito* more than somewhat resembles a scene in a drama of this kind, presumably a familiar kind by Plato's time.

Before we proceed to Crito's more overtly moral case, there is a further general point to be made on the question of Crito's intelligence or lack of it. We are told at the outset (43a7–8) that Crito had frequently visited Socrates in prison. If, as some suppose, Crito has frequently tried to persuade Socrates to escape, then on at least one such occasion he is likely to have started off with, or at least included, the obvious argument (ii) above, and to have had it duly rejected. If not, it is hard to see why not.[75] Such a sequence of events might make Crito look foolish on the occasion of the actual dialogue. But two alternative possibilities require consideration. The first arises from dramatic technique. Dramatists sometimes do, out of necessity, begin dramas with speeches one would have expected to be made before the action opens: witness, e.g., the outline plans offered in the prologues to Sophocles' *Electra* and *Philoctetes* to people who might have been expected to ask about them beforehand. No reputable Sophoclean critic labels the recipients of the relevant information 'stupid'. Plato may have done something dramatically similar. The second possibility is that Crito's previous visits, if any, have been concerned with other things; this possibility arises from examination of the evidence put forward for the scholarly hypothesis that Crito has previously attempted to persuade Socrates to escape.

This evidence consists of two expressions, one of Crito's and one of Socrates'. The former is ἔτι καὶ νῦν (literally 'still even now') at 44b6–7. This is used at Ar. *Frogs* 1236 and Thuc. VI 40.1 in a 'final appeal' in cases where the speaker himself has been trying to persuade his addressee(s).[76] That is a natural situation for an expression meaning essentially 'even now at this late hour'. But it is surely not the only situation in which it is relevant. The expression is perfectly appropriate to a case where the speaker knows that other people have made their appeals, and is bent on making the last, eleventh-hour, appeal himself. It might also be appropriate to a situation in which the eleventh hour has been reached without any series of previous appeals having occurred. Such is apparently the case at *Gorgias* 495a2; there Socrates has not explicitly put the question concerned to Callicles before, so that it is not explicitly the latest of a series; and when Socrates has put similar questions (e.g. at 494d7), Callicles has given him an answer, but has not stuck consistently to it. Ἔτι καὶ νῦν in these circumstances means simply what it says, 'even at this late hour…'; this is hardly the final appeal, and is not one of a clear-cut series. A similar use of the phrase with no series and no eleventh-hour appeal occurs in Xenophon's *Apology* at §26.[77] The same expression here in the *Crito* certainly does not prove that Crito and Socrates are going over old ground.

The second relevant expression is used by Socrates at *Crito* 48e2–3: '...cease now, my dear friend, uttering many times (πολλάκις) the same remark, that I ought to leave this place against the Athenians' wish'. This could indeed refer to Crito's use of previous visits to exhort Socrates to escape. But it need not: several times in the course of the present dialogue Crito has said things which amount to telling Socrates to escape: see 44b7, 45a3, 46a8–9, to say nothing of the actual arguments Crito brings, all in the course of a few minutes' talk. Accordingly, readers could very well take Socrates to be referring to Crito's verbal behaviour on the present occasion. Whichever of the above two possible explanations of Crito's *apparent* obtuseness is correct, whether dramatic technique or a different conception of Crito's previous visits, either would give us a Crito less unintelligent than the text might otherwise make him appear.[78]

There is, however, a further problem with this passage, as Gabriel Danzig has kindly pointed out to me. *Socrates* is not going to suffer anything further at the hands of the multitude than his condemnation and prospective execution. The idea that the mob will rise up and do *Crito* an injury for *failing* to rescue Socrates from them and for *not* breaking the law would be far-fetched. So why does Crito, encouraged by Socrates, so irrelevantly bring the power of the multitude into the discussion? Or, to put essentially the same question in another form, why does Plato so irrelevantly drag in the mob? The sequel exacerbates the difficulty: if Crito *does* rescue Socrates, the sycophants, Crito admits, will attack him – naturally by rousing the rabble against him as a law-breaker; Crito does his best to play down this prospect. The harm the multitude can do, in Crito's as in most normal eyes, seems accordingly irrelevant. So what is going on? Ordinary readers might not have seen any problem; readers who could see one would have had the materials in front of them to work it out.

Percipient readers could perhaps see something like this going on: (1) Crito says (44b–c) that 'πολλοί ('many people') will think, who don't know you and me, that...', and that his reputation will suffer accordingly. But we do not have to believe that what Crito meant by 'many people' was the mob. They could simply comprise Crito's un-Socratic friends and his business associates and rivals. To be thought by such people to prefer money to friends would be a serious setback, causing one to be deeply distrusted in ordinary business affairs. (2) Socrates then refers (44c7) to οἱ πολλοί, 'the many' meaning 'the many people you're talking about'. (3) Crito picks this up as if given a cue, and uses the same phrase to mean 'most people' or 'the multitude' or even 'the mob', in order to construct a quick argument in rebuttal of Socrates. It was doubtless true, moreover, that most people wouldn't, as Crito has it, 'believe that we were eager for your escape but you refused to go'; 'most people' (οἱ πολλοί) sounds better in this context than 'my business associates'. Crito's expression also has the effect of turning his appeal into an argument about Crito's *general* reputation, and there is no doubt of the high value, not only or necessarily material, placed on one's general reputation in classical Athenian society. But (4) Socrates, having given Crito this opportunity, uses the results to make the point that he attaches no value or weight to general reputation *per se*, only to the opinion of those he respects. (5) Crito's retort, that a bad general reputation can result in the greatest harm, illustrates not what may happen to Crito in particular if he should on this particular occasion let down a particular friend, but rather the importance in general attaching to one's general reputation. But (6) Socrates does not accept that death is the greatest harm; and Crito, whether mindful of the *Apology* or of Socrates' evident present equanimity, does not broach that subject. Plato here manipulates his Socrates into manipulating Crito, presumably to bring out his point that popular reputation in itself was not an important factor in sound moral thinking. That point would be clear, whether acceptable or not, to both ordinary and accomplished readers, whether or not they perceived the *non sequiturs* in this passage of conversation.

A striking omission from Crito's worldly case, an omission which imposes itself, one would have thought, on a minimally careful reader, points again to Crito's general awareness. Just as Socrates does not try to convince Crito that we do not know whether death is a good thing or a bad, so Crito does not attempt to frighten Socrates into escaping. He does not suggest that Socrates might find death an uninviting prospect, worse than any other. One might have expected from him a plea along the lines of 'At least the alternative I'm offering is better than *death*, isn't it?' But such pleas, if indeed they appear at all, are muted. The nearest Crito comes to such a plea is in the course of his *more overtly moral* argument, at 45c6 ff. It seems appropriate to desert the order of the text and deal with these points here. At 46c6 ff. Crito says (1) that Socrates is betraying himself, when he could be saved; and (2) that Socrates is pursuing the same sort of aims as his enemies would, in their attempt to destroy him.

Of these, (1) implies that he is refusing 'to be saved', when he could be. Evidently he is to be saved from death, but Crito does not make that explicit, perhaps because he, like any alert reader, knows already of Socrates' attitude to death. Nor does he make clear here what Socrates is to be saved *for*: merely to remain alive? To pursue his mission as portrayed in Plato's *Apology*? Crito mentions neither of these: he speaks elsewhere of Socrates' friends and here, in a nearby sentence, of Socrates' sons; of Socrates' own prospective gains from staying alive he says virtually nothing. He appears indeed at this stage more interested in his *moral* point, that Socrates is behaving unjustly, in 'betraying' – a very moral word – himself. All this is remarkably little compared to what he might have said, on worldly lines, about Socrates' approaching end.

The above (2) implies, on the surface, that Socrates is destroying himself. But it takes a long time to suggest that implication, and by a roundabout route which fails to reach its destination. Socrates' enemies wish to destroy him (and, to that end, to put him to death). Socrates is, in effect, pursuing his own death. But is that death actually Socrates' destruction? Crito does not say it is. He avoids any philosophical discussion on the nature of death, whether it is truly the end or not, and whether it is a good thing for Socrates or not. Now *Plato* may merely have been reserving these topics for other dialogues; but whether he was or not is a question whose answer does not affect the impression made on the attentive reader of the *Crito* by the character of Crito in this dialogue.

Should Crito have mentioned the gods, and Socrates' divinely ordained mission as it appears in Plato's *Apology*? Perhaps so, but no uninitiated reader would desiderate such an argument, nor would those who have not read in particular the *Apology*, in which alone the tale of that 'mission' appears. Yet those who have read the *Apology* will have observed that in that work Socrates, while acknowledging the 'mission', does not think that it justifies him in suggesting exile as his penalty in opposition to his accusers' proposal of the death penalty. One reference to the gods does appear in the opening scene of the *Crito*: at 43d Socrates, on hearing that the sacred ship which has been holding up his execution will arrive 'to-day', replies 'Well, Crito, good luck! If the gods wish so, so be it!' Socrates here clearly views whatever happens to him as the will of the gods, and is prepared to submit to it. This chimes so harmoniously with popular views on the gods and fate that Crito, who does not appear to entertain any special religious beliefs or zeal, would be hard put to it, as would Plato's ordinary readers, to find anything wrong with it.

So, what does this analysis tell us about Crito's character? It shows him capable of at least some degree of argumentative tact. We need not suppose him to have listened to, and taken in, previous discussions on the goodness or badness of death, even if already published when the *Crito* appeared. How far Crito has, in his Platonic past, understood and taken on board what Plato's Socrates is driving at is doubtful. More decidable, and more immediately relevant, is the question what Crito has seen and expressed verbally in this dialogue. Almost from the start, when Socrates wakes up, Crito (43b3) draws a sharp contrast between his own sleepless grief and Socrates' ability to have a good sleep and confront his fate with imperturbable equanimity. Another contrast backs this up. When Socrates points out the incongruity of a man at his age rebelling against a death sentence, Crito retorts that other old men in similar situations do rebel. In the face of this attitude in Socrates Crito admits that Socrates will not find the news of his approaching death hard to bear, grieved though his friends are. This third contrast, adding in all Socrates' friends, reinforces the main point here. Not only is Socrates calm of bearing and of speech; Crito is deeply aware of that calm. A lesser man might indeed have tried to frighten Socrates; Crito in this early moment of their meeting offers only the oblique approach by reference to what other old men feel when confronted with death.

When Crito thus avoids using the bugbear of death to argue for Socrates' escape, he is not merely deploying a friend's tact in leaving Socrates' calm undisturbed. That might conflict with his purpose of rousing Socrates to save himself. He is implicitly recognizing that it will do him no good in his argument to speak of death as annihilation or as something to be feared. This persuasive tact may seem obvious or, philosophically, trivial. But very little in Plato's dialogues is entirely trivial, and this particular apparent triviality will gain in importance. Indeed we shall find below that the recognition of Socrates' complete calm at the prospect of death actually cuts off one way in which Crito could have evaded Socrates' – or the Laws' – final argument.

4

CRITO'S OVERTLY MORAL ARGUMENT

(a) Negative points rebutted

It has naturally not escaped notice that Crito *has* a moral case.[79] But I have seen no account of quite how far Crito's morality goes on this occasion. You're surely not worrying, he asks Socrates at 44e2 ff., about the possibility that for their part in the escape, your friends might (44e5) lose all or a goodly amount of their wealth, *or suffer something else in addition* (ἢ καὶ ἄλλο τι πρὸς τούτοις παθεῖν)? Crito goes on to tell Socrates not to worry about that, 'for we would be acting justly in saving you and running this risk and if necessary *one even greater than this*' (καὶ ἐὰν δέῃ ἔτι τούτου μείζω). A fine, then, *or something worse*, is acceptable to Crito; he thinks such penalties for him or other friends ought to be acceptable to Socrates, because (γάρ 45a1) they would be acting justly in rescuing Socrates [all emphases mine]. It is impossible to be sure how much is covered by 'even greater [sc. risk] than this'. Private prosecutors in Athens were apt to demand the death penalty, and Athenian juries could notoriously be capricious.[80] There were a number of accused persons – perhaps most notably the historian Thucydides – who fled into exile before they could be brought to trial. On the other hand, an accused could in certain circumstances be executed by the 'Eleven' magistrates without trial.[81] Could a normal condemned man, even if wealthy like Crito, rely on buying his way out before execution? In Socrates' exceptional case he had long enough in prison for arrangement of an escape, and there is no doubt that Crito and his friends had prepared the ground. It is doubtful whether normal procedure would have allowed time enough: I have found no example of a prisoner in classical Athens escaping between sentence and execution. Crito might, if his prosecutor proved resistant to bribery, have found himself either choosing between exile before trial if not summarily executed, and the genuine risk of his life if he did stand trial. We are dealing here with uncertainties, but very possibly Crito would have been dealing with uncertainties too: he accepts at 48a–b the ability of the masses to kill. Crito would not lightly, in arguing with Socrates, be explicit about the risks: it makes sense for him to minimize the risks to himself, as he subsequently does, in order to persuade Socrates. But Crito places no actual limit on the risks he is prepared to run, and thinks he ought to run rather than fail to do the just thing in this case. To pay lip-service to justice was conventional, and Crito is a conventional man. But so high an opinion of the ultimate significance of justice goes beyond conventional lip-service. Heroes were willing to die for justice; and Socrates in Plato's *Apology* (28d5–9) ranks nothing, not even life, before what is morally fine. But would an ordinary Athenian gentleman place his life in some danger? Perhaps, if he cared enough, either from a moral or a selfish point of view, about the particular case at issue. From our present point of view, we observe that the Crito who goes as far as he does here will land in some dialectical embarrassment if he at any subsequent time tries to backtrack on the high, if not essential, importance of justice in human life.

Is Crito sufficiently alert to realize what he is saying? It is normal, in charity, to assume the alertness of Plato's characters – and those of other dramatists – to what they are saying. Crito has not been shown to need an exception to be made for him. On the contrary, a similarly charitable interpretation of Crito on Socrates' dream has also yielded good sense. It would appear so far that Crito is not without some dialectical, or indeed ordinary mental, alertness. What is more, alert readers might well be expected to notice his alertness.

(b) Positive points

Up to now Crito has shown no more than the moral inadequacy of certain reasons for Socrates' staying to die. He now turns, as critics note, to a moral argument, admittedly with emotional overtones, in favour of Socrates' escape.[82] He uses again the word just, δίκαιον. He insists that Socrates' staying would be οὐδὲ δίκαιον, 'not just', and indeed voluntarily so, in that:

(i) Socrates is betraying himself, and seeking to destroy himself, as his enemies have – and that when there is an alternative, viz. accepting rescue;

(ii) Socrates is betraying his sons by leaving them orphaned – and that when there is an alternative, viz. [accepting rescue and] bringing them up himself.

Crito must be counting these betrayals as voluntary, since he offers Socrates an available alternative to each. He adds that Socrates' sons, left thus in the lurch, will, τὸ σὸν μέρος ('so far as Socrates is concerned'), be left to fare however they may chance to fare. That is to say that, so far as Socrates is concerned, their welfare will be a matter of chance – ὅτι ἂν τύχωσιν – and the chances are not necessarily in their favour. Crito's language here at once recalls Socrates' at 44d9–10. The phrase ὅτι ἂν τύχωσιν is repeated. There Socrates had said that the many are not able to make a man prudent or foolish, but their effect is a matter of chance.[83] Crito's point is that no collection of Toms Dicks and Harrys can reliably make a man reliably prudent, or even reliably imprudent; and those who bring up Socrates' boys in his absence through death will be no better. Crito is again demonstrating, for readers advanced enough themselves to perceive it, his ability to respond in a manner essentially dialectical to Socrates' words, using them against him. In argument he is neither stupid nor too suggestible, but presentably alert. Naturally it takes a presentably alert reader to notice that, and only those familiar with Platonic dialectic are likely to have seen the whole point; but other less well-informed readers will have felt the emotional force behind the moral appeal, and Plato could rest content with that.

When Crito labels Socrates' apparent determination to die 'not just', he must mean that it is unjust. It is an essential part of his argument that Socrates will be doing something morally wrong, not merely morally neutral, and it is an essential part of Socrates' subsequent response that escape would be morally wrong. Can 'not just' mean 'unjust'? Yes, it can. At *Ap.* 35b10–c1 Socrates says, 'Nor does it seem to me to be just to beg...', when he clearly regards the non-justice of begging as a clear reason for not begging. Also to be actively avoided are 'things not just', μὴ δίκαια, at *Ap.* 32c1–2. In the *Crito* itself, at 48b11–12 πότερον δίκαιον...ἢ οὐ δίκαιον , 'whether it is just...or not just', stands parallel to 48c8–d2, πότερον δίκαια πράξομεν ἢ...ἀδικήσομεν, 'whether we shall be doing just things...or...committing injustice'. Similarly, 49a5–8 has οὐ δίκαιον, 'not just', in parallel with ἀδικεῖν, 'to commit injustice'. These passages show that where actions are up for moral appraisal, the distinction between the contrary and the contradictory of 'just' is insignificant. It does not follow from this that thinkers like Socrates and Plato were unable at the relevant period to make the distinction between contrary and contradictory, or incapable of imagining anything to which neither 'just' nor 'unjust' would apply. It is more likely that Plato's Socrates is assuming an ethic in which it is just to do what justice *permits* and unjust to do what justice does not permit. In non-technical contexts, an action that is not just is unjust.[84]

(c) Manly or unmanly?

Crito, then, imputes injustice to Socrates, if he stays to die. To that imputation Crito adds that of unmanly weakness. Socrates ought to choose, he says, not the lazy path of declining to bring up his sons, but the path a good and manly (ἀνδρεῖος) man would choose. This is a reversal of norms: 'manliness' was very commonly courage, in particular the soldier's virtue of facing up to death. Here, on the contrary, it is to be shown in escaping from death and persisting in the education of Socrates' sons. In the unphilosophical language of Laches in his dialogue (192b9), it is a kind of endurance, καρτερία τις. Crito's choice of expressions is interesting for a further reason, perceptible in Plato's day only to advanced and careful Platonists. Socrates ought to choose as a 'good and manly man' would; that closely associates, if it does not equate, manliness with the quality of a good man. Crito points out with a tinge of sarcasm that Socrates says he has cared about goodness all his life. This leaves problematic, as several of Socrates' Platonic interlocutors do, the relation between justice, 'manliness', and goodness.[85] The point does not detain Socrates here, and would certainly not detain any unpractised reader of Plato, but it is worth observing that Socrates gives to the Laws of Athens at 53e6 the similarly problematic expression 'justice and the rest of goodness'. Socrates, and his creatures the Laws, can in dialectic use an opponent's explicit or implicit doctrine against him, even if the doctrine evinces what Plato's Socrates might call confusion. Crito is in this respect typical of Socrates' interlocutors, and Socrates' treatment of him is characteristic. One thing, however, which distinguishes Crito from some others, such as Thrasymachus in *Republic* I, is the high value he appears in practice to put on justice.

(d) An argument from reputation

It has surprised some readers that Crito should next turn to an argument looking somewhat like the one from reputation which Socrates had earlier rejected, with Crito's reluctant acquiescence, at 44b–e. Many modern scholars[86] seem to roll into one that earlier argument together with the argument developed here at 45d9 ff.

'Since', Crito says at 45d9, 'I am ashamed for you and for us your friends, in case the whole matter concerning you should be thought to have been conducted in an unmanly way by us, both the coming of the case to trial when it was allowable to avoid its coming to trial, and the actual fighting of the case, and the climax, as it were the reduction of the affair to absurdity, that it should be thought to have slipped through our fingers because of our own cowardice (κακία) and unmanliness, when we did not save you, nor did you save yourself, when it was possible and achievable if we had been the slightest use. So, Socrates, see to it that this behaviour isn't, not only bad, but also shameful both to you and to us…'

Reputation is concerned here in the expressions 'you should be thought', 'it should be thought', and 'shameful' (αἰσχρόν). It not only might seem surprising that Crito should thus advance an argument here from reputation after Socrates' rejection of the previous similar one; it might surprise also that *Socrates* should not point out that he has already rejected a similar argument, but should rather launch into a further, and different, argument about the 'many', especially from 47a to 48b.

Plato, however, has engineered certain material dissimilarities between Crito's original argument at 44b–d and its successor at 45d–46e. The former argued explicitly from the opinions of many people, and, at Socrates' prompting, of 'the many'; the latter does not, and indeed does not specify at all the holders of the opinions it mentions. The earlier argument explicitly labelled 'the many' as ignorant of certain relevant particulars; the later does not, and indeed says nothing of the ignorance of the unidentified holders of the relevant opinions. The earlier said nothing of the badness of any conduct of Socrates' or of his closest friends; the later urges Socrates to take care that his conduct is not [*not*, here, 'is not thought to be'] shameful as well as bad.[87] This implies, conversationally speaking, that it is indeed bad. The particular vice or bad quality hinted at is, in context, unmanliness. This is not merely hearsay, or the opinions of others; it is apparently at least in part Crito's own opinion of the matter. There is enough here to give Socrates pause, enough to make his earlier rejection of an argument from people's opinions, or public opinion, inoperative in the new context. There are enough dissimilarities, too, to show how Crito, and even unphilosophical readers, could believe that he was offering a substantially new argument, not affected by his abandonment of the earlier one.

Indeed, in the absence of any mention by the later argument of '(the) many' or of their power, or of their ignorance, or for that matter of giving priority to money over friends, there is no obvious reason why the unphilosophical reader should have conflated the two arguments. One wonders why attentive and scholarly readers should ever have conflated them. There is room for substantial doubt whether Plato even reckoned with the possibility of their conflation. We do not have here a piece of writing on two levels. We have rather, in my judgment, a straightforward composition which some have misinterpreted.

Crito's values are not Socratic, but conventional, so far as the reader can tell.[88] Some spots the leopard cannot change. What Crito means by 'virtue' or 'goodness' (ἀρετή) need not be, and in the end turns out not to be, what Socrates would call 'goodness'. As many commentators have remarked, even though Socrates would accept that 'manliness' or courage is a virtue – perhaps even the whole of virtue – his notion of courage seems, at least in Plato's writings, very different from anything likely to be in Crito's mind. Nevertheless, Crito does here advance, in C. Emlyn-Jones' useful words on 45e2, a 'direct moral argument', even if Crito returns at once to the question how Socrates' behaviour will look to someone unspecified. The argument remains in part directly moral whatever the morality may be. The nature of Crito's morality and the meanings he gives to moral terms do not make it, for him, any the less a directly moral argument. If it is for him a directly moral argument, then Socrates is behaving quite normally in examining the morality of it. The 'early' Platonic Socrates spends much of his time countering moral views differing from his own even though couched in language he could have used himself.

But we need, as ever, to analyse the relevance in the new context of Socrates' subsequent fresh arguments, including the one about opinions. We should also seek reasons why, in the course of the dialectical discussion, Crito gives Socrates the answers he requires – unless, that is, Plato has arbitrarily manipulated Crito, in which case philosophical analysis might as well cease forthwith. The analysis inevitably touches on the reactions of the careful and philosophically alert members of Plato's intended readership. The precision with which he writes would no doubt escape a reader reading only for the drama. To keep him interested, this unphilosophical reader could enjoy, as we shall shortly see, some splendid rhetoric. The style of argument Socrates thus adopts needs examination to prepare for comparison with that of the 'Laws of Athens' later.

5

SOCRATES' ATTACK: FIRST WAVE

(a) **General**

My reader might expect to find here a summary of the characterization of Socrates in the *Crito*. But little in the argument hangs on that, as opposed to the perception of Socrates we can attribute to Crito. We may therefore let Socrates' character emerge gradually in the course of the discussion. To do this is, after all, to follow Plato's example. Some traits will have emerged already, e.g., Socrates' indifference in the face of death. There is little point in rehearsing here characteristics appearing in dialogues only doubtfully available to the *Crito's* original readers. R. Blondell and M. Burnyeat have recently offered lists of them.[89] Of Burnyeat's list only one – Socrates' staying in Athens all his life – appears in the *Crito.* Famous characteristics such as Socrates' ugliness, his habit of swearing 'by the Dog', his sexual interests and behaviour, appear in Plato only sporadically. They are not obviously either presupposed or presented in the *Crito.* His indifference to death, however, in *Crito* and *Apology*, squares well with his military prowess mentioned in the *Laches.*

(b) **Argumentative style**

In reply to Crito's long and rhetorically styled speech trying to persuade him to escape, Socrates in his turn launches into a harangue.[90] True, the harangue takes, characteristically for Plato's Socrates, a partly interrogative form. The questions, though, are in a sense rhetorical and he does not stay for an answer. The simile of the bugbear (46c3–6), the triad of abstract plurals 'imprisonments, deaths, and deprivations of money' (46c5–6), and above all the hammer-blow repetitions, mark out this speech as impassioned rhetoric. 'Was it well said…?' recurs in one grammatical form or another at 46c8–d1, 46d3, 46c2–3, and, with 'adequately' for 'well', 47a2, to say nothing of 'Is this not well said?' at 47a5; 'on each occasion' is repeated from 46d1 to 46d8; 'some opinions…and some not' recurs at 46d1–2, 46e1–2, 47a3–4; the contrast between 'all' and 'some' hits the reader twice at 47a 3–4; ideas are repeated in the pairs 'vainly for argument's sake' and 'childishness and nonsense' at 46d3–4, as previously in the doublet 'respect and honour' at 46c1. Socrates in dialectical flow does not always, or even usually, speak with this kind of emphasis, as practised readers of Plato would have known. But Crito has just concluded a similarly emphatic speech. In Crito's passage 45c6–46a9, observe the repetitions of ἔξον, 'when it is allowed' at 45c7, 45d1, and 45e4; of the root σπευ- at 45c8–9; of parts of τυγχάνω at 45d1–2; of ὀρφαν- in 'in orphanhoods concerning orphans' at 45d4; of the word 'choose' in αἱρεῖσθαι, ἕλοιτο, and αἱρεῖσθαι again at 45d7–8; the antithesis (at a distance) between a good and manly man (ἀνὴρ ἀγαθὸς καὶ ἀνδρεῖος) at 45d7 and some badness and unmanliness (κακία καὶ ἀνανδρία) at 45e6, the latter phrase recalling 'unmanliness' (ἀνανδρία) at 45e2; the repetitive 'entry' (εἴσοδος) with corresponding verbs 'entered' and 'to enter' (εἰσῆλθεν and εἰσελθεῖν) at 45e3–4; the repeated root δικ- (roughly 'just-') at 45e3–4; the repeated idea of possibility (οἷόν τε ὂν καὶ δυνατόν) at 46a2 and correspondingly at 46a7 of impossibility (ἀδύνατον καὶ οὐκέτι οἷόν τε); the repeated root βουλ- ('counsel, decision') at 46a4–5. Socrates well speaks of Crito's ardour, προθυμία, at 46b1; his own contribution begins immediately and obviously in the same vein.[91]

Two consequences flow from this. The first is that Crito's ardour should not be read by anyone as the result of an emotional distraction which Socrates does not share. It does not form part of the contrast between Socrates and Crito at all. Both are speaking forcefully and with rhetorical emphasis; neither, in all probability, is driven by emotion to incoherence of syntax or of thought. Moreover, it would be a curious emotional distraction which lent itself to the careful shaping of Crito's whole speech. The speech begins at 44b7 with 'Even now, be persuaded by me and escape'; it ends at 46a7–9 with the similar but much more vehement 'But by all means…be persuaded by me and do not act in any way otherwise'; it is punctuated at 45a3, also at paragraph-end, by the moderately vehement 'But be persuaded by me and do not act otherwise.'[92] Moreover, it is Crito's persuasive cunning rather than mere emotion which repeatedly joins both Socrates and his friends in the potential blame for what Crito dreads will happen: at 46a1 'I am ashamed…for you and for us…we who did not save you, nor did you save yourself…lest it be both bad and shameful both to you and to us.'

The second consequence, accordingly, is that Socrates, before embarking on the more evidently dialectical portion of his response to Crito, feels himself entitled to emulate the kind of persuasive technique, by no means dialectical, which his interlocutor has availed himself of. Crito, as we saw, is sufficiently alert to dialectical possibilities to throw Socrates' words back at him. He does not, however, deploy the other weapons in the Platonic Socrates' usual armoury, and, for a single paragraph here, neither does Socrates. Accordingly, if and when Socrates, later in his response, reverts to a rhetorical manner, even Platonically experienced readers have no right to be surprised; what Socrates can legitimately do once he can legitimately do more than once. Confronted with a Crito who, despite singular pronouns, addresses him rather as if he were a crowd, Socrates, too, is entitled to express himself with rhetorical force. Does not Socrates actually say at 46b1–2 that Crito's ardour [which is clearly audible in his style] would be very valuable if only Crito were right? Socrates in this dialogue shows at this relatively early stage his propensity for casting back at his opponent not only the opponent's phraseology and specific argument but also his style of argumentation.[93]

Socrates himself makes another preliminary point. Starting at 46b4 he says: 'This is not the first time for me. I have always been the kind of man to obey nothing and nobody else of mine other than the argument which seems best to me in discussion.' *Socrates* thus makes clear that (1) he is going to follow the *argument* which seems to him best, and not (for example) either fears or worldly desires; (2) he is going to follow the argument which seems to *him* best, and not to his friend(s); and (3) such has always been his practice. *Plato* could hardly have made it clearer by any words than he does by 'I have always been the kind of man…' that he regards the argument here carried on between Socrates and Crito as paradigmatic for his Socrates' arguments about single particular moral decisions. Since it is indeed paradigmatic, Plato never again needed to have his Socrates deliberate, or rather argue about, a single specific practical and moral decision. Indeed, as portraying such a deliberation and decision, the *Crito* is unique in Plato's writings. One thing fitting it for this uniqueness is Socrates' confrontation here with what one may call the ultimate choice, between justice and life itself. Its uniqueness is not, of course, a reason for suspecting the authenticity of the dialogue.[94] What the passage does suggest is a motive – not necessarily the sole motive – for Plato's having written the dialogue at all. One motive in Plato's mind may have been to show his Socrates resting a specific decision on his own general ethical arguments, regardless of other considerations, and to suggest that this was his Socrates' normal practice. He would thus avoid any possible charge that his Socrates talks in abstractions irrelevant to actual problems of conduct. This would remain a valid point even if, as is plausible, the Platonic Socrates' actual solutions to moral dilemmas, including the one depicted in the *Crito*, did not commend themselves readily to ordinary citizens.

(c) Dialectic begins

Socrates' rhetorical paragraph leads up to his question for Crito at 47a2–5, where dialectical analysis of the first wave of Socrates' attack on Crito should begin. He asks, then, whether all opinions should be respected, or only some; and whether the opinions of all human beings should be respected or only those of some. Evidently practised readers would find here two questions, not one; it might or might not be the case that everybody has at least one opinion deserving respect and at least one opinion not deserving respect. The antecedents of this pair of questions in the dialogue earn the attention not, one may suspect, of ordinary, first-time readers, but of experienced, studying and remembering ones. In an earlier exchange, at 44b–d, Crito argued that one ought to pay attention to certain opinions and to the opinions of certain people in particular ('the many'), because of their power. Socrates in reply did not reject either the notion of certain opinions deserving respect or that of certain people's opinions deserving respect. Indeed he suggested fairly explicitly (44c7–8) that the opinions of the most reasonable people, the ἐπιεικέστατοι, merited at least *more* attention or respect than those of the many. Crito subsequently abandoned his side of this argument. In doing so, he left Plato's more philosophical readers and doubtless, in Plato's imagination, Socrates too, in some doubt as to precisely which propositions he had abandoned. In his later argument at 45d–46a Crito certainly means that some opinions should be attended to but he does not say whose, or why they deserve attention. If he is sensible, he will be hoping that Socrates will take him to be attending to the justifiable opinions of those reasonable and qualified to have them, conceivably including Crito himself. Yet, though Crito is assuredly no fool, neither Socrates nor we can be sure how sensible Crito is on this particular issue. It is thus quite natural for Socrates to ask his opening double question, couched in general terms to take account of Crito's vagueness at 45e1 ('seems', δόξῃ, without mentioning to whom); and it is natural also for Crito to elucidate his views as he does. Readers unaccustomed to such niceties will have had the rhetoric, the characterization of Socrates as steadfast in consistency, a touch of sarcasm at Crito's expense and much else to entertain them. They may also have wondered how the argument will proceed that starts with such seemingly artless and obvious questions.

Crito's next answers, at 47a6–11, show his acceptance that good, but not defective, opinions deserve respect, and that good opinions are those not of the powerful but of the intelligent, φρόνιμοι. These people are clearly related to the most reasonable or best qualified, ἐπιεικέστατοι, mentioned by Socrates at 44c7 in contrast to 'the many'.[95] Crito has changed approach or general position from his formulation in the earlier argument. Such a change offers to readers with exact memories the choice between a pair of perfectly acceptable hypotheses. Either the earlier argument was *ad hoc* and did not represent Crito's considered views after most of a lifetime as Socrates' friend, or Crito, having perceived that he was getting nowhere with the earlier argument, has decided to adopt a line more likely to prove persuasive in *ad hominem* argument against the master of *ad hominem* argument. If Crito is adapting his argument to his interlocutor, he has at least been given a recent incentive to do so: at 46c3–6 Socrates rejected the 'bugbear' deployed by the many; it was on the power of the many to deploy it that Crito based the earlier argument from opinions. This would show us a Crito who abandons views or propositions not just because Socrates suggests contrary ones and he does not have the wit or the strength to say 'No', but rather because he is alert to the requirements of his argument in a changed situation created by Socrates' reactions. It is not easy to see why scholars do not in charity give Crito the benefit of any doubt there may be here.

Socrates needs and requests further clarification. Who are these 'intelligent' people? How numerous are they? Are they 'many'? The question might arise in general because some Athenians held, though not all of them will have articulated, the view that any Tom, Dick or Harry had a right to an opinion on questions of right and wrong.[96] The range of 'intelligent' or perhaps of 'sensible' people on such questions might accordingly be wide enough to lead us back to 'the many'. More specifically to this dialogue, the range of people Crito would call 'intelligent' is not clear from his remarks at 45d–46a. Clearly he must refer to people whose moral judgment he respects or thinks Socrates will respect. But who are these people, even if they include himself, and how numerous are they? In the process of clarification Socrates advances some tendentiously expressed arguments based on leading questions and difficult choices. Plato cannot have expected his more naïve readers to detect just how tendentious, leading, and problematic they are, but will rather have hoped to sweep them along with what may fairly be called the rhetoric of Socrates' dialectic.

A case in point is the choice he offers Crito to start with at 47a12–b11. Take a practising athlete: does he attend to the opinion of every Tom, Dick or Harry, or to that (literally) 'of that one man alone whoever happens to be a doctor or trainer' [and is therefore knowledgeable or expert in the field]? In Greek the last part of this is ἑνὸς μόνου ἐκείνου ὃς ἂν τυγχάνῃ ἰατρὸς ἢ παιδοτρίβης ὤν; It seems on analysis to be three questions telescoped into one: does the professional listen to experts only? Is he prepared to listen only to a single expert? Or does he listen to everyone, whether expert or not? Not many, now or in Plato's time, would hesitate before agreeing that high-class athletes seek expert advice. But beyond this there are complications, and Plato's Greek here is not, to non-native speakers, immediately perspicuous; indeed it may have caused some initial difficulty to the more attentive of his Athenian contemporaries.

The tricky clause just quoted could conceivably, in the Greek, be read in any one of three different ways:

(a) 'of whichever single, only man, happens to be a doctor or trainer';

(b) 'of that single, only, man who is a doctor or trainer, whoever he may be';

(c) 'of that single, only, man, whoever he may be, who is the athlete's own personal doctor or trainer'.

It is necessary to look at each of these three possibilities.

Reading (a), one can very easily make sense of what is being said in the sentence as a whole. The athlete takes advice from any expert. Barring conflict between experts, a kind of conflict Plato seldom if ever recognized, athletes listen to experts. But the expression of what is thus meant leaves, on this reading, something to be desired. For the words 'single' and 'only' (ἑνός and μόνου) are now wholly redundant in logic. There is no logical reason for their presence; they are there only for rhetorical reasons, to constitute a sharp antithesis with 'every man' in the preceding clause. Taking this sentence in isolation, one could easily accept this. But its consequences for the context are perhaps harder to bear. Crito answers simply 'of one man alone', suggesting that for him the words 'one, alone' or 'single, by himself', are the key words in Socrates' question's second alternative. Socrates' next speech mentions the praise or blame 'of that one man [that we mentioned] rather than those of the many', (τοῦ ἑνός ἐκείνου ἀλλὰ μὴ . . . τῶν πολλῶν), suggesting that for him too the singleness, the uniqueness if you like, of the expert in question was the cardinal point. Socrates continues in the same vein in his next speech too, and, in the other half of the analogy he comes up with, at 47d1. To adopt reading (a) we should have to suppose that Crito bases his reply, and Socrates his argument, in large measure on an accident of rhetoric.

This is a somewhat unprepossessing supposition; there remains, however, a question whether Plato simply went with the flow of his own rhetoric, and another question whether novice readers would have seen anything wrong in his doing so. Crito certainly shows no sign of detecting the problematic nature of what is being put to him here. The unphilosophical Crito is in fact in a very similar position to the unphilosophical reader. Socrates' shrewd questioning will lead such readers, if they persist, away from a simple reliance on untrained, uneducated opinion to consideration of a truth not necessarily in tune with inexpert opinion. It will persuade Crito, and is no doubt intended to persuade any philosophical novice, that deeper reflection, going beyond superficial commonplaces, is a proper requirement of moral decision-making. Plato's philosophically mature readers, on the other hand, will have spotted at least some of the rather cleverly laid snares that Crito falls into. Spotting them, they will perhaps have seen looming up a rather delicate question: has Plato's Socrates, and has Plato himself, the right to deploy arguments which, to be polite, are less than cogent, in order to obtain people's attention for more serious, more strenuous, and more exact philosophical reasoning?

This question confronts also the modern interpreter: should we continue to read and admire a thinker who can perpetrate such fallacious arguments? Which would be the more attractive prospect for Plato's admirers, to suppose him to have set these snares knowingly, or to suppose him to have found, himself, no fault with the argument? It might be fair to say that by the time a reader has learnt enough to detect the fallacies the argument will have achieved its aim, to interest the reader in philosophy. For better or worse, the present analysis rests on the belief that Plato did know what he was doing, did lay traps on purpose, and was not scrupulous in the means he used to draw people into philosophy, but that once drawn in, he took them seriously and subjected them, as his Socrates subjects Crito in the second half of this dialogue, to serious reasoning. That reasoning, in order to be serious, does not have to be 'philosophical' in quite the modern sense. It could be dialectical, basing itself on the words and whole position of the respondent; but that need not make it anything but serious.

To continue the analysis: in order to make sense of alternative (c), which looks like our better bet of the remaining two, we have to supply in some way personal possessive pronouns which are not actually present in the Greek. We have, in other words, following talk of an athlete, to make Plato's Greek talk of 'his' doctor or trainer, the athlete's personal expert to whom alone he defers. One could support such an understanding of the Greek by reference to 47b10–11: there the definite article in the phrase τῷ ἐπιστάτῃ καὶ ἐπαΐοντι could, at least at first glance, be rendered, as often, by a personal possessive: 'his overseer and expert [literally 'knowing person']'. The possessive goes better with the noun 'overseer' than with the participle 'knowing', though one could perhaps stretch a point. But such expedients would not help other definite articles in this passage: the first one, at b10, in τῷ ἑνί, 'the one man', surely does not refer to 'his' one man, but refers, in the normal 'anaphoric' usage,[97] to 'the' one man mentioned earlier; and in any case the articles at 47b10 come two speeches after the phrase at 47b3 which particularly interests us here. If Plato's Socrates had meant 'his' doctor or trainer, the place to introduce an article or other potentially possessive expression was in the phrase under discussion, that is at 47b3. If this argument stands, then the Greek offers no support for the otherwise plausible-looking alternative (c), which we must accordingly rule out on linguistic grounds. No reason is visible for any even passably exact ancient reader to want to read the passage in this way.

Linguistic grounds here receive reinforcement from dialectical ones. The purpose of this whole argument must be in context to refute the notion of a group of φρόνιμοι, of 'intelligent people' whose opinion deserves respect. But as every athlete knows, expertise in the field is not restricted to his own trainer, and the opinions of any competent trainer deserve respect. In order to wean Crito by dialectic away from the notion of a group of intelligent and knowledgeable people to whom reference may and should be made, Socrates cannot legitimately use an illustration which treats expertise as belonging to members of an indefinitely large group. If Socrates is indeed talking of an expert group, while concealing his point from Crito with a smokescreen of words, then, as on the view adopted below, Socrates is using shady tactics in his questioning.

So, ruling out (c) thus, and perhaps feeling uncomfortable with (a) as we read on, we ask ourselves whether the alternative (b) might be what Socrates intends after all, implausible though it may sound to us. There is no doubt of its implausibility: there are of course many doctors, many trainers; to suggest that there is one unique expert in the field is, on the face of it, nonsense.[98] And yet this seems to be what the context demands, and what both Crito and Socrates appear to think has gained Crito's assent. How did Crito land in this mess? Regrettable though it may seem, it was because Socrates asked him a tricky question which he did not see through. Socrates laid before Crito a choice between the athlete's deferring to one man and his deferring to every man. Crito can see that 'the many' – whose relationship to 'every man' is sufficiently obvious – are ignorant. He has spoken of 'many' as ignorant on a relevant topic at 44b ('who do not know you and me well'). When challenged on why one should attend to 'the many' he spoke of their power; but their power is not relevant to the athlete in his choice of trainer: the 'many' are not about to kill the athlete.[99] The contrast Socrates draws between 'every man' and the 'expert' strikes a chord in Crito's mind. Faced with the stark choice between the ignorant many and the single expert, Crito chooses, since choose he thinks he must, the single expert.

Why does Crito not say: 'Socrates, that's a tricky question, and I don't want to make either choice you lay before me'? Perhaps because he lacks the necessary quickness of mind; he is alert, as we have seen, but not *that* alert. If one is inclined to suppose that that makes him a fool, or that Plato is arbitrarily switching Crito's alertness on and off as it suits him, one should perhaps ask how many modern scholars have noticed this particular point. A partial excuse for Crito's lapse here is that he may hear in Socrates' potentially ambiguous second choice echoes of interpretations (a) and/or (c) above, which are relatively harmless, and he may thus fail to realize quite what he is letting himself in for. In this failure he will doubtless have been not unlike many of Plato's intended readers, whether more or less philosophically sophisticated. The way Socrates has expressed his question is tricky in more ways than one; it is easily understandable that Crito should fall into his trap. What we have here is a Crito less skilled in dialectic than Socrates, not a mere un-philosophical fool. We find Plato relying on at least some readers' being also less skilled in dialectic than his Socrates, which does not make them merely stupid either.

In itself the general proposition that disregard for expert advice is dangerous would have found widespread agreement. Disobedience to, or failure to attend to, expert opinion or advice can reasonably be expected to have consequences harmful to the athlete. Bodily fitness will indeed suffer for disobedience to an expert trainer incapable, being an expert, of mistakes, in obedience instead to the inexpert majority. The body will suffer at least to the extent that the athlete will end up less fit than he would otherwise have become, and, relatively speaking, will be ruined.[100] This much Plato can have Crito accept without compromising his common sense or intelligence. Plato leaves out of account only the trainer's contribution to his athlete's morale, which we value so highly nowadays.[101]

(d) The single moral expert

Even the immediate leap at 47c8 to a generalization, 'Then in the other cases, Crito, the same applies', is not in this instance obviously hard to swallow. But, nevertheless, the particular case Socrates turns out to be interested in, that of moral judgments, presents some difficulties, better known to modern readers than to those of Plato's time. Should one, in moral questions, or other questions of value, respect the opinion of 'the many' or of 'the one man, if there is any expert, whom one ought both to respect and fear more than everybody else'? Socrates loads the question by adding the description of the single expert, if there is one, 'in disobedience to whom we shall destroy and harm what we used to say was improved by justice and destroyed by injustice; or is there no such thing?' The general difficulties of supposing there to be a moral expert have been expounded in our time by no-one more clearly than J.R. Bambrough.[102] Noticeably to the modern reader, Socrates (a) hedges his bets here, with the condition 'if there is one', and (b) hedges his bets the other way at *Ap.* 23a, '*Probably* [my emphasis] only the god is wise.' Although Plato's less practised readers will certainly not have been conversant with these points, and even his more practised ones will presumably have been at best a little vague about them, both classes of ancient reader will have found relevant the question *who is* the 'single expert' in the *Crito.* The following considerations are relevant to their choice:

First, the suggestion that the 'moral expert' is the personified Laws of Athens who appear later exhibits little plausibility.[103] For unphilosophical first-time readers it exhibits even zero plausibility: the Laws would not, at this moment when they first come across the single expert, enter their heads. For those reading the dialogue again, the Laws cannot be 'the one who knows', partly because they are plural. They refer to themselves as 'we', and the alternative, singular designation (50a8) at 'the community of the city', τὸ κοινὸν τῆς πόλεως, occurs less frequently and with less emphasis. This might in a different context be a trivial point, but not here, where Socrates makes so much of the expert's singularity. Moreover, at least experienced and thorough readers would discard the suggestion that the Laws or the community of Athens are repositories of moral wisdom. They would be aware that the suggestion would be repugnant to Plato's Socrates in general and to Crito. For Crito, the Laws and the city, when they eventually appear, would seem at first to represent the voice of the 'many'. Moreover, he believes that the city treated Socrates unjustly – one cites 50c below, but Crito's whole attitude from the start proclaims his rejection of the court's verdict on Socrates. That Plato and his Socrates would in general find this suggested identification repugnant is evident from, among other places, Socrates' vain search in the *Apology* for just such a repository of moral wisdom. This search explains Socrates' noticeable caution in his expressions at *Crito* 47c11–d3, whether that caution was actually noticed by readers or not.

But R. Polansky offers a modified version of the theory that the Laws of Athens are the 'one expert'.[104] On his version, 'in the coming argument Socrates can introduce the Laws as a *stand-in* for the knower as expert. The law may oversee and direct deliberation about what is just and unjust'. Polansky supports this with (1) *Politicus* 292–302, where, as he says, 'it is in part the absence of a completely wise ruler to serve everywhere that makes the rule of law necessary and appropriate'. He adds (2) 'The rule of law is not a merely external authority because citizens have agreed to it.' Now (2) seems to me irrelevant: the Laws do not possess knowledge or some slightly lesser epistemological grade because the citizens have agreed to their rule – even if they have so agreed, a question which must keep till later. To Polansky's (1) one could add that in *Apology* (19a6–7) Socrates says he ought to obey the law (τῷ δὲ νόμῳ πειστέον). Again at 32b9 he prefers on the occasion of the trial of the generals after Arginusae to stand 'on the side of the law and the just' (μετὰ τοῦ νόμου καὶ τοῦ δικαίου). Certainly the Platonic Socrates has a considerable respect for the law, however we construe the Laws' harangue at the *Crito*'s end. One might suppose that the Laws could *stand in for* the singular hypothetical knower even if not themselves singular. But if they do, then again *at the place in the dialogue where the single knower is mentioned*, Crito is not going to think of them as such, or accept their authority. What should make Crito, or readers like him, think *here* of the laws of Athens as stand-in experts? So far as Crito at this juncture is concerned the laws of Athens (if he thinks of them at all) have allowed Socrates' unjust condemnation; and these are experts on justice? And *later*, we come up against the obstacle that a stand-in for the one man who hypothetically knows can only be someone who, also hypothetically, does not know. But if someone or something does not know the relevant field there is always, according to the argument, a risk of harm from obedience to him, her or it. Further, the risk may be extreme, for Socrates and Crito have acknowledged no degrees of ignorance: they speak only of the knowledgeable and the ignorant.

Secondly, if the Laws are ruled out, is Socrates himself the 'one who knows'? Against this, it is difficult to find examples of Socrates in the 'early' dialogues claiming openly to be a moral expert: e.g., at *Ap.* 37a6–7 Socrates says he *believes* or 'is persuaded' that he has not *deliberately*, i.e. (in this context) knowingly, wronged anyone. At *Ap.* 41c8–d5 he does offer the jury a hint that he is a good man, but without actually saying so, and without laying claim to the kind of moral expertise he attributes to 'the god'.[105] Further, if Socrates were to present himself in the *Crito* as the one moral expert, nothing guarantees that Crito would accept him as such. Socrates never speaks to Crito with that kind of authority; he seeks rather to obtain Crito's agreement in discussion (48e). Indeed, Socrates speaks as if his judgment in the matter were provisional, even tentative: 'Let us consider the question together,' he says at 48d9, 'and if you have any counter to what I say, counter it, and I will do as you say...'; far from laying down the law to Crito, he asks him to consider the acceptability or otherwise of what he terms at 48e5 τῆς σκέψεως τὴν ἀρχήν, 'the beginning of the inquiry'. Within this dialogue as a whole, let alone in Plato's 'early' dialogues at large, it would make little sense for Socrates to assume the air or the airs of a moral expert. Whatever Plato may have intended his readers to think, his Socrates cannot consistently refer to himself as possessing moral expertise. Some readers might, at this early stage of the *Crito*, suppose Plato to be setting up his Socrates, and perhaps by implication himself, as an expert in morals. We cannot know how far Plato himself would have wished such readers to think thus. But even if Plato does mean the words here to apply to himself or his Socrates, he must still, as a dramatist, have had in mind another reference for Socrates' words as those of a character in the drama, and perhaps another reference also for his practised readers.[106]

Thirdly, if Socrates does not think himself a moral expert, *a fortiori* he does not think Crito is one either. Socrates has already by now pretty clearly rejected Crito's declared respect for the opinions of 'the many', and is going to reject the opinions of many respectable people. Later on, for students of the dialogue as a whole, Socrates actively controverts, through the personified Laws, Crito's initial perception of how justice stands in the case at issue; and, whether Socrates is speaking through the Laws or not, in the end he does not act on Crito's initial perceptions. He does not therefore at any point in this dialogue treat Crito as an authoritative expert on questions of morality, to be obeyed on pain of dire consequences. The same argument shows that Plato too cannot have in mind for Crito the status of moral expert.

Fourthly there remains the interesting suggestion of E. Benitez that the 'one who knows' is perhaps a divine person.[107] For Platonically innocent readers this would not work; there is no reason why they should think of it in this context, even though the Greeks tended when thinking about gods to think of them as knowing everything. For those readers who knew at least Plato's *Apology*, the divinity of the one who knows would at least make sense for both Plato and his Socrates. Benitez well cites *Ap.* 23a, and one may add a reference to the last sentence of the *Crito*, referring to the god's guidance. But neither for Crito nor for ordinary readers of this whole context in the dialogue should one suppose that the god who knows is relevant here. For how should Socrates and Crito even in principle gain access to any indisputable divine message in their quandary? Or indeed, under normal circumstances, how should the readers? The dream of Socrates, as we have seen, is not clear beyond dispute; and what else is there in this dialogue which helps here? If the single expert is the god, then he could be of no practical use to the participants in or the readers of the dialogue. It is too late to send even post haste to Delphi.

These considerations suggest that the 'one who knows' is no personage, but rather a dialectical device. But a dialectical device may have a serious purpose – and indeed for Plato's Socrates dialectic is a serious activity. The purpose here could include, but need not end with, Socrates' intention, irrespective of his own commitment or lack of it, to commit Crito to entertainment of the notion of a single expert, one expert only, in each relevant field. Why? Because, I suggest, it will help in driving Crito out of *any* position relying on shame before a group of more persons than one. In this context Crito will then not be able to appeal even to the ἐπιεικέστατοι, the reasonable people, of 44e7 or the φρόνιμοι, the sensible people, of 47a9. In default of any obviously identifiable single moral expert this will force Crito back on the argument between himself and Socrates, as it develops. Plato drives his readers also in the same direction. This has the useful effect that when at the very end of the dialogue Crito is silenced there is, as it were, no-one left to take the discussion further; it is truly finished.

One way, indeed, in which 'the single expert' is a tendentious expression is that if there is a single, sole expert[108] then any plural group will be unreliable. It is instructive, for the student of Socratic dialectic, to observe how Socrates pushes the argument towards this point. At 47a9 Socrates asks whether good opinions are those of the sensible or wise (φρόνιμοι) and defective ones those of the foolish (ἄφρονες). Here the 'wise' are plural. Socrates arrives at the singular by contemplating in his next question a single athlete, who may naturally lead to the thought of a single doctor or trainer. Socrates is thus making use (illegitimately, as we have seen) of the association of a single athlete with a single trainer in a normally one-to-one relationship, even if he does not use any possessive pronoun which would clarify the relation. Having brought into play the single doctor or trainer, Socrates at b1–2 in the same question builds a contrast between every [and any] man (παντὸς ἀνδρός) and the single doctor or trainer from whom we started this discussion. The following question[109] takes the easy step from 'any and every' to 'the many', τῶν πολλῶν. This Socrates follows up by 'all the rest' in the plural, σύμπασι τοῖς ἄλλοις. A further easement of this transition would be the earlier words about paying attention to the opinions of the 'many' at 44c6–7 and 44d1–2, words still echoing in the reader's, and presumably in Crito's, mind. Hence the reference at 47b6–7 to 'the praises of that one man but not of the many'. Moreover, when at 47b6–7 the singular expert is placed in strong antithesis with the necessarily plural 'many', the introduction of both the single man and the 'many' is facilitated by the antitheses. By this time Crito, and the unphilosophical reader, could scarcely be expected to feel any tension between his previous acceptance of 'sensible people' in the plural and the singular expert. Indeed, if Crito thinks about this at all, he might be supposed, in a reader's imagination, to think that the earlier plural referred to experts in different and plural fields. More of the same sort follows. The question or statement[110] contrasting the single expert with 'everyone else' (σύμπασι τοῖς ἄλλοις) picks up on 'any/every man', παντὸς ἀνδρός at 47b1, while firmly tying down the singularity of the expert. That accomplished, Socrates can refer to the 'many' at 47c2–3 as 'knowing nothing' (μηδὲν ἐπαϊόντων). Since there is only one man who 'knows', clearly the 'many' do not know, and indeed do not know anything. This makes it all the more plausible that to attend to the views of any but the expert is harmful.

But it is not obvious that no-one but the expert knows *anything*; that is true only if one cannot really know any item within a subject (ἐπιστήμη or τέχνη) without grasping the whole subject. Now Crito and his like might accept, or at least let pass, this not wholly untenable view. But in *Ap.* Plato's Socrates, for what another dialogue is worth on such a question, does not. There, after disclaiming knowledge of 'human and citizenly goodness' (20b4–c3), he claims to *know* that it is 'bad and shameful to act unjustly and disobey a superior' at 29b6–7. Evidently the point about expert knowledge is not obvious. It seems less likely that Plato makes Socrates in the *Crito* rely on Crito's acceptance of a far from obvious point than that Socrates is deliberately leading Crito on, step by step, to a conclusion he need not accept, and would not have accepted without such a gradual extension of what he is being asked to agree to. The extension would be imperceptible to an average man arguing 'on his feet' or reading casually.

That Crito does agree here is less of a tribute to his stupidity, which is not abnormal, than to Socrates' dialectical skill, which is. The point needs emphasizing, since there exists – though it is not universal – a scholarly tendency to pick holes in Socrates' dialectical arguments and then to suppose the interlocutor stupid, thick-headed, or at least intellectually slow, because he has not spotted the flaw in the argument. What Plato portrays in passages of this sort is not a stupid or easygoing respondent failing to see the obvious; it is Socrates deploying all the techniques of the skilled interrogator to drive the victim to the conclusion Socrates desires. Unsophisticated readers also would naturally be expected to succumb to this Socrates' skills, though real philosophers *should* have seen through the complications Socrates introduces. But surely such techniques are disreputable, and ought to form part of no serious philosophical discussion? It is not my purpose at this point to renew discussion of the general question whether Plato ought to have made his Socrates descend to the disreputable; more germane to the present passage in the *Crito* is a different question: what function in the dialogue does the present argument fulfil? The answer to this is, in brief, a subsidiary function. The main argument, as we shall see in due course, is a great deal tighter. The present argument does not lead Crito to any substantive conclusion about the rights and wrongs of escaping from prison, or of helping an escape. It leads him rather to the point where he is prepared to start thinking about those rights and wrongs rather than merely rely on half-baked opinions drawn from popular views and feelings. As we saw, Plato may, and with some justice, have been less scrupulous about arguments of this protreptic kind than he was about substantive moral arguments.

Plato's Socrates has, anyway, a particular purpose here in guiding Crito's responses and commitments. Plato and his Socrates are constructing an analogue for a point about the moral part of Man. The point is that the opinions on moral matters of even respectable, reasonable and intelligent or sensible people (οἱ ἐπιεικέστατοι or οἱ φρόνιμοι) may safely be ignored. Such people are reduced to a single expert, who is not to hand, and all other opinions than his may be deemed unworthy of attention. Unpractised readers are probably not even intended to notice the dialectical, or rhetorical, sleights-of-hand leading to this reduction, any more than Crito does. If Plato troubles any of his prospective readers hereabouts it can only be the practised ones, experienced in analysing dialectic – and these will by definition have been convinced beforehand that the philosophical or dialectical enterprise is worth pursuing. It is a question whether Plato meant his readers to conclude that they should seek out the best possible teacher. That seems to be Socrates' conclusion at the end of the *Laches* (201a2–7). But one cannot read the end of the *Laches* directly into the *Crito.* And did Plato think of himself as the best possible teacher of right and wrong?

Once Socrates has achieved this reduction of the morally expert to one person, he can afford to relax, as it were. We no longer need for any dialectical purpose the singular sole expert on matters medical and gymnastic, 'singular' in more senses than one. But of course to abandon the sole expert at this juncture would be to demonstrate to sophisticated readers that the function of the sole expert in medical gymnastics was dialectical, that he was designed simply to found the argument for a single sole expert in morals. Now Socrates does exactly that: he abandons the single sole expert in medicine and gymnastics at 47d10. There those who know are plural: 'following not the opinion of those who know' (μὴ τῇ τῶν ἐπαϊόντων δόξῃ). One observes, with the editors, that Plato according to the MSS did not write, and there is no reason to suppose he intended, 'following the opinion of those who do not know', which would have been, with a different order of words, τῇ τῶν μὴ ἐπαϊόντων δόξῃ. The abandonment of the single knower of medicine and gymnastics the moment we have a singular expert in morals demonstrates indeed the dialectical purpose of the single expert in medicine and gymnastics. It also demonstrates that for both Plato and, presumably, the Socrates of the dialogue the purpose of introducing the single expert was mainly dialectical, though Plato *may* have had ulterior motives. Neither is unaware of the implausibility of supposing there to be only one expert trainer for the aspiring athlete.

Both use this implausible thing to confound Crito, and no doubt also the philosophically naïve reader.

(e) 'The one man and the truth'

The single moral expert re-appears a few lines later at 48a7, with the expression ὁ ἐπαΐων περὶ τῶν δικαίων καὶ τῶν ἀδίκων, ὁ εἷς καὶ αὐτὴ ἡ ἀλήθεια, 'the man who knows about things just and unjust, the one man and the truth itself'. Now by the time we have reached 48a7 Socrates has made his dialectical argument against Crito that 'the many' – that is to say, any plural group – are not worth serious attention.[111] The words Οὐκ ἄρα, 'not *accordingly*', at 48a5 signal arrival at the argument's conclusion. Having thus finished with the 'single-expert' idea in morals no less than in medicine and gymnastics, Socrates immediately drops it, and introduces a companion notion, that of the truth.[112] From now on, as we shall see in a moment, he operates not with the single expert, but with the truth. The suggestion that the single expert is a dialectical device again draws strength from this fact, that Socrates drops the 'single expert' *immediately* he announces his success in driving Crito out of his reliance on 'the many'. The thing is done in this one brief and neat phrase, 'the man who knows...the one man and the truth itself'. It is again extremely unlikely to be coincidental that the supersession of the single expert by 'the truth itself' should occur exactly at the very point where the single expert becomes dialectically otiose. Clearly the 'single expert', 'the knower, the one man', is a dialectical device.[113]

What is more, the *subsequent* argument of the dialogue is tested, not against the elusive single expert, but against the truth – however illusory the notion of truth may appear.[114] Thus:

48a10–b2: Socrates (if the MSS have rightly distributed the parts) or Crito (if Schanz's distribution is right)[115] sets the ball rolling by acknowledging the truth of the suggestion Socrates offers to Crito, that 'the many' can kill.

48c4–5: Socrates says that 'perhaps, in truth', (μὴ ὡς ἀληθῶς) Crito's considerations, or queries, are those of 'the many'.

48d2: The only question is whether escape will be just 'or in truth we shall act unjustly' (ἢ τῇ ἀληθείᾳ ἀδικήσομεν).

49c9: Crito, too, falls into this way of speaking: 'What you say is true' (Ἀληθῆ λέγεις).

51a6–7: 'And will you say,' the Laws ask with heavy irony, 'that in doing this you are acting justly – *you who in truth care about goodness*?' (ὁ τῇ ἀληθείᾳ τῆς ἀρετῆς ἐπιμελούμενος;).[116]

51c3–4: Socrates asks Crito '[Shall we say] that what the Laws say is true or not? ([φήσομεν] ἀληθῆ λέγειν τοὺς νόμους ἢ οὔ;).'

51c6: Following on, the Laws say, '*Consider* then, Socrates, *whether these things we are saying are true*, that what you are undertaking is not just' (Σκόπει...εἰ ἡμεῖς ταῦτα ἀληθῆ λέγομεν...).

52d4–6: At the end of this paragraph the Laws put it to Socrates, 'First, then, answer this very question, *whether what we say is true, when we declare* that you have agreed..., or untrue' (εἰ ἀληθῆ λέγομεν φάσκοντες...).

In most of these it is Crito to whose judgment of truth the steps of the argument are submitted. An apparent exception is 51a6–7; but this passage alludes verbally to, and in effect addresses, Crito's earlier words at 45d8 φάσκοντά γε δὴ ἀρετῆς...ἐπιμελεῖσθαι ('when you declare that you care about virtue'). 51c6 is addressed by the Laws formally to Socrates; but this is a Socrates who has, hypothetically, taken up Crito's position and undertaken the action Crito recommended. At 52d the Laws again put their question to Socrates, but Socrates passes it on to Crito, saying, 'What shall we say to that, Crito? Shall we not agree?'; and Crito takes the responsibility of answering in the affirmative.

These facts do not supply a good reason for identifying the 'single expert' in morals, and the possessor of the truth itself, *in Plato's mind*, or indeed in his Socrates' judgment, with Crito. Nor do I see any good reason for any reader, practised or unpractised, to make that identification. The reasons against the identification are as strong as before. Rather, Plato's Socrates would appear to be weaving together (a) the dialectical argument for the need for moral expertise, necessary to confute Crito on what is thought by many to be good or right, with (b) the at least occasional Socratic-Platonic requirement that the respondent in dialectic answer with what he believes, whether firmly or fleetingly, to be the truth.[117] One could possibly, but not charitably, suppose that the result is to bamboozle Crito into imagining that his answers accepting the Laws' arguments are based on his own moral expertise; or perhaps one could even suppose the bamboozlement to be reserved for Plato's readers. But 'bamboozle' is perhaps not quite the right word. Crito at 45a1 and c6 offers his own view about what it is just to do; he does not speak of knowledge, but nevertheless, knowledgeable or no, he expects Socrates to act on that opinion. More significantly, his solid οὐ χρή at 45d5 and χρή at d7 ('ought not' and 'ought') assume an authority in the matter which *should* only be that of knowledge.[118] Since Socrates questions that authority at 46b1–3 and throughout the dialogue, an appeal to Crito's judgment of the truth as authoritative has an ironic piquancy. The appeal has also a fitting place in an argument designed to convince Crito, who has never formally abandoned his first easy assumption of authority. Ordinary people everywhere think they know right from wrong.

On this interpretation, 'the truth itself' becomes a dialectical device no less than the 'single expert'. Now it helps a dialectical device if the victim does not notice it. If he does, then resistance naturally follows. Crito cannot therefore be allowed by his author to notice what we have elucidated here. At the same time Plato could not make his Crito simply stupid, for reasons already seen. So Plato had to construct an argument which Crito as characterized could fall for, without making it too obvious. At the same time Plato's protreptic purpose, his aim to draw the victim into serious philosophical argument, was surely not confined to the character Crito in the dialogue. He will also surely have intended to draw in also his unpractised, uninitiated, unphilosophical readers. For them too, he had to create an argument which would persuade them, not so much that any given proposition was true, but that argumentation itself was important and indeed necessary. If they were serious enough to unravel the flaws and complexities of the argument concerning the single expert, then already willy-nilly they were engaged in philosophical argument. It was therefore not necessary at this point for Plato to produce a fully cogent and convincing piece of reasoning; all he had to do was to produce one that such readers would have to think about. On the other hand, if they were not capable of unravelling the argument, then they were, hopefully, going to wear it. They were then – given a certain level of intelligence and intellectual energy – going to try and follow the substantive moral argument Plato is about to lay before them. Plato has, vis-a-vis readers of this kind, nothing to lose.

(f) The moral part of Man

But however that may be, and whoever the 'single expert' may be, the argument of the dialogue continues. On a different point, at 47e–48a Socrates persuades Crito to accept an analogy between the body and the moral part of a man. We must see whether Crito's affirmative answers to Socrates' questions about the moral part suit his character as, apart from wealth and Socrates' friendship, an ordinary honest and intelligent man. At 47d3–6, is it plausible for a man like Crito, who is not a philosopher, to accept that there is a part of a human being which justice improves and injustice damages? Or is there a Socratic-Platonic tinge to such a belief, coloured, perhaps in advance, with tints of the *Gorgias* or the *Republic*? The answer to these questions lies in common Greek thought and language about justice. Justice, δικαιοσύνη, ranked for most ordinary Athenians as a good quality or virtue, ἀρετή. Ἀρετή functions as the abstract of ἀγαθός, good. Goodness, indeed, was for many and diverse people a good thing: see *Rep.* 335c1–7, *Meno* 87d1–2, *La.* 190b4–5, and for goodness being beneficial see *Meno* 89a2.

It is not a long step from here to the notion that there is something in a human being which goodness, and hence justice, is good for and of which justice is a good quality. It is not immediately obvious that this 'something' is the soul, and Socrates accordingly does not so designate it here; what *is* obvious is that the part of man justice is *directly* good for is not the body. The gods may (or may not) see ultimately to the prosperity and the bodily cossetting of a just man;[119] but that is at best an indirect benefit of justice to the body. One might expect Socrates, given that the body is ruled out, to mention the soul. The identification of the moral part of man with the soul is un-obvious, but might prove acceptable, to a normal Athenian.[120] Socrates' reluctance to mention the soul here may be partly due to the fact that ψυχή, the Greek for 'soul', can also mean 'life': life or death is the question before Socrates in the *Crito*, and he chooses death. Weiss is right that a philosophical disciple of Socrates would have accepted 'soul' here.[121] But though Crito is a friend, we have seen reason not to believe him a convinced disciple. Socrates does not have to suppose that every non-disciple is, in ordinary parlance, the fool Weiss takes Crito for. However that may be, goodness or virtue makes a man – but not his body – better or good, and justice has to be a virtue or good quality for Crito. Otherwise he could not urge considerations of justice on Socrates or imply so high an evaluation of such considerations as he did at 45 a1–3. Crito appears indeed to be a typical highly respectable man, not a Thrasymachus (as portrayed in the *Republic*, especially 348c–d) who would deny that justice is a virtue. One surely did not have to take on board 'Socratic' baggage concerning the soul to accept that goodness is good for you, at least for the moral part of you. Once again, in this Crito will stand in for an averagely intelligent non-philosophical reader: the latter could also have been confused by the word 'soul', is better off without it, but need have seen no obstacle to acceptance of what Crito agrees to.

It is not hard to imagine that a man so respectable, though not necessarily absorbent of all the moral inclinations and beliefs of Plato's Socrates, would accept the next step, that a man's moral part is more important to him than his body. The whole introduction to Plato's *Protagoras*, especially 313a–b, depends on the greater importance of the soul being accepted by the unphilosophical young gentleman Hippocrates. The combination of analogy and *a fortiori* works just as well there as in the *Crito.* Youth apart, Hippocrates resembles Crito in being a well-off friend of Socrates who has not taken on board much of his Platonic teaching, but thinks of himself as respectable. In this context again it is also important to remember that Crito (44e–45a) has already suggested that justice, as he sees it, is for him more valuable than riches.

Crito, then, is not responding to Socrates' questions in the way he does *merely* because he is an old friend of Socrates', or *merely* because Socrates reminds him of past conversations they have had; he responds thus at least in part because of the kind of person Plato makes of him. There is nothing in what he has agreed to so far to arouse scepticism in the mind of a reader interested in the dialogue as drama. But if Crito is so respectable, then why does he propose, no doubt illegally, to spring Socrates from gaol? The text suggests that he thought, on balance, that this conduct was not only the best thing for Socrates and himself in all the circumstances, but that it was the *right* thing to do. His opinion that it was just, more just than the alternative, stands firmly in the text. We know so little about imprisonment, or escape from it, in classical Athens that one must resort to some conjecture. It is a plausible conjecture that to spring a friend condemned to death from gaol would in some circles not destroy, though it might still in certain circles endanger, the respectability of those responsible. Crito at least, in this dialogue, gives the impression – and who are we to say it is false? – that he thinks *not* to spring Socrates from gaol would attract more obloquy than admiration, at least from people whose opinion he values. There is no obvious reason to suppose that the obloquy would be based on practical rather than on moral considerations.

(g) The 'many' again

Plato allows Socrates next, at 48a10–11, to raise again the point that 'the many' can kill people. Do 'the many', and does Crito, still have this bullet in their magazine, or has Socrates already dodged it? Socrates had earlier denied flatly (44d6–10) that 'the many' could inflict the greatest harm, but not, of course, their ability to kill. In the course of an argument with, primarily, another target, Socrates (47e7–48a2) has got Crito to admit, unsurprisingly in view of Crito's own earlier pronouncements (44e1–45a3), that life is not worth living with a corrupted moral part. From this, with assumptions we have justified, it follows that death is better than injustice. In effect this shot from 'the many' has been neutralized. But this neutralization took place when Crito was concentrating on other issues. Crito, like many a reader unused to long stretches of argument, might need this reminder that death is a lesser harm than injustice, before Socrates proceeds with a lengthy argument to show Crito that escape will indeed be an unjust act, and not the just one that Crito thought it.

C. Emlyn-Jones finds a contradiction here;[122] this time, between the assertion that 'the many' have the power to kill and what Crito and Socrates have just agreed, namely that they should pay attention not to what 'the many' will say, but to the expert and the truth. Against this finding, there is no formal contradiction. The power to kill is a *fact, undeniable.* Socrates has never denied it, but has denied only the judgment that 'the many' can do the greatest harm. Nevertheless Emlyn-Jones' comment raises a question: why does Socrates choose this moment to bring up again the power of 'the many' to kill? One answer is: if we give Socrates and his creator credit for sound reasoning, then Socrates will have seen that Crito's acceptance of what he said about experts and 'many' à propos of the athlete's body is understandable at least partly because what he said did not seem relevant to the discussion at large. Evidently 'the many' will not in any case kill an athlete for disobeying them, whereas they may, and can, kill anyone who, as they see it, has committed injustice. To deal with this point would be unnecessary if Plato had only novice readers in mind, who would scarcely notice so negative a point. More advanced readers, however, capable of analysis and criticism of the earlier argument, could well have wanted to raise it. Crito's response, whether to 'the many's' actual power or only to the likelihood of someone's raising the question, indicates that Plato thought, very reasonably, that the matter was worth dealing with.[123] The answer I just gave, though it might have occurred to Plato himself or to some advanced readers, is assuredly not the sort of thing to enter the head of a newcomer to Plato or of any less philosophical reader. The less advanced, then, if they asked at all why the power of 'the many' comes up again, will perhaps have had a vague feeling of disquiet assuaged, a vague feeling that for all Socrates' dialectic, he had somehow not adequately dealt with the necessity, if one wished to survive at all, of paying attention to the dangerous 'many'. For Plato as an author, this passage supplies a neat transition from the merely protreptic argument we have been discussing to the substantive moral question which forms at least the ostensible main subject of the dialogue. From the power of 'the many' to kill, to the greater importance of a good life than of mere living, is an easy step. Plato had to forge some such link between the protreptic argument and the central moral issue.

6

SOCRATES' STRATEGY

Before delving into detail about the tactics followed in each phase of the assault on Crito's proposal, it will be useful to outline the strategy of Socrates' whole line of argument from this point to the end of the dialogue. In this context it deserves re-emphasis that Socrates directs the argument as a whole, and not merely in certain details, at Crito as he has appeared so far; he does not necessarily aim at proof by ineluctable deduction from inescapable premisses. The argument is *ad hominem.* Both Socrates and the Laws of Athens, whom I believe to be pursuing his argument further, are responding to Crito and to *his* arguments and to the way he expresses them. To convey here a sense of Socrates' strategy over the argument as a whole it will be necessary to make controversial statements without immediate justification about some sections of the argument. The justification will follow later.

(a) *Ad hominem* argument illustrated

Some illustration of the *ad hominem* nature of the reasoning may form a helpful preliminary. We may begin with three passages whose mutual resemblance editors have often noted without further comment. The first of these, at 45c–d, has Crito saying that Socrates' staying to die is unjust. 'In addition,' he says, 'I think you are betraying your sons by passing on and leaving them behind, when you could rear and educate them right through – and so far as in you lies, τὸ σὸν μέρος, their welfare will be a matter of chance.' The phrase τὸ σὸν μέρος recurs in the mouth of the Laws of Athens twice, the second a mere recall, in transparent ring-composition, of the first. The first time the Laws use it is at 50b, at the outset of their series of arguments, when they accuse the hypothetically escaping Socrates of undertaking their destruction, as they put it, 'so far as in you lies', τὸ σὸν μέρος again. The nature and force of the apparently implied argument here have been the subject of considerable debate. Are the Laws deploying a kind of generalizing argument, to the effect that, since if everyone did this it would be disastrous, no-one ought to do it? Several versions of the implied argument have appeared, notably from

David Gallop.[124] It is at least doubtful whether any formal version of such an argument would hold water in isolation. As readers of Plato, however, we do not have to deal with formal logic, certainly not at any likely date for the *Crito.* In informal, conversational logic, the Laws' reasoning here bears a resemblance in its faultiness to Crito's when he used the phrase 'so far as in you lies' earlier. Crito's argument about Socrates' sons' welfare omitted to mention – as the Laws themselves make explicit later at 54a7–10 – that if Socrates leaves his sons in the lurch by dying plenty of Socrates' friends will look after them. The Laws' argument, on the other hand, omits to mention that even if Socrates does his bit to destroy the Laws, plenty of good citizens will continue to uphold them. The phrase 'so far as in you lies' serves in each argument to exclude a number of relevant people other than the argument's addressee. The Laws are thus indulging in dialectic, or *ad hominem* argument, in that they employ a form of argument, doubtfully cogent, which the interlocutor used. The interlocutor accordingly cannot indicate the escape-route from the argument without having to offer an escape-route from his own argument. The Laws' later indication of the gap in Crito's argument, and the conspicuous verbal repetition of τὸ σὸν μέρος, 'so far as in you lies', suggest very strongly that Plato knew exactly what the Laws were doing. Whether it was philosophically reprehensible in Plato to make the Laws argue *ad hominem* against a '*homo*', a person, Plato had himself in some measure created as an author remains debatable. It would have been more clearly reprehensible if Crito's original argument were not such a natural one for a reasonably intelligent man in Crito's position to construct.

A further illustration of the kind of thing I call dialectical, though some might call it eristical, occurs in the run-up to the argument for the citizen having an agreement with the Laws. The Laws point out that they allow any Athenian who has inspected them with displeasure to leave. This lays them open to the retort, and scholars have not missed the retort, that exile in ancient Greece involved difficulties and dangers, as indeed it did, and even a native city one had reason to dislike might seem preferable.[125] But could Crito leap to point this out? Certainly not. He was himself trying to persuade Socrates to escape into exile. Could Crito not at least say, 'Socrates, exile may not be up to much, but at least it's preferable to *death*, isn't it?' Perhaps he could, but he has himself remarked at some length and with emphasis at the beginning of the dialogue how completely tranquil Socrates remains in the face of death. Thus he has good reason to know that such a retort will cut little or no ice with Socrates. Crito's *situation* here inhibits him from disarming the Laws' argument.

(b) A strategically important passage: 49a4–c3

The two examples above perhaps straddle the rather vaguely drawn boundary between tactics and strategy. But we consider next a third, strategically most important, interaction between the Laws and the admissions Crito makes to Socrates in the part of the dialogue before they appear. Discussion will have to range fairly widely in the dialogue, but will focus on the exact meaning and dialectical ramifications of the central passage 49a4–c3. In the first and last paragraphs here Socrates offers Crito the choice whether or not to agree that one should never, in any way, anyhow, commit injustice. This absolute prohibition is the *only* thing Socrates certainly claims to be derivable from his and Crito's agreements in the past. It needs renewed emphasis that even this prohibition is not only derivable from past conversations with Socrates of whose detail the dialogue tells us nothing; it is also a useful and perhaps vital plank in Crito's own platform. For Crito had accused Socrates of behaving unjustly in not escaping. Hence it is obviously in Crito's interests at this early stage in Socrates' argument to maintain that one should never in any way anyhow commit injustice. For if Crito were to allow any exceptions his argument might be fatally undermined – and there is no reason why we should not credit the Crito we are reading about with enough shrewdness in argument to see that.

The next step is more difficult and more controversial. With a deductive question, one following on from the previous prohibition on committing injustice, Socrates asks whether one ought then, contrary to public opinion, to refrain from returning injustice for injustice suffered. With a certain reluctance, Crito agrees. What does it mean, to return injustice for injustice suffered? This is a surprisingly complex question, on which T. Irwin has shed much light,[126] but which still needs more illumination. The fundamental question at issue is: what *counts as* injustice when injustice has previously been inflicted on the agent? Irwin produced two principles of non-retaliation, which he called (R1) and (R2). One can add to these possibilities another pair I shall call (R3) and (R4). For a more formal statement of these four principles of non-retaliation see p. 106 below. Here we may inspect informal statements of principles (R1)–(R4). The four principles are different ways of stating what counts as unjust or unjustified retaliation.

Under (R1), then, what counts as unjust retaliation is whatever, being a retaliation, would be unjust for the initial victim to do if un-victimized. Under (R2) what counts as unjust retaliation is whatever, being a retaliation, cannot be justified by moral reasons other than *or* in addition to the fact of the initial victim's having been victimized. Under (R3) what will count as unjust retaliation is only whatever, being a retaliation, would, if the initial victim had remained un-victimized, be a greater injustice than the initial injustice. What would be unjust here is, in Dover's memorable expression, 'a head for an eye'.[127] Under (R4) what would count as unjust retaliation is a head for an eye that cannot be justified by moral reasons other than *or* in addition to the loss of the eye. We may observe that (R3) and (R4) are not mere special cases of (R1) and (R2). (R3) and (R4) do not respectively rule out, or rule out in default of further justification, the taking of an eye for an eye; (R1) and (R2) do respectively rule out, and rule out in default of further justification, the taking of an eye for an eye.

Given these alternative readings of a veto on unjust retaliation for injustice suffered, what, at the end of the injustice-argument at *Crito* 49a4–c1, do the two speakers know about each other's views on what it would mean to commit injustice in return for injustice? The answer to that is, virtually nothing. The questions put and the assents given are so potentially polysemous that fine though they sound, their informational content is low.

This state of affairs, however, could be radically altered by the next section of the argument on some readings of that next section. One popular reading is to take the key verb κακουργεῖν, *kakourgein*, etymologically 'bad-work', to mean 'harm'. In that case, Socrates at c7–11 asks Crito if he will equate doing injustice with doing harm to people, and Crito accepts that equation. This would require us to read also the injustice part of the argument (as distinct from the κακουργεῖν or 'bad-work' part) as prohibiting all harm, and in particular retaliatory harm, to people. It is clearly this reading which encouraged for example V. Harte in a recent review to refer to this whole passage as 'the well-known bar on retaliation'.[128] But it is not necessarily the right reading, and it leads, as we shall see, to a number of difficulties in understanding the Laws' argument at the end of the dialogue, difficulties which Harte has indeed skilfully exploited so as to divorce the Laws from their presenter Socrates.

But does κακουργεῖν, *kakourgein*, necessarily mean 'harm'? C.H. Kahn and others have taken the word to mean 'do *wrongful* harm' (my emphasis).[129] This in effect means 'do wrong [to someone]', for it is hard to imagine an ordinary man like Crito thinking up a kind of wrongdoing not involving at least the intention of harming. So could κακουργεῖν, *kakourgein*, in the *Crito* mean 'do wrong' or 'work wickedness'? It would be very difficult to prove philologically that it *must* mean that; we are dealing here with possibilities, not deductive certainties. But I shall argue below with some philological detail that to read κακουργεῖν as meaning 'do wrong' here is indeed a possibility. The upshot of this would be to make of 49b–e an argument not against harming but against wrongdoing. If that is right, κακουργεῖν, 'bad-work', is here assimilated to injustice, ἀδικεῖν, rather than ἀδικεῖν, 'do injustice', to κακουργεῖν in the sense 'harm'. This possibility will, as we shall see, help us to resolve the difficulties leading Harte to dissociate Socrates from the Laws.

(c) Ought one to dissociate the Laws from Socrates?

Should one mind if the Laws are divorced and dissociated from Socrates? After all, they indulge in longer continuous harangues than Socrates normally allows himself elsewhere in the dialogues usually called early, and they say some things Socrates could not possibly say in his own person: that they in effect procreated him, for example. But these points are by no means decisive: Socrates in this dialogue allows his adversary Crito longer speeches than he normally would let go without interrupting, and if Crito can make long speeches, in fair dialectic Socrates and his creatures the Laws should be permitted the same licence. And as part of the furniture of their appearance, as it were, on stage they may be allowed some remarks in character which their puppetmaster could not utter. They are indeed puppets rather than mere dummies to Socrates' ventriloquist. Considerations of this sort would fade into insignificance if there were serious discrepancies of doctrine between the Laws and Socrates, but I shall attempt to show that major discrepancies depend on the reading of 49a–e as ruling out all harm done to other persons. And I shall treat discrepancies arising from that reading as providing an argument – not the only argument – against that reading.

That might seem an arrogant procedure, since it appears to take for granted that the Laws continue Socrates' argument against Crito by other means, and that there is only an external discontinuity at the introduction of the Laws, and no essential discontinuity within the argument. But it is not necessary to take the continuity of the argument for granted; there are two major structural considerations within the dialogue telling in its favour.

The first such consideration is that Crito at 49e9–50a5, like various characters elsewhere in Plato,[130] expresses incomprehension of two questions Socrates puts to him, and duly, as is normal in Plato, has the questions explained to him. It is the Laws who explain them. This creates a strong presumption in Plato's reader's mind that the Laws represent Socrates, albeit in a different mode of speech. If they do not represent Socrates, then we nowhere come upon Socrates' own explanation of his questions. This would not only be a literary clumsiness in itself; it would, I suggest, be unique in Plato.

The second structural consideration is philosophical. Socrates brings Crito, before the Laws start, to the admission that one should never commit injustice. He does not, however, (*pace* R. Weiss, for whom see Appendix below) explain intelligibly why his escape would be unjust; the Laws convince Crito that the escape would be unjust, but do not argue or even state that one should not do what is unjust. Yet evidently, both the general premiss that one should not act unjustly and the particular premiss that escape would be unjust are needed for the conclusion that Socrates should not escape.[131] If the Laws' arguments are not dialectically, as against Crito, convincing arguments for that conclusion, then the dialogue offers no reason in dialectic why Crito at the end should be silenced. Which would be extraordinary. If, however, the Laws' arguments are dialectically convincing as against Crito, then those of us who believe that much Socratic argument is *ad hominem* will find no reason to dissociate the Laws from Socrates, and much reason to suppose them in essentials to be one and the same person. The best parallel for this in Plato is the *Symposium*, in which the imagined or recounted argument of Diotima against the youthful Socrates continues the argument of Socrates against the poet Agathon.[132] It seems natural to suppose that similarly the argument of the imagined Laws against the hypothetically escaping Socrates continues the argument of Socrates against Crito. Part of the motive for Plato's procedure in each case may have been to have his Socrates urbanely lift some of the burden of defeat from a friendly or respected interlocutor and shoulder some of it himself. Part of it may have been to allow his Socrates the more easily to make a longer speech or speeches than usual because he is either reporting or imagining someone else's speech or speeches. But the motivation may be left in doubt; the structural arguments are clear.

(d) Apparent discrepancies between Socrates and the Laws

It is high time to mention at least one apparent doctrinal discrepancy between Socrates against Crito on the one hand and on the other hand the Laws against the hypothetically escaping Socrates. The most apparently glaring particular discrepancy appears in the Laws' argument that, as in effect Socrates' procreators and masters, they have a special status;[133] Justice is not equal, they say in effect, between them and him (50a4–7), and he has no right to treat them in the same way as they are treating him. That is to say that he has no right, that it is not just for him, to try to destroy them as they are trying to destroy him (50e7–51a7). Harte argued successfully in 1997[134] that – on her assumption that 49a–e prohibits all harm to any person(s) – the detail of this argument conflicts with what is agreed at 49e.

This argument of the Laws' against retaliation by Socrates rests mainly on the claim that justice is unequal between the two parties.

The Greek sentence at issue is 50e5–51a2:

> ἆρ' ἐξ ἴσου οἴει εἶναι σοὶ τὸ δίκαιον καὶ ἡμῖν, καὶ ἅττ' ἂν ἡμεῖς σε ἐπιχειρῶμεν ποιεῖν, καὶ σοὶ ταῦτα ἀντιποιεῖν δίκαιον εἶναι; ἢ πρὸς μὲν ἄρα σοι τὸν πατέρα οὐκ ἐξ ἴσου ἦν τὸ δίκαιον καὶ πρὸς δεσπότην, εἴ σοι ὢν ἐτύγχανεν, ὥστε ἅπερ πάσχοις ταῦτα καὶ ἀντιποιεῖν κτλ...

> Do you think that the just is equal between you and us? And do you think it just for you to do to us in return whatever we set out to do to you? Or was it the case then that justice between you and your father, or between you and your master, if you had happened to have one, was not equal so that you should do in return [to them] whatever you suffered [at their hands] etc.?

The negatives in this sentence, especially in the section at the end not yet quoted, are confusing; but Harte is surely right – always on her assumption about 49a–e – in saying:

> The principle of non-retaliation which emerges from this may be stated as follows: in certain morally asymmetrical relationships the subordinate person must never retaliate. This principle of non-retaliation is clearly different from Socrates'. Socrates' principle of non-retaliation makes no issue of the relative status of the persons involved.

Indeed this passage from the personified Laws of Athens does imply that if justice were equal, if the playing field were level, between Socrates and the Laws, it would not be unjust for him to retaliate in kind. If the earlier passage was rightly construed as a general bar on all retaliation, then we would have a pretty direct contradiction between the Laws here and Socrates and Crito earlier. But was that construal right? We surely have to choose: unless Plato made a very serious error, either 49a–e does not mean to bar all retaliation; or we have to dissociate the Laws from Socrates. Disregarding the somewhat arbitrary supposition of Platonic error here, and noting the strong structural arguments for the proposition that the Laws do represent Socrates, we should already be inclined to doubt whether 49a–e prohibits all harm and hence all retaliation. And we have seen already that at least the injustice-argument in that earlier passage is multiply ambiguous, or, if you like, polysemous.

If that earlier passage did prohibit all harm and in particular retaliatory harm, that would create another difficulty or two for my – and the traditional – Socratically arguing Laws. The Laws begin by accusing the escaping Socrates of attempting to destroy them, which is of course attempting to harm them. If Crito were to agree, the argument would then be over. Crito is prevented dialectically by the 'so far as in you lies' point of dialectic, mentioned above, from disagreeing; so the Laws could indeed rest their case here. But perhaps Plato wanted to have the Laws argue the point that they are the persons Socrates ought *least* to harm? Possibly. That is a possibility hard to refute, and we should not labour this particular point.

We should however labour another issue, relating to the question Socrates himself – not the Laws, and not the hypothetical escaping Socrates – puts to Crito after the Laws' initial outburst. Socrates asks Crito whether Crito and the escaping Socrates, confronted with the Laws' accusation of attempting to destroy them, will say in their own defence, 'the city treated us unjustly, and decided the case wrongly'. Crito eagerly assents to their putting up this defence (50c1–3). On the 'bar-to-all-retaliation' view of 49a–e, this is obviously a stupid and by implication self-contradictory defence for Crito and the escaping Socrates to put up. To compound this difficulty, Socrates fails completely to point out that this defence implies a contradiction with what they have agreed earlier. Socrates, of all people, lets pass a glaring implied – even immediately implied – contradiction? Without a murmur? Suppose he politely ignores it and proceeds to allow the Laws their next points. Why then is the question there – with Crito's eager assent – if it is to be ignored? To make Crito look simply foolish? On the contrary, though Crito is certainly no philosopher, he is not (again *pace* R. Weiss) a fool; and if Plato meant to demonstrate or illustrate Crito's folly it would have made sense to have Socrates gently remind Crito here of what he had agreed earlier. One may add that if Plato's average reader was supposed to notice for himself the stupidity of Crito's assent, then why should the averagely intelligent Crito not notice it too?

There is, however, a way out of the difficulty of this offered and accepted defence of the projected escape, if what was said above about the ambiguity of the injustice-argument at 49a–e holds good. For in that case Crito has, by agreeing to offer the defence that the city had behaved unjustly to Socrates, shown that, whatever he meant to agree to in that injustice-argument, he did *not* mean to agree to (R1). Under (R1), the city's injustice is irrelevant, since in retaliation for that injustice Socrates is then forbidden to do in any case anything that would be unjust if he had *not* been the victim of the city's injustice. So, with (R1) by implication rejected by Crito, Socrates through the Laws cannot argue sufficiently against escape simply by showing that what he would be doing would be an unjust action even if he had not been the victim of the Laws' injustice; he has to go further. How much further may depend on whether he thinks Crito has agreed (R2), (R3), or (R4). Crito's 'Yes' to Socrates' question thus establishes an important point for the nature of the argument to follow. It is reasonable to suppose that Plato gave the question to Socrates in order to have Socrates clarify and elucidate this significant detail of Crito's views before launching him on the tide of argument that follows. It is indeed important for Socrates to have some notion about what counts for Crito as unjust retaliation before trying to argue through the Laws that escape would be unjust.

My readers will notice that this interpretation treats Socrates' question to Crito as a genuine question, seeking elucidation; also that it does not treat the question as a barely concealed announcement of Socrates' own commitment to a position from which to refute Crito. I am unpersuaded that any of this tells against the interpretation.

(e) The Laws' argument in outline

The Laws now have to persuade Crito that in attempting to destroy them Socrates is attempting an unjust retaliation for their attempt, as they admit, at 51a, in good faith to destroy him.[135] How does their attempt, in broad outline, measure up to our principles (R2), (R3), and/or (R4)? 'In broad outline' because the arguments' cogency in detail, or lack of it, is beyond the scope of this section and will be dealt with below. There are three main phases to the Laws' argument. First what S. Panagiotou has called the superior-status argument (50c–51c);[136] second what is called the agreement argument, that Socrates in escaping will be breaking a just agreement he has with the Laws (51c–52d); and thirdly an argument that Socrates has nothing worthwhile to gain by escape (52d–54b). The third argument answers in its course, whether effectively or no, most if not all of the points made by Crito earlier and in particular his accusation of injustice in Socrates' staying to die.

(e1) *The superior-status argument in relation to the Laws' other arguments*

The superior-status argument in part elicits the admission that the Laws are in a position at least analogous to parents of children and also (in passing) to masters of slaves, and hence treats justice between them and Socrates as not being equal, not on a level playing field. As we have seen, they imply that if the playing field had been level, Socrates would have been justified in returning Attempted Destruction for Attempted Destruction. Accordingly, in part, the argument must be aimed at the confutation of someone who, like Crito, rules out (R1). Could Socrates use the whole superior-status argument against a Crito who accepted (R2)? The whole argument runs, schematically expressed, as follows: Since (p) Justice is not equal between Socrates and the Laws, therefore (q) It is not just for Socrates to return Attempted Destruction for their Attempted

Destruction of him. But would returning Attempted Destruction for Attempted Destruction count as unjust under (R2)? It would so count as unjust if and only if no other considerations than the Laws' action justify Socrates in returning Attempted Destruction for Attempted Destruction. Crito earlier advanced considerations tending to justify Socrates' escape; even after having labelled his escape as Attempted Destruction of the Laws, the Laws still have to demolish Crito's points to be sure that no considerations are left which would justify Socrates' Attempted Destruction of them. The final demolition of Crito (53a ff.) holds its place on this view. Where does the intervening argument, to the effect that Socrates has broken an agreement, fit in under (R2)? Under (R2), Socrates' having broken an agreement is simply another act which would be unjust if the Laws had not unjustly treated Socrates. So again, under (R2), Socrates is not justified by the Laws' behaviour in breaking his agreement with the Laws, but still needs to demolish Crito's other considerations. If the reader asks why the agreement argument, and the superior-status and attempted-destruction arguments, are both necessary, the answer is clear: they are not both necessary, but piling up arguments that escape is unjust does neither the Laws' nor Socrates' case any harm.

There is nevertheless a major difficulty with the supposition that the Laws are treating Crito as if he had accepted (R2). This is that under (R2) the Laws have no need to argue, as I think they mean to do, that Socrates' Attempted Destruction of them is a greater injustice than their Attempted Destruction of him. Under (R2) all that the Laws needed to do was to set one Attempted Destruction beside the other. All the kerfuffle about their superior status making Socrates' escape actually impious like an attack on a parent (50c–51b) is logically superfluous.[137] It is a bit too much, I think, for an interpretation to render superfluous not just the agreement argument but the superior-status argument as well. The conclusion must be that Socrates has set the Laws a tougher task than confuting a Crito who has implicitly accepted (R2).

So what about (R3)? Under (R3), the kerfuffle about the Laws' special status analogous to parents' falls neatly into place. Under (R3) Socrates' escape counts as unjust retaliation because, since Justice is unequal between Socrates and the Laws, his Attempted Destruction of the Laws would have been, if Socrates had been un-victimized, a greater injustice than the Laws' Attempted Destruction of him. The implication of the special-status argument is that retaliation in exact kind against parent, master, or city *counts as* 'a head for an eye'. Further, though the agreement argument now remains superfluous, it does fit in rather better. Any extra injustice Socrates in escaping does to the Laws serves to widen the margin by which his injustice is greater than theirs; one supposes that a head and an arm for an eye would be a greater injustice than a head for an eye if it were not for the awkward contingent fact that loss of one's head is fatal anyway. What under (R2) was a mere piling up of arguments remains a piling up of arguments, but the size of the pile is at least helpful to the *overall* drift of the Laws' reasoning.

Under (R3) one could argue that Crito's 'other considerations' advanced earlier made no difference and do not need the answer Socrates puts into the mouth of the Laws (53a–54b).[138] No such 'other considerations' will serve to justify Socrates' escape, if the escape involves him in a greater injustice than the Laws are doing to him. But one might also want to argue that Crito has accused Socrates of injustice in not escaping, and that that might serve at least to narrow if not obliterate the margin by which Socrates' Attempted Destruction of the Laws is a greater injustice than what they are doing to him. This line of argument, however, will not work. The injustice Crito alleges against the non-escaping Socrates is not one committed against the Laws. So, whatever the relevance of Crito's 'other considerations' is, it does not consist in reducing the margin mentioned above. So Socrates' final demolition of Crito's other considerations would be strictly irrelevant against a Crito who accepted (R3). If it were strictly irrelevant, why would it be there? Two possible answers raise their heads. One is purely literary, saying that as a literary structure the dialogue would be incomplete without a rebuttal of Crito's earlier pronouncements and arguments. So it would, and Plato was a most careful literary artist. But if his artistry led him to tack on something that was philosophically or dialectically otiose, would that not represent in itself a failure of artistry? Surely it would, and one should be reluctant to give much weight to this particular literary consideration. The second answer to the question why Socrates should under (R3) produce a strictly irrelevant demolition of Crito's points is more philosophical. At the end of the dialogue Crito admits he has nothing to say against the Laws' arguments; but if his own points had remained un-rebutted it would have been open to him to say: 'Socrates, I appreciate your and the Laws' points to the effect that you will be doing them an injustice by escaping. But you will also be doing an injustice, as I showed, by staying. You still haven't shown that the injustice you will be doing to the Laws outweighs the injustice you will be doing to yourself, family and friends by staying to die.' Against this answer, however, Plato has, doubtless cunningly, provided a retort. For, especially at 51a–c, he has made the Laws argue, un-rebutted, that they, the Laws, are the people that Socrates ought least to 'try to destroy', ought to 'try to destroy' even less than he ought to 'try to destroy' his parents. Weighed in the balance against attempted destruction of self, family and friends the attempted destruction of the Laws brings down the scale. The upshot is that attempts to justify under (R3) the inclusion of Socrates' final demolition of Crito fail, unless after all Plato was *merely* indulging in ring-composition, bringing his literary composition round to its starting-point.

So we are left with (R4) as the way in which Socrates chooses to interpret Crito's agreement to ban unjust retaliation. Under (R4), the Laws must not only show that the escaping Socrates' retaliation against the Laws is a case of a head for an eye, and hence a candidate for injustice. They must also show that it is a definite case of injustice in that any other considerations Crito may have advanced are inadequate to justify that retaliation. And that is what the Laws finally do. By the end they have argued a dialectical case for regarding the escape as a case of a head for an eye. They have also shown dialectically against Crito that there are no other relevant considerations which will justify the escape. They have fulfilled the obligations of one arguing on the basis of (R4), and they have left Crito with nothing to say. But, you may want to quibble, what if Crito were to think up more reasons to justify escape? This is indeed a quibble and nothing more; for it is in the highest degree improbable that Plato would allow Crito to pull any punches or leave out anything he could think of in his initial attempt to persuade Socrates to escape; so *as against Crito* the argument is complete.

At this point my readers might be tempted to label the selection of (R4) as a basis on which to argue as 'purely arbitrary'. That would be a mistake. (R4) is the most moderate principle of non-retaliation – if you can call it that – which I can devise. Now the more moderate the principle of non-retaliation underlying the discussion the harder it becomes to show that a particular retaliation is unjust. It follows that in selecting as his underlying principle the most moderate one, Socrates has given the Laws the hardest possible task; and he has after his lights taken them through to its accomplishment. This is no arbitrariness; this is rather an arguer pursuing (in outline at least) a thoroughly honest argument. This point explains in large measure why Socrates and the Laws fail to interrogate Crito further on what he meant by ruling out unjust retaliation. To do so would probably have confused Crito to little purpose. To rule out, however, his having meant (R1) had some importance, since if he had meant (R1) the argument could have been swift indeed; and Plato could reasonably expect this point to occur to an intelligent reader in his own day. The actual course of the argument, my readers should observe, enables Socrates or the Laws to confute Crito whichever of (R2)–(R4) the latter adopted; by undertaking and accomplishing the hardest task he has undertaken and accomplished them all. The one demolition in a sense includes the others.

(e2) *A difficulty in 49a–e?*

Let us now return to 49a–e. On returning there we find a possible difficulty confronting the present analysis. If Socrates is later prepared to allow for a Crito who adopts the relatively innocuous veto on 'a head for an eye', and one who admits that other considerations might justify even taking a head for an eye, then why the striking emphasis at 49c–e? Why labour the point that Crito should answer in this context only what he truly believes? Why emphasize that only a tiny minority do now, or will in future, hold the opinions on which Socrates and Crito have agreed? On my interpretation it would look like a simple falsehood to say that few people would accept that it is unjust to take a head for an eye, especially if other considerations are allowed to outweigh that *prima facie* injustice. Nor in my view is it possible to claim that few *ancient Greeks* would have thought a head for an eye unjust, though Greek literature does contain some instances.[139] This kind of consideration has perhaps led notable scholars such as G. Vlastos to interpret the passage as the veto, shattering in classical Greece, on any retaliation, or even on doing any harm to a person.[140]

But no, Socrates is not telling a falsehood, nor does one have to believe that he is giving expression to any such paradox. I suggest that Plato's readers should look at the *absolute* way in which Socrates phrases the questions in this passage which receive Crito's assent. Ruling out injustice, 'In no way', οὐδενὶ τρόπῳ, he says at 49a4, in emphatic contrast with 'in some way yes, but in some way no', τινὶ μὲν…τρόπῳ τινὶ δ' οὔ; 'Nohow', he continues – οὐδαμῶς – is it either good or fine to commit injustice, ἀδικεῖν. And at the end of that same speech he turns the sentence round with equal emphasis: 'Injustice is both bad and shameful for the unjust agent παντὶ τρόπῳ, *in every way*.' And look at 49d7, where it is *never* right to commit injustice etc. I suggest that Socrates' division here between the majority and the small minority is the division we are all well aware of between those on the one hand whose integrity and aversion to unfairness are fallible and in varying degrees easygoing, and those very few on the other hand whose integrity is unwavering and absolute. The same point is being made about 'the many' at 49b10 and at 49c10: ordinary Greeks did not think that all and any unjust retaliation for injustice was right; the doctrine that is opposed to that of 'the many' is that it is *not* right *in any way*, οὐδαμῶς – another absolute which at 49a4–5 was in turn opposed to 'in one way…but not in another', τινὶ μὲν…τρόπῳ τινὶ δ' οὔ. Does Crito, Socrates is asking, acknowledge that there can be *no* exceptions to the rule forbidding injustice? Does he really cleave to that in every way? And Crito is constrained to say 'yes' he does, because otherwise, as we have seen, his own argument from justice may fall. What is more, in any given moral choice there can be, as Socrates has it, no joint deliberation between those whose integrity is absolute and those whose integrity is not absolute; they come at the decision from totally different angles. It is not hard to believe that each will feel a degree of contempt for the other.

(f) Interim conclusion

Now all this, and our return just now to 49a–e, suggest a rather neat fit. There is a neat fit between the outline of the Laws' argument and the argument a skilled dialectician such as Socrates might develop against a Crito who did not rule out all retaliation or all harm to persons, but only unjust retaliation, where 'unjust retaliation' may be defined according to any one of our (R2) (R3) or (R4). However, this neat fit vanishes if one construes 49a–e as prohibiting all harm to persons. That seems in itself a powerful argument against taking 49a–e as prohibiting all harm to persons. We shall support below, as we have suggested above,[141] the philological possibility of taking the passage as prohibiting not all retaliation but rather all injustice and wickedness and hence all unjust and wicked retaliation. This enables us to fit our account of the rest of the argument against Crito round the ambiguities of 49a–e, and conversely to fit 49a–e into the present version of Socrates' strategy. In the process of getting this far we have lost the embarrassment caused by the supposed bar at 49a–e on all retaliation. We are now in a position to see, as we explore the *Crito* further, the way in which Socrates' dialectical arguments not only dovetail with each other as a single whole, but also fit neatly together with Crito's admissions and agreements throughout. We can accordingly observe the interaction in dialectic between on the one hand Socrates and his puppets the Laws, and on the other hand the respondent Crito – that interaction which forms the principal theme of this book. Hopefully such observation will help us to understand more of what Socrates is doing in this dialogue and how he is doing it.

7

SOCRATES' SECOND WAVE

(a) Justice the paramount consideration?

Before turning attention to Socrates' general strategy, we considered his reminder to Crito of the power of the 'many'. This reminder was helpful even though Crito earlier laid himself open to Socrates' subsequent attack with his argument at 44e–45a for Socrates' friends' doing the right thing at whatever risk. Crito's endorsement of the reminder evokes a response in the form of Socrates' two questions at 48b. Does our argument still stand, the first asks, that the highest value is to be set not on living but on living well? In case of any misunderstanding of 'living well', the next question elucidates it. This question is well-nigh untranslatable: Τὸ δὲ εὖ καὶ καλῶς καὶ δικαίως ὅτι ταὐτόν ἐστιν, μένει ἢ οὐ μένει; Socrates inquires, roughly speaking, whether Crito's identification still stands of 'well' with 'admirably' and 'justly'; the point of this is to ask whether Crito still identifies the good life with the moral one.

It is tempting to suppose that the argument which may 'still stand' here, μένει, is nothing but the repeated arguments of Socrates over a lifetime that moral goodness is paramount. But that is not a necessary supposition; and Crito is not merely knuckling under as Socrates browbeats him. A repetition or a browbeating might or might not satisfy a casual or novice reader; it would leave an experienced student of dialectic unmoved. More significantly for such a student, Crito has in the present dialogue, over the course of the present discussion, admitted that to live with a corrupted moral part of oneself is not a life worth living. Crito has also (44e–45a) implied a high esteem for justice in his own life in volunteering to take any punishment for what he deems the just act of helping Socrates to escape. If he now denies that living justly is more important than merely staying alive, Socrates could in turn deny that Crito and his other friends were justified in taking risks, possibly with their lives, in the attempt to rescue him.

Justice is not quite, for Crito, the only consideration; he thinks Socrates may be concerned at costing his friends material trouble or damage; but even for Crito it is the dominant consideration. Dominant, that is, as far as his words in the dialogue go. How sincere he is, as opposed to how clever at devising arguments likely to appeal to Socrates, is a question certainly opening up a documentary fallacy. It is a question impossible to answer and vain to ask. Sophisticated readers might have their suspicions of what Plato is up to with Crito; that is all. Crito, anyway, urged upon Socrates at 45d7 ff. the conduct appropriate to a good man, and taunted him with a lifetime devoted to talk of goodness. And it will bear repetition that Crito, though hitherto vague on the relation between justice and goodness, has every incentive, given his thesis that escape would be a just act and not to escape would be unjust, to agree in answer to the second question, as many of his fellow-Athenians would have, that the good life is the just one. A similar argument comes from Crito's view at 45a that to rescue Socrates would be a just act. It is not at all hard to conceive Crito as capable of seeing what would improve his argumentative stance. Nor is it hard to imagine him or a decently intelligent reader being expected to discern that Socrates has said nothing whatever up to this point that would even tend to refute Crito's thesis that staying to die would be an unjust act, or to diminish the confidence Crito feels in that thesis. At this stage Crito need have no qualms whatever about accepting the equation of the good life with the just life.[142]

(b) Does Crito give in too easily here?

At 48b10–c2, having thus secured Crito's explicit and timely assent to points that – unbeknown to Crito – will become the foundation of a counter-argument, Socrates draws the important conclusion that the only point remaining to be decided is whether escape would be just. At the end of the speech Crito offers his assent to this conclusion, being still, obviously, confident in his own moral judgment that escape would be just. He then proceeds without more ado to the practicalities: 'See what we should do!' (ὅρα δὲ τί δρῶμεν). Yet in the middle of the speech Socrates has said things to which Crito's assent might be found problematic, and C. Emlyn-Jones in his commentary does indeed so find it. These things need a brief explanation.

In his zeal to exclude all considerations from their choice other than those of justice, Socrates suggests to Crito at 48c2–6 that questions such as Crito raised earlier are such as to appeal to 'the many' who kill, and would resurrect if possible, lightly and without intelligence. The questions cover money spent, reputation and the nurture of children. Crito himself wanted Socrates to ignore the possible monetary cost to his friends of arranging escape. Crito would also have to admit, following the thrust of Socrates' earlier argument about 'the many', that mere reputation without the reality is irrelevant to the question of the justice or injustice of an action. So the first two of the three considerations Socrates thus dismisses Crito has himself played down or already abandoned. So far, at least, Emlyn-Jones' contention on 48d7–8 that 'Crito supports without protest – indeed enthusiastically – a conclusion which consigns his key arguments about money, reputation and childcare…to oblivion' is unfair: money Crito himself played down; the matter of reputation Socrates and Crito have dealt with. So far, then, this passage offers no firm support to the view that Crito is prepared to accept anything Socrates chooses to put to him.

But do Socrates' children not have some moral claim on their father? This question is reserved, in part, for the Laws to answer at 54a2–b2. 'In part', because only part of the question is raised here at 48c3–4. Here, in the passage we are discussing, Socrates speaks only of παίδων τροφή, the 'nurture of children', a phrase which could refer simply and literally to their nourishment, the provision for them of the necessities of life.[143] This much Socrates could regard as *merely* material. Crito would have shared with many of Plato's readers – if the latter had read, seen or heard about Aristophanes' *Clouds* – the knowledge that the Socrates of dramatic literature has not been the best of material providers for his family; and in any case Crito himself and other friends are clearly, from this dialogue, able and willing to provide the necessary resources. What readers entirely new to Plato and Socrates would think of these things is unclear. But Plato has given his Socrates an excellent piece of rhetoric to sweep them along. Practised readers of Plato with the required sharpness of memory should have noticed the difference between the present passage and Crito's ἐκθρέψαι καὶ ἐκπαιδεῦσαι, 'nurture and educate to the end', at 45d1. For what Socrates does not mention here explicitly and separately, and presumably would not have regarded as so obviously irrelevant, is the children's education. That is a paternal function which Socrates might have been expected to regard as significant, a subject which incidentally he refers to obliquely at the end of the *Apology*, and a subject indeed which the Laws of Athens broach later (54a). Crito has raised both questions, of nourishment and education, at 45d1 and d6; Socrates dismisses here explicitly and separately only the question of nourishment. That would seem to leave Crito with some hope of interesting his friend in playing a part in the children's future moral and intellectual upbringing, and need not discourage him at all from assenting to the generality of Socrates' contentions in this speech.

But is this distinction in accord with the usage of the two terms παιδεία ('education') and τροφή ('nurture')? The two or their grammatical relatives are conjoined eight times in this dialogue, of which three are at 54a. There is little doubt that these families of words *could* behave like near-synonyms: at 50d6, for example, the Laws appear to make no distinction; and in their final summary the Laws at 54b3, as earlier at 51e7, use only the single word τροφεύς, 'nurturer', to cover all their quasi-parental functions for the child once born.[144] But nevertheless the fact remains that *Crito*, in the two references to the topic of Socrates' sons which he makes in the course of his attempt to persuade Socrates (45d1 and d6), not only uses verbs belonging to both word-families but also conjoins them with καὶ…καὶ…, 'both…and…', which mostly conjoin different things rather than synonyms. Moreover, it would indeed make sense for Crito to accuse Socrates of abandoning, by staying to die, both material and educational provision for his sons. In these circumstances Socrates' employment only of the word used for material provision in his dismissal of Crito's arguments does leave Crito with a ray of hope. It does accordingly absolve Crito from the charge levelled by Emlyn-Jones of feebly giving up all his key points at one fell swoop. This passage offers no firm prop to the view that Crito will accept anything Socrates chooses to put to him, however conflicting with Crito's previous position. It does support the idea that Plato allows his Socrates at one and the same time to bludgeon the innocent reader with rhetoric and pierce the experienced with the rapier of precision.

(c) Back to justice

Now that Socrates and Crito have acknowledged the paramountcy of justice, for Crito the only question remaining at 48d is, 'What is to be done?' Crito does not doubt – and Socrates has given him so far no reason to doubt – his judgment that for Socrates to stay and die would be to commit injustice. Socrates and he are apparently agreed, each for his own argumentative purposes, on the high importance of justice. So fortified, Crito is now in a hurry, the same hurry as he was in before at 46a4–7. But Socrates is not. To the question, 'What is to be done?' the latter replies Σκοπῶμεν, 'Let us consider…' How he proposes to consider the question will have worried Crito. For Socrates makes rather clear that he is still minded to stay and die rather than escape against the Athenians' collective wish. But he does at least attach importance to persuading Crito rather than acting against *his* wish. He does also offer Crito the chance to respond persuasively to whatever considerations Socrates may bring up. Crito has as yet, we may repeat, no reason to believe that Socrates will be able to overthrow the apparently solid moral considerations Crito presented to him earlier, which apparently show that the only just course of action is escape.

Nor does Crito have *at this juncture* any reason for refusing assent to the question Socrates puts to him as τῆς σκέψεως τὴν ἀρχήν, 'the beginning of the inquiry'. This is, in effect, 'Are there any exceptions to the rule that one should act justly?' Socrates' reminder that this is a question they have often agreed upon in the course of their long friendship has only rhetorical force. The rhetorical force is, one readily admits, considerable. Yet one can both suppose that Crito can accept the rhetorical push in the direction Socrates wants him to take and continue to acknowledge the constraining force of Crito's own present position.

Thoughtful readers whose first experience of Plato this is might imagine Socrates, given any exceptions to the rule against injustice, wriggling out of doing what Crito thinks, and has no reason to doubt that Socrates thinks, to be right and just. Practised and proficient readers would realize that Crito cannot believe that Socrates, given the possibility of an exception to that rule, will argue that that lets him off the hook, and he can for once commit an injustice. But such readers would easily gather also that Crito has no reason to withhold his assent, and that he can therefore, at this stage in the argument, readily give it. Crito is thus, at least externally, committed to a universal rejection of injustice.[145] Such a universal rejection can in any case only add to the rhetorical force of Crito's plea that Socrates treat his family, his friends and himself justly. It will turn out, for readers sharp enough of memory, that from Socrates' point of view it was worthwhile to extract this universal rejection from Crito at a point where he has no reason to dissent, in order to prevent him from turning round at the end of the argument and saying something like: 'Ah, yes, Socrates. You show that it's unjust for you to escape; but aren't we all allowed the occasional peccadillo, a single injustice – especially in a good cause?'

On this reading, Socrates might seem to be over-egging the pudding, or to be closing loopholes hardly visible to the naked eye. But Plato is working, presumably with the goal clearly in view, towards a conclusion in which Crito has '*nothing* to say' (emphasis of course mine). Anything that closes even the tiniest of loopholes is a means to that goal, whether or not it is perceptible to a first-time reader. For such a reader, the passage rhetorically reinforces the characterization of Socrates as a hero with *absolute* moral integrity.

(d) Why no definition of justice?

Before we proceed to the next section of the dialogue's argument there is a rather fundamental matter requiring, as John Glucker has kindly impressed upon me, serious discussion. Crito has based his arguments partly on the claims of justice. Socrates has agreed that the claims of justice are overwhelming, and will make that agreement into the foundation of his counter-argument. At no stage, however, do Socrates and Crito discuss what they mean by (τὸ) δίκαιον, 'just(ice)'. They might, for all the drama itself shows us, hold very similar views on the meaning of these words;

they might hold very dissimilar views. Socrates proceeds with the discussion as if it did not matter what these vital terms mean. Indeed, for the unpractised reader unversed in Socrates' habit of asking for definitions, it does not matter. For such a reader, Socrates argues that what he is doing, by staying in prison to die, is just; and that is all. But the practised reader of Plato will want to ask how Socrates can be sure that what he is doing is just unless or until he knows what justice is.

The question strikes the modern reader with added force because the *Euthyphro* is so close in the printed Platonic Corpus to the *Crito* and has usually been attached to much the same period of Plato's life. Now in the *Euthyphro* Socrates attacks Euthyphro for claiming that he is doing something pious when, as it turns out, he cannot say what piety is. Should we then turn our backs on the *Euthyphro* and other definition-dialogues when reading the *Crito*? Certainly, the practice of interpreting one dialogue out of the others is dangerous. But could Plato afford to ignore in the *Crito* a point he rammed home in several other works? If he could, why could he?

The answer to this might conceivably be chronological. Conceivably when Plato composed the *Crito* he had not yet thought of the philosophical importance of definitions. To believe this one would have to believe that the true historical Socrates had not thought of their importance either. In that case one would be forced to suppose that Plato's definition dialogues were the purest of fiction, that Xenophon *Memorabilia* IV vi was also pure fiction, and that Aristotle in his *Metaphysics* (987b1–4 and 1078b17–30) was totally mistaken about Socrates' interest in definitions. Now all these beliefs might possibly be true, but an answer based on them would need – to put it mildly – a great deal of argument by way of foundation. Nor am I convinced myself that they are all entirely true.

An argument from character might help. Crito is not, as we have seen, a philosopher. So he is not likely, even if he has the time, to endure an argument as long as, say, Books II–IV of the *Republic.* Plato portrays him as a practical man. Crito lays stress on *doing* as he says, at 45a3 and 46a8–9. His arguments constitute less an intellectual challenge than an appeal for action. Instant decision (46a) is what he requires. The case he advances with no small rhetorical skill seems designed to result in action rather than intellectual conviction. One finds it difficult to imagine him at this juncture allowing Socrates to enmesh him in a complex web of argument. Given this character not many readers will have expected Socrates to engage him in lengthy philosophical discussion of what justice is. Of course it was Plato who chose or fashioned him the character that he is in the dialogue. But if experienced readers of Plato came to the *Crito* with expectations that terms such as 'justice' would eventually have their definition looked into, Plato in his portrayal of Crito has done his best to dampen down such expectations.

But to deal with readers' expectations does not abolish the philosophical difficulty. It is hard to picture Plato, whenever he wrote the *Crito*, and whatever characteristics he gave Crito, as having no conception of the complexity of the terms 'just' and 'justice'. The political discussions of Plato's adolescence and early manhood bandied these words about, using them to justify many and varied types of constitution, public policy, or individual behaviour. The right interpretation of 'justice' can surely never have seemed to the adult Plato a simple matter on which gentlemen could agree in silence. So why did he create in the *Crito* two gentlemen, one of them his inquiring Socrates, who pass over any complexities that might appear?

The question gains in sharpness from the general nature of what Crito urges upon Socrates as being just. From what Crito labels as unjust in his main harangue some have supposed, not without justification, that he adopts – if he cared to think about it – a view that it is right not to harm one's friends, those who are close to one, including oneself, and not to help one's enemies.[146] Crito does not actually say that one should help one's friends nor that one should harm one's enemies. These propositions are not necessary to his argument. They stand, nevertheless, in the background of his implication that one should neither harm friends nor help enemies. This nexus of propositions is for Crito apparently the criterion of justice. On the other hand, Socrates' criterion of justice does not emerge at all from the dialogue. It will be shown in more detail below[147] that Socrates does not commit himself, as many have supposed, to the doctrine that to do any harm to anybody is wrong and unjust. He is committed, one would naturally suppose, to the earlier suggestion that justice benefits, and injustice harms, the moral part of a human being. Even that commitment is not beyond dispute; at least, however, on reading as far as 48b, one finds that Socrates has, as he says, been through this argument before, and still cleaves to it. From that suggestion he and Crito proceed together to ultimate agreement that, in deciding what action to take, justice is what counts. They make no attempt to define justice here, and there is none in what follows. The personified Laws, at e.g. 49e6 and 50a3, join Socrates in taking the concept of justice for granted, and argue simply that what Socrates proposes – if he acts on Crito's advice – is unjust and wicked. Within this dialogue, whatever may happen elsewhere in Plato or indeed in any other Socratic literature, Socrates operates with the word 'justice' while leaving undefined what justice is.[148]

Those who came to the *Crito* by way of intelligent perusal of other dialogues, in particular the definition dialogues, would have to content themselves with the reflection that the *Crito* must aim simply at refutation of a particular character in a particular situation, and that it fulfils that aim. Confronting the further question why they should read, or Plato write, a work so narrow in its application, they need not fall back on the supposition that it was all a matter of biography, of fact or propaganda about the real Socrates who had died in 399. They could at least consider the question whether the application of Plato's drama was so narrow after all. Many people will have shared Crito's morality – or something like it, as Crito is vague.

To this way of looking at the *Crito*, its exhibition of some by no means simple philosophical dialectic is an apparent obstacle. The dialogue can be read as a drama on more than one level, yes; but this is a difficulty on a single level, that of the relatively experienced and capable reader. This reader is expected to combine dialectical insight with lack of interest in definitions so long as Socrates emerges as the dialectical victor. The way round this obstacle resembles the escape-route we took when confronted with the dubious logic of Socrates' argument about the single expert. Plato seems to expect the advanced reader to make allowances for the way in which he caters for those less practised or less alert. As an author, he is capable of tempering the wind to the shorn lamb entering Platonic pastures for the first time. Crito does not, as Plato's unpractised readers do not, make progress so fast that he or they can take on board a lengthy discussion of the meaning of 'justice'. Socrates' refutation of Crito presents in any case matter of great intellectual interest even to those who want to ask what justice is.

There is another avenue of escape, too: the descriptions of unjust actions to be avoided in the *Crito* lack the controversial quality of Euthyphro's proposed prosecution of his own father for homicide. Breaking promises or agreements, for example, which themselves entail no injustice, or undertaking the destruction of those one ought least to treat badly, were hardly contentious cases of injustice. In the absence of easily disputable cases there is certainly less and perhaps no need to seek laboriously a definition of justice before proceeding to the actual moral issue. Moreover, it is possible to read the dialogue, as it stands, initially for the drama, find it moving and uplifting, and on subsequent re-readings be drawn into the argument and analyse it. One can gain satisfaction and profit from each stage of one's study.

8

SOCRATES' LEAD-IN TO THE LAWS

(a) 49a–e: injustice and wickedness

(a1) *Justice*

At the risk of some repetition, it is worth stressing that, before Socrates can launch the Laws' final arguments on the unsuspecting Crito, it is normal for him, without being a great surprise to any reader, to find out what specific moral beliefs and attitudes Crito is maintaining on this particular occasion. He does not need to know the general attitudes of his old and gentlemanly friend, with which he is thoroughly familiar. He needs to know rather what his friend is thinking now, or at least what he is saying in his attempt to persuade Socrates, and precisely how far he is prepared to go in support of his arguments for escape. Crito has based his arguments partly on the claims of justice. What Socrates can do is to explore the precise strength of the claims of justice that Crito accepts. By way of exploration he asks certain questions which turn out to display multiple ambiguities, though the unphilosophical Crito is hardly the man to perceive so technical a point. Having obtained the answers he needs in the first instance for his dialectical purposes, he then has to find out what Crito means, or thinks he means, by his ambiguous answers to the ambiguous questions. He must up to a point disambiguate Crito's answers. Over the whole of the rest of the dialogue some of Socrates' questions could appear bewildering. Some of the questions he puts into the mouth of the Laws are more rhetorical and less carefully dialectical than is Socrates' custom in Plato's 'earlier' and shorter works. But, as usual, Socrates has first to find out what his interlocutor thinks on the subject at issue before he can show that the interlocutor must on his own say-so abandon the beliefs, or in this case the course of action, he previously advocated. As elsewhere in Plato, and as apparently recommended in Aristotle's *Topics* VIII 1 (especially 156a23–6), Socrates chooses the matter, manner, and order of the questions not in a spirit of disinterested inquiry but in a way designed to make it difficult for the interlocutor to resist the conclusion Socrates wishes to reach. Here in the *Crito* this process has already begun: the question already asked, in effect, whether there are any exceptions to Crito's rule that one should behave justly, had to be asked *before* there was the least possibility of Crito's perceiving that the projected escape is in Socrates' eyes unjust, and *while* Crito is still at least externally committed to its essential justice.

The question and answer at 49b7–8, then, give Socrates the first premiss he needs: one ought not ever, in any circumstances, to commit injustice. By the simplest of syllogistic reasoning Socrates asks for, and obtains, Crito's agreement to the proposition that one ought therefore not to commit injustice in return if treated unjustly. This proposition is already ambiguous, as we have seen. We shall examine its ambiguity in detail. Meanwhile we must note two preliminaries and one major point. The first preliminary is that Socrates immediately, at 49b 9–10, declares, or admits, that this debatable proposition as it stands is not popular doctrine or common belief: 'It is not right to commit injustice in return... (ἀνταδικεῖν) as "the many" say [it is].' The view of 'the many' here may assist clarification. It may itself need clarifying: it is not quite clear what 'the many' actually would say if they were there to be interrogated. Next, Crito himself appears somewhat reluctant to accept this unpopular proposition. Οὐ φαίνεται, he says at 49c1: 'It seems [it is] not [right].' This diffident reply contrasts strongly with Φάμεν, 'We do say [that]', at 49b6 and Οὐ δῆτα, 'Indeed not', at 49b8. But it is no good Crito pressing his reluctance. In 'Socratic' dialectic he can do only one of two things: he can ask Socrates to disambiguate his expressions, which he is not philosopher enough to do, or he can accept the conclusion which on the surface follows so smoothly.

The above-mentioned major point about the passage is already clear: Crito has not so far agreed that no retaliation is legitimate. He has indeed agreed so far only that unjust retaliation is to be excluded. The argument so far, from premiss to conclusion, says nothing in general about retaliation *per se*, says nothing in particular about retaliation *per se* being unjust, and does not even tend to the conclusion that all retaliation is illegitimate. The whole thrust of Socrates' argument, so far, is against *injustice*, and so far Crito has not agreed that all retaliation is unjust. If he did so agree, he would have to re-orient himself with regard to the whole criminal law by abandoning all retaliatory elements in its prescribed punishments. This, however suitable for a Protagoras,[149] one might think implausible for an ordinary unintellectual Athenian gentleman, even one who had a recent bad experience of a criminal court. It is all the more implausible in the light of recent work by G. Herman suggesting that at least by the early fourth century BC Athenian gentlemen were accustomed to treat law-court redress as a civilized alternative to personal revenge – and redress often took the form of a criminal prosecution.[150]

(a2) *The* κακουργεῖν *(kakourgein) section of the argument*

The ground seems to shift beneath us when we look at the next few lines. These culminate in a conclusion, at 49c4–6, followed by its justification at 49c7–9. The conclusion is that one ought not to ἀντικακουργεῖν (*antikakourgein*), 'wrong [someone] in return' *or* 'act wickedly in return' *or* 'harm [someone] in return'; the justification is that κακῶς ποιεῖν (*kakōs poiein*), 'treat badly', very commonly interpreted to mean 'to harm' someone, is no different from committing injustice – and Socrates and Crito have already agreed to reject injustice. On this common view, the total conclusion to this argument and the preceding one taken together is, at 49c10–11, that one ought not to return injustice to or κακῶς ποιεῖν, *kakōs poiein*, 'treat badly', normally 'harm', any human being, no matter what one suffers at their hands. Taken thus, with this sense of κακῶς ποιεῖν (*kakōs poiein*), 'treat badly', or κακουργεῖν, *kakourgein*, (left untranslated for the moment), these lines, in ruling out any retaliation of any kind, or indeed any harm to any other human being, go well beyond the first part of the argument. They present, indeed, as G. Vlastos emphasized, a shatteringly original thing to say nearly four centuries before Christ. Moreover, it is not subsumed by the conclusion Socrates arrives at in the *Gorgias*, that it is better to suffer injustice than to commit it, but goes further; and for good measure, as Vlastos himself pointed out, it is actually contradicted, *if* one may hold the Socrates of another dialogue to be in contradiction of the Socrates of this one, at one place in the *Republic*.[151]

Let us admit that so startling a new departure in ethics as is sanctioned by this common interpretation of our *Crito* passage *could* be justified in the loftiest Socratic-Platonic terms. One has only to suppose, e.g., that the only real harm one can do is moral damage to the soul, and that to damage someone else's soul or virtue is unjust. In *Republic* I Socrates at 335b–336a does argue a thesis that for practical purposes, though without explicit mention of the soul, amounts to that. The *Republic* argument is adapted to a different dialectical situation from the one in the *Crito*, but there it stands. But at the same time (a) the Crito of this dialogue has shown no previous sign of prior deep appreciation of Socratic philosophy – witness his initial attention to the opinions of the numerous but ignorant (44b–c), and (b), as we shall see, the supposed new departure neither follows logically or dialectically on what has gone before in the dialogue,[152] nor forms a necessary foundation for arguments to come. Nor, for good measure, does Plato mention it or argue for it more than just once in the *Republic*. We shall see that the kind of harming at issue in the *Crito*, insofar as harming becomes an issue, is not this kind of moral harm to a human being, but more mundane. When we come to the 'superior-status' argument of the Laws of Athens, for example, we shall find (at 50e) that 'justice is not equal between parents and children'. What is not equal there is a justice involving the trading of blow for blow or harsh word for harsh word – nothing to do with the soul or with the total virtue of a human being. Before Socrates even begins his attack on Crito's whole position, Crito speaks (45c–d) of what is unjust in his eyes about Socrates' behaviour – and it is clear that he has no high 'Socratic' considerations in mind, but only ordinary notions of betrayal, including self-betrayal. Vlastos seems to treat the apparent assimilation of 'harming' to 'treating unjustly', which forms the premiss to the present argument on his interpretation, as 'a powerful intuition whose argumentative backing remains unclear in Plato's presentation of Socrates' thought'.[153] A major Socratic paradox, then, mentioned only twice at most, and backed with argument only in a rapid dialectical refutation of a possible way out for the Polemarchus of *Republic* I? And that in a sense which seems irrelevant to the *Crito*? The notion should arouse at once the deepest suspicion.

More problems arise in the *Crito* itself to enhance that suspicion. If 'harm' in this supposed paradox means what an ordinary gentleman like Crito would mean by it, then Socrates himself would hardly accept the paradox. Socrates regards, e.g. pecuniary disadvantage as a consideration only of 'the many' (48c), and would not accept, e.g., that unjustly fining somebody was harming them. But if the 'paradox' does say that the just man may not, *qua* just man, do what Socrates would call harm, then the principle becomes yet more irrelevant to the *Crito.* There is no open suggestion in the text that 'harming those one ought least to harm' (50a1–2, κακῶς τινας ποιοῦμεν, καὶ ταῦτα οὓς ἥκιστα δεῖ) means 'causing those one ought least to harm to commit injustice'; a recent attempt to find such a suggestion fails to convince, as requiring too much and too hard work from Crito and/or from Plato's readers.[154] Rather, 'those we ought least to harm' are, in the text, the Laws of Athens, and they have apparently committed one injustice already before the dialogue begins, and cannot therefore be made unjust by anything Socrates and Crito do. Further, there is no clear reason why Crito should agree to be bound by any such principle, being, as he is, a friend and not, because he is no intellectual, a disciple. He has shown no genuine understanding of Socratic moral philosophy hitherto, and may be presumed not to accept a Socratic paradox here assumed out of the blue, and consequently not to interpret a word meaning 'harm' as meaning or implying 'make unjust'.

If Socrates takes Crito to accept the paradox and to interpret thus, then Socrates is seriously at fault. Either he has misjudged his old friend or he is deliberately pulling wool over his eyes. The second is in principle by no means impossible. On this occasion, however, there is no obvious reason why a reasonably intelligent Crito should not perceive the wool being pulled. Readers deeply imbued with Platonism will have been at liberty, one supposes, to understand Socrates and Crito as agreeing to treat 'harm' as meaning here 'make unjust'. But the readers can have done so only by (a) temporarily forgetting that they are reading a drama with presumably a reasonable level of consistency in characterization, or (b) neglecting what follows, which contains no further allusion to this Platonic kind of 'harm'.[155]

Still in the deep suspicion mentioned above, we should attend to the two persistent strands in the scholarly interpretation of the simple verb κακουργεῖν, *kakourgein* (still not translated), and its compound ἀντικακουργεῖν, *antikakourgein*, at *Crito* 49c–e. One of these lines of interpretation is certainly the older, has probably been, over the history of the dialogue's scholarly reception, the commoner, was still supported by Vlastos (with reservations), and is upheld most recently by V. Harte and L. Brown.[156] But the other has behind it now the weight of critics such as R.E. Allen, D. Bostock, R. Kraut, C.H. Kahn and T. Irwin,[157] and it will receive my support, too. The former group treat the *Crito* passage as ruling out all retaliation that consists of harm done to somebody. The latter group, in various ways, take the *Crito* to rule out only wicked retaliation, or, in Kahn's terms, 'wrongful harm'. Socrates asks at 49c2, 'Ought one to κακουργεῖν, *kakourgein*, or not, Crito?' Κακουργεῖν, *kakourgein* and its relatives are capable, as the Lexicon says, of being translated by two very different types of English locution. Κακουργεῖν, *kakourgein*, may, on the one hand, mean 'do evil' or 'work wickedness', or, on the other hand, 'injure'. Similarly, the abstract noun κακουργία, *kakourgia*, may be rendered either 'wickedness' or 'villainy', or, on the other hand, 'injury', and the other nominal form κακοῦργος, *kakourgos*, either 'doing ill', 'mischievous', 'knavish', or, on the other hand, 'harmful'. This potential ambiguity, pointed out explicitly with reference to the *Crito* by R.E. Allen, has led to the above-mentioned scholarly disagreement.

Before trying to resolve that disagreement or the underlying ambiguity, let us once more imagine a reader untutored in Platonic writing and coming to the *Crito* for the first time. Such a reader would pretty certainly take every expression in the dialogue at face value, as the older school of modern interpreters do here. The failure (as will be seen below) of the results to make philosophical or dialectical sense would not have disturbed a reader unversed in the niceties of argument. Whether Plato's Socrates and Crito are prohibiting all harm done to anyone else or only unjust harm *might* be of some concern to any reader alert enough to be startled by a prohibition on all harm done to a fellow human being. Yet even a reader so startled might construe his feelings as a normal response to the somewhat exaggerated heroism of a drama's central figure. As for the question what, philosophically, κακουργεῖν, *kakourgein* ('bad-doing') and related expressions may or may not mean, Plato's untutored readers could as they pleased have taken κακουργεῖν, *kakourgein*, as 'harm' or as 'behave wickedly' and in either case appreciated the high moral standards Socrates persuaded Crito to adopt. For that kind of appreciation it would not matter whether κακουργεῖν, *kakourgein*, as 'behave wickedly' is a synonym and functions as a rhetorical doublet of 'do injustice', or whether Socrates is labelling all 'harm' done to another as unjust. This standard of appreciation would and need take no account of philosophical difficulties still to come, of which the relevant type of reader would be, and would for some time remain, blissfully unaware.

But the untutored are surely not the only readers Plato had in his sights. He will also have aimed at a more sophisticated and/or more studious readership. The philosophical difficulties arising out of face-value reading should direct *these* readers to work out ways of understanding the text so as to circumvent the difficulties and make sense of the whole as a continuous and cogent piece of dialectical argument. They will, I believe, have found themselves unable to justify Socrates' arguments without digging below the surface of what he says, whereas less sophisticated readers will have skated cheerfully over the surface.

Where does this leave Crito himself, always as a character in the dialogue? The short answer is that it leaves him far behind. But that answer needs two qualifications. First, in a strong sense it does not matter to seriously philosophical readers that the character who assents to Socrates' questions in the right places could not, consistently with earlier characterization, have seen all the implications of his answers, or himself have threaded his way through the labyrinth of ambiguity and subtlety Plato has constructed. Crito's actual answers to the questions as he would naturally have understood them are nowhere inconsistent with his character as a normally, but no more than normally, intelligent Athenian gentleman; there was nothing new in Greek drama about a character agreeing to more than he or she knows. Secondly, there is in any case in Platonic drama at least one example of a character being drawn into philosophy by a set of highly dubious arguments but then, once involved, displaying a surprising dialectical acumen and insight. The example is that of Clinias in the *Euthydemus*, on whom Socrates foists initially some distinctly shaky arguments at 278e ff. (esp. 279c9–280b5). Clinias advances by 290b7 ff. to some remarkably Socratic-sounding arguments of his own – though another character doubts if they are truly his. Certainly by then he is capable of giving Socrates clear and appropriate answers. Whether or not readers of the *Crito* were familiar with the *Euthydemus*, they need have felt no inconsistency between a man's initial impercipience in an unaccustomed form of discussion and his later perception, once initiated, of a thread of argument. Indeed, if one purpose of the *Crito* was protreptic, then a degree of progress by Socrates' interlocutor would, for the more intelligent readers, have contributed to that purpose, as it certainly does in the *Euthydemus*.

One must accordingly be prepared, in interpretative charity as a reasonably sophisticated modern reader, to use the sequel in the dialogue to elucidate ambiguities that the uninitiated would not even perceive. The sequel forms part of the context in which one has to make philosophical sense of the argument as a whole. It will be helpful to resolve the ambiguities in such a way as to sharpen and clarify the argument as Plato might have intended it for more philosophical readers in his own day. Plato, we may safely assume, would have expected these readers to puzzle out the argument in a spirit of interpretative charity on the assumption that it made sense.

To elucidate in this spirit the ambiguities of our present passage at the beginning of Socrates' second wave of argument demands careful attention not only to the sequel but also to material earlier in the dialogue which may point in the right direction. The material may demand more attention than the uninitiated will have been inclined to give it, but it is there. For the modern reader, elucidation requires also the examination of certain philological points in our present passage itself. We may start with some neglected philological evidence.

(b) The meaning of κακουργεῖν (*kakourgein*) here

So, does κακουργεῖν (*kakourgein*) here mean 'be wicked [to]' or 'harm'? Some linguistic and stylistic considerations come in here. When it means 'be wicked' or 'behave wickedly' κακουργεῖν (*kakourgein*) is an intransitive verb. In this sense it has no proper passive till long after Greece fell to Rome.[158] In classical Greek, that is to say, it can take an accusative, but the accusative is always of the crime committed, an 'internal' accusative. If the whole is turned into passive mode, the subject, given or implied, is always the crime, and not the person(s) against whom the crime or wickedness was committed. Where such person is mentioned, a preposition intervenes, such as εἰς, περί, ἐπί ('to, about, against') etc. As a transitive verb, with an external object and, in the passive, with an external subject, the verb κακουργεῖν (*kakourgein*) means 'harm', 'damage', or, in military contexts, 'ravage'. It does not appear to mean, in these syntactic contexts, 'work wickedness'. In a verb Plato uses 27 times, these points will have been well ingrained in his idiolect.

Some facts about κακῶς πάσχειν (*kakōs paschein*), 'suffer harm' or 'suffer wrong', and about its correlative κακῶς ποιεῖν (*kakōs paschein*), 'do harm', or 'do wrong', are also, as we shall see, relevant. Κακῶς πάσχειν, 'suffer…', appears in Plato outside the *Crito* only twice, once in the mouth of Aspasia at *Menexenus* 244b5–6, once in the mouth of Pausanias at *Symposium* 184b1: on neither occasion, therefore, on Socrates' lips. Xenophon never has it on Socrates' lips either: of eight occurrences only one is in the *Socratica*, given to Charmides at *Symposium* IV 30. Our other principal source of conversational classical Attic, Aristophanes, has it only once, at *Plutus* 900. In Plato κακῶς ποιεῖν, 'do…', is also relatively rare: once in Lysias' speech, *Phaedrus* 231c6, once given to Anytus at *Meno* 94e; on Socrates' lips only at *Gorgias* 480e and *Republic* I 332d, both tinged with a kind of irony in expressions of Socrates' interlocutors' views or conclusions. We have accordingly very little control over what this pair of expressions might mean in Plato's idiolect, or over their function in Plato's Socrates' vocabulary. It would therefore be unwise to reject out of hand the possibility, if occasion should arise to consider it, that Plato could give the words to Socrates in the *Crito* in a sense different from what they mean elsewhere.

Why are these phenomena, quite different from the usage of ἀδικεῖν, 'commit injustice' or 'treat unjustly', relevant? Because of certain asymmetries, one of them important, in our passage: in the first place, there is an unimportant asymmetry at 49b–c between the injustice- (ἀδικεῖν-) argument which leads off and the harm- or wickedness- (κακουργεῖν-, *kakourgein-*) argument which follows. If we look at 49b–c, there is in the first part of the argument, the injustice-part, an *internal* symmetry:

(U1) One ought not to behave unjustly (U).
Therefore (U2) One ought not to U in return for U
because [reprise of (U1)] One ought not to U.

Compare with this the internally asymmetrical second (κακουργεῖν, *kakourgein*, 'harm' or 'behave wickedly') part. With W for 'behave wickedly' or 'wicked behaviour', we have:

(W1) One ought not to W.
Therefore (W2) It is not just [= one ought not] to W in return for suffering evil [SE]
because (W3) To do evil (DE) to human beings = U.

In this second part, we perhaps expect, firstly, in (W2) 'one ought not', but we find instead, at 49c4–5, a question-and-answer about 'just or not'. This variation is not hard to account for: Plato will have wanted verbally to connect, somehow, the unjust and the wicked. He is able to do this partly because Socrates and Crito have already agreed, as most people would have, that one ought not to U. So U stands in for what one ought not to do.

But there is in (W2) a second disappointment of expectations, far more important for our purposes, and more confusing. By symmetry, as mathematicians say, we expect 'W in return for W'; we find instead SE substituted for the second W. To account for this it is necessary to start by accounting for the presence here of κακουργεῖν, *kakourgein*, 'harm' or 'behave wickedly'.

Earlier in the dialogue, at 46a3, Crito made bold to suggest that Socrates' behaviour was κακόν, *kakon*, 'bad' – and that suggestion occurs in a speech he began by saying the behaviour was unjust and continued with a hint (45d7–9) that it lacked virtue (or 'goodness') and (45e2) appeared cowardly. Socrates stands accused by Crito not only of injustice but of doing something bad, κακόν, *kakon*, even though Crito fails to clarify the relation between the two, and 'bad' in the earlier passage could have meant either 'wicked' or, more narrowly but still morally, 'cowardly'. As with injustice, Socrates can be sure that Crito will accept, for good dialectical or argumentative reasons, that one should not *do evil, kakourgein.* But κακόν, *kakon*, 'bad', in the earlier passage had at most a hint of 'harmful'; it follows hard on the related noun κακία, *kakia*, ('badness' or 'cowardice') in a pretty straightforwardly moral context. So Socrates does not have the same dialectical incentive, or indeed the same dialectical justification, for talking about 'harm' as he does for use of the intransitive κακουργεῖν, *kakourgein*, in the sense of 'do evil'. Crito has said nothing about 'harming' that would tend to commit him to agreement with any proposition concerning it, let alone with the startling proposition the older interpretation makes Socrates put forward.

Suppose, then, that Socrates' first question in the W-argument, at 49c2, means 'Ought one to do evil, Crito, or not?'. Now (U1–2) has the active ἀδικεῖν, 'act' or 'treat' 'unjustly' and the passive ἀδικούμενον, 'being treated unjustly'. The symmetry we naturally expected between (U1–2) and (W1–2) would produce in (W2) κακουργούμενον, *kakourgoumenon*, a form from the passive of κακουργεῖν, *kakourgein*, meaning 'being done evil' – and there is no such passive in the classical period of Greek with an external subject. Κακουργούμενον, *kakourgoumenon*, would have to mean 'being harmed', which is not to the point in the wider context, as we have just seen, of the preceding argument, or, as we shall see below, of the dialogue as a whole. What is more, if 'harming' and 'being harmed' *were* what Plato meant here there would have been no serious reason for Plato to change verbs in the middle of the W-argument as he has. What Plato needed was a passive expression meaning 'to suffer', or 'be the victim of', 'wickedness', and one which has a corresponding active and transitive form. So far as I know, normal and common classical Attic prose supplies no such expression, except the verb ἀδικεῖσθαι 'be treated unjustly' with its active, 'treat unjustly', ἀδικεῖν, which he has just used. So Plato, in default of any better word from his normal idiolect, hit on expressions which in addition look as if they are – and indeed actually are – related to κακουργεῖν, *kakourgein*, namely, κακῶς (*kakōs*) πάσχοντα and κακῶς (*kakōs*) ποιεῖν. These are not ideal for his purpose, because they too normally mean 'suffering harm' or 'do harm', rather than referring to wickedness; but no ideal solution was available. Κακῶς (*kakōs*) πάσχοντα, 'suffering harm/wickedness', preserves the intransitive nature, and can be adapted to preserve the moral sense, of κακουργεῖν, *kakourgein*, 'act wickedly', as the passive κακουργούμενον, *kakourgoumenon*, 'being harmed' in context would not. Κακῶς (*kakōs*) ποιεῖν, 'treat badly', normally meaning 'harm' but now 'treat wickedly', follows naturally on κακῶς (*kakōs*) πάσχοντα, 'suffering evil', being a form of its obvious correlate, and again avoids making κακουργεῖν (*kakourgein*) transitive in the wrong sense.

On this view the whole passage, including 49c7–8, does not assimilate harming (of whatever sort) to injustice; it merely makes use of the common or garden equation of unjust behaviour to somebody with treating them wickedly – a commonplace equation Crito need have no difficulty in accepting as a premiss. The conclusion of this second, W-argument is now for practical purposes the same as that of the first, injustice-argument. It is not a revolutionary doctrine such as Crito would more naturally refuse to accept. Its difficulties are purely verbal, in that κακῶς (*kakōs*) ποιεῖν does not normally mean 'treat wickedly'; but the context is sufficient guide for Crito in this difficulty. Furthermore, and this is an important corollary, we may reasonably suppose that Crito allows Socrates, now that he has started, to use κακῶς (*kakōs*) ποιεῖν and κακῶς (*kakōs*) πάσχειν in this same way, meaning 'treat wickedly' and 'suffer evil', throughout the rest of the conversation. On the assumption that this is indeed the correct understanding of the κακ-, (*kak-*) 'bad-', 'wicked-' or 'evil-' words in this context, we may now understand Socrates' speech at 49c7–8, not as equating injustice with harm, but rather as equating injustice with wickedness. The reason why Crito will now, at 49c7–9, accept that κακουργεῖν, *kakourgein*, wickedness, is to be ruled out is that wickedness is the same thing as injustice, which they agreed to rule out a moment ago.

Rhetorically, ἀδικεῖν, 'behave or treat unjustly' and κακουργεῖν (*kakourgein*), 'behave or treat wickedly', may indeed serve as doublets; in some contexts κακουργεῖν (*kakourgein*) (intransitive) is the more general word of the two, but there is nothing out of the way in Plato's Socrates and Crito setting them very close together. One notes, for example, Xen. *Hiero* 10.8: κακὸν μὲν οὐδὲν ποιοῦσι τὸν μηδὲν ἀδικοῦντα, τοὺς δὲ κακουργεῖν βουλομένους κωλύουσι, βοηθοῦσι δὲ τοῖς ἀδικουμένοις, 'They do no harm to the man who does no injustice, but constrain those wishing to do wickedness, and help those treated unjustly.' (One observes here that Xenophon also, like Plato, avoids the passive κακουργουμένοις (*kakourgoumenois*) in the sense 'treated wickedly'.) But why in Socrates' next speech (49c10) does Plato use both terms, linked with neither...nor..., if they are nearly, and in the present context virtually, synonymous?[159] The answer is not only that Crito had used both terms or their relatives in his attack on Socrates; it is also that doublets do help the rhetoric along, and the *Crito* is one of Plato's most rhetorical works. Crito was pulling out rhetorical stops when he used both terms, and Socrates does likewise. There is a rhetoric to dialectic, too. Rhetorical reinforcement of a point never comes wrong.

So far, at least, we have not shown that the 'face-value' interpretation of the whole passage is mistaken. Still less have we shown that an uninitiated fourth-century reader of Plato could not have so interpreted it. Nor have we shown that Plato did not envisage some of his readers following the 'face-value' interpretation, and thus taking the passage as a whole to forbid all harm to another human being on the grounds that all such harm is unjust. What we have on offer is the availability to more practised readers of a different interpretation of this deeply ambiguous piece of dialectic. On this interpretation the passage forbids, instead, all injustice and all wickedness, even in retaliation. The prohibition of wickedness and injustice arises more naturally, for practised and alert readers, out of the preceding conversation. That it fits better, philosophically speaking, with the rest of the dialogue, and makes Crito appear to philosophical readers less foolish, still requires proof.

(c) Principles of non-retaliation

On this different reading, then, this passage of rapid dialectic formally obtains Crito's agreement, helpful to his general argumentative position, to rule out all unjust or wicked action, and specifically all unjust or wicked retaliation. But there is a major question still up for discussion:[160] what *counts* as unjust or wicked retaliation for wicked or unjust treament? So far as I know T. Irwin was the first to raise this question in any systematic way, and certainly he has shed the brightest light on it – without closing off further discussion.[161] He produces the principles (R1) and (R2) below for inspection. I have not intentionally altered anything in Irwin's statement of them, except for a change in Irwin's note's very dense lay-out on the page, and the making of certain additions, placed in square brackets.

'The extreme principle of non-retaliation is this:

(R1) If (1) A has done injustice to B
and (2) B's doing x to A would be unjust if A had not done injustice to B,
Then (3) B is not justified in doing x to A.

'The moderate principle is:

(R2) If (1) A has done injustice to B
and (2) B's doing x to A would be unjust if A had not done injustice to B,
Then (3) the fact that A has done injustice to B does not justify B in doing x to A.' [But other considerations *might* justify B in doing x to A.]

To this pair of Irwin's I add a third, more moderate even than (R2):

(R3) If (1) A has done injustice y to B
and (2) if A had not done injustice y to B B's doing x to A would be a greater injustice than A's doing injustice y to B,
Then (3) B is not justified in doing x to A.

And here is a fourth, more moderate still, differing from (R3) in the same way as (R2) does from (R1):

(R4) If (1) A has done injustice y to B
and (2) if A had not done injustice y to B B's doing x to A would be a greater injustice than A's doing injustice y to B,
Then (3) The fact that A has done injustice y to B does not justify B in doing x to A. [But other considerations *might* justify B in doing x to A.]

These are obviously alternative and various ways of describing types of action (symbolized by x in each principle as rendered above) which might *count* as unjust retaliation. Whatever philosophical cunning they may exhibit is Irwin's, not mine. The question at issue in what follows below is not what counts as unjust retaliation either for me, or for my readers, or for anyone alive to-day. Rather, the question to ask here is what counts as unjust or wicked retaliation for the characters in Plato's *Crito*, or for Plato's intended readers. We have already discussed that question briefly in the chapter on Socrates' strategy. Further detail has to be postponed till we reach the arguments in the dialogue to which it is relevant. But a reminder is in order here that, so far as we and the two principals are told by the language of Socrates' questions and Crito's answers at 49b–c, neither they nor we are any the wiser at this stage in the dialogue (say 49c11) on the question which (if any) of the above four principles of non-retaliation either Socrates or Crito has endorsed or would endorse.

(d) 'Few would agree' – a possible objection

Here there arises a problem.[162] What becomes of Socrates' immediately following, un-contradicted assertion that the views he and Crito have just agreed find acceptance only by a tiny minority (49d2 ὀλίγοις τισί)? 'I know', he says 'that [sc. only] few people hold or will hold these opinions.' He adds that joint deliberation [sc. about what is to be done] is impossible, and mutual contempt inevitable, between those holding these opinions and those not holding them. Any interpretation of the preceding agreement must therefore satisfy two conditions: (1) it must result in a doctrine few would accept; (2) it must divide those discussing moral choices into two classes such that the one cannot fruitfully debate a moral choice with, nor even respect, the other.

To fulfil these conditions, do we not need the revolutionary equation of any harm with injustice? Or, failing that, do we not need the extreme principle (R1)? Or, at the least, the somewhat more moderate, but still fairly strict (R2)? One way of approaching this question would be to say that we do not have here a clear statement of any principle at all; we have unclear questions, and answers also unclear because the questions are. Socrates says he agrees with Crito's answers; but what it is that thus receives Socrates' assent is still unclear. What is more, it is doomed to remain unclear until or unless the parties to the discussion agree on what should count as injustice or wickedness in B retaliating against A's injustice. That would, logically, involve them in a lengthy discussion of the proper meaning of 'justice' and 'injustice' as applied to actions. Unpractised readers would not expect or miss such a discussion. Practised ones, as I argued above,[163] would recognize (a) that Crito has been characterized as in haste and impatient to a degree making such a discussion implausible, and (b) that Socrates refutes Crito on his own terms without digging into the meaning of τὸ δίκαιον, 'just(ice)'. How, despite the unclarity, can Socrates say that few people would agree with them?

One way of explaining how Socrates can say this would be to suggest that few intelligent people would have accepted the wording of what Crito has agreed to without asking further questions about what they were supposed to be agreeing with. If they thought they might be agreeing with something like (R1), most people would have had strong reservations. But Crito, it would seem both to him and to Plato's more acute readers in his lifetime, could not enter those reservations without imperilling his previous admissions. He could not weaken his advocacy of justice or opposition to injustice, nor enter upon quibbles about the meaning of 'justice' or 'injustice', without imperilling his previous argument for escape, namely, that it is just for Socrates to escape and unjust for him to stay and die. Once he allows Socrates to start quibbling about justice he is lost. We may presume him to be imagined as capable of realizing that. The last thing he should want to do is to *discuss* justice with Socrates. On this explanation Crito is willing to believe, or not openly to disbelieve, that people will reject the principles offered them here on account of their vagueness. But this explanation has three drawbacks: first it gives Crito credit he probably does not deserve for the philosophic or dialectical ability to spot the vagueness of the principles he and Socrates have agreed on; secondly it runs counter to the high moral tone of the passage at large by suggesting that people in general will reject these principles merely on account of their vagueness; thirdly, as Gabriel Danzig pointed out to me, the text says nothing to highlight the vagueness of the offered principles.

If we cannot fall back on the vagueness of these principles to help us out, we face a difficulty still. But another approach may make matters easier.[164] Socrates insists that the opinions round which he and Crito have crystallized agreement are absolute: 49a4 'In no way' (Οὐδενὶ τρόπῳ), 49d7 'never' (οὐδέποτε), etc. The absoluteness of the propositions accepted, and the absence of any exception made, make a great difference to the number of people who would in practice act on any of the various principles we have been canvassing. Since the setting of the dialogue requires and indeed sets up deliberation with a view to action, and Crito is trying to persuade Socrates to *do* something, mere lip-service to an absolute principle would not suffice. Plato does not make this quite explicit. But he does make Socrates insist that Crito must not answer contrary to his real opinions, which makes sense as his way of insisting that mere lip-service will not do. The interpreter of the principles arrived at by Crito and Socrates does not therefore have to show that his or her version is one to which few would have paid lip-service. It is necessary to show only that one's interpretation offers principles which few would have accepted in practice without any exception. These points are not special pleading; they derive from the text and setting of the *Crito.* But they do make the interpreter's task easier than it may have seemed earlier.

How elastic, or how tightly drawn, were the limits on revenge? We have to deal with limits which would have appealed to those living not in today's West but in the late fifth or early fourth centuries BC. Which people alive at that time? The question is awkward. Does Socrates, or did Plato, have in mind people living in the Athens of his day? Or people in the Greek-speaking world at large? Or does Plato's Socrates believe, after all, that the moral division he mentions is so fundamental as to apply to everyone everywhere at all times? I suspect the last, since Socrates says 'few hold *or will hold* these opinions' (49d2). But this discussion will stick for the most part to Greece, and largely to Athens, in Plato's time. Hopefully any conclusions reached will not seem too absurd for present-day readers to swallow.

On retaliation and reciprocity in general in classical Athens recent scholarly work has shed much light. The following brief discussion does not attempt to shed more. If it shines at all, it shines by reflected light alone, in this resembling moonshine. It owes much not only to the older work especially of K.J. Dover,[165] but also to a series of articles published in the 1990s by G. Herman and to critics of them.[166] Though works on reciprocity in ancient Greek contexts tend to treat positive reciprocity between friends more extensively than negative reciprocity between enemies, Herman himself, and M. Whitlock Blundell too,[167] have done much to redress the balance. It needs emphasis that the following brief sketch would have been very difficult to put together without these scholars' collections of relevant passages and stimulating commentary.

On retaliation, then, in the ancient Greek world at large, there were many voices singing of the acceptable, almost obligatory practice of helping one's friends and harming one's enemies. As one's friends were largely those who had helped one, and one's enemies those who had done one an injury, this practice and the underlying principle naturally involved reciprocity or retaliation. Whitlock Blundell in her chapters I and II presents a collection of passages not needing repetition here. Retaliation of some sort for injury was almost *de rigueur.*[168] If Socrates and Crito had, as the older interpretation of *Crito* 49a–e has it, agreed a veto on returning harm for harm, then there would be – and indeed scholars found – no difficulty in supposing the veto to be very rare and paradoxical. On the present interpretation, however, the interpreter needs to decide whether it was acceptable in practice to do your enemy an injury that would in normal circumstances be a greater injustice than he had done to you. Would there have been *in practice* anything controversial and unusual about Socrates' limiting retaliation to what is proportional? G. Herman's work suggests that in fourth-century Athens, though revenge might still be sweet, it was part of the democratic ideal to postpone and transmute it into legal punishment. This might require us to argue that revenge still played a prominent role in Athenian life, and indeed that revenge was still hard to limit to precise requital.

In the Greek world in general, 'a head for an eye' was sometimes acceptable, though only, I think, within limits. Herman himself says that it is 'by no means ruled out'.[169] There is nothing to suggest an unbridgeable gap between those who found 'a head for an eye' acceptable and those who did not. To the suitors' families in the *Odyssey* it is material for a feud.[170] In the *Iliad* Achilles was entitled, even obliged to kill Hector to avenge Patroclus; it is fairly clear that the poet does not approve of Achilles' further act of revenge, the mutilation of the corpse. Gloating over the dead was blameworthy in theory and in practice from *Od.* 22, 411 to Lysias 2.28, as Whitlock Blundell remarks.[171] Whether Herodotus found excessive and culpable or apt and admirable the terrible vengeance he describes at IV 205 he does not reveal – at least not to me; 'in accord with a just law', δικαίῳ νόμῳ, in that passage is not Herodotus' direct authorial comment. But the proposition that some vengeances are excessive does not entail the proposition that *any* vengeance beyond precise requital would be excessive. It is not Homer's or Herodotus' job to be clear and exact about moral principles. That job is at least less inappropriate for the didactic poet Hesiod. On one point he is clear: *Works and Days* 710–11 enjoins, if a friend take the initiative in doing or saying something unpleasant, double retaliation. Theognis 1089 echoes this. But even this does not clarify whether retaliation should be doubled because harm from a friend is double harm or because lacerated feelings require the extra retaliation or both. The double penalties for theft mentioned by E. Fraenkel[172] are perhaps subject to the same ambivalence. But there is certainly nothing in these poets and laws to discourage over-retaliation. Nor is there anything to discourage it in such later prose passages as:[173] Isoc. I 26, which recommends, in effect, at least equal retaliation; Xen. *Mem.* II 6, 35, which has Socrates, of all people, attributing to Critobulus without a hint of disapproval the realization that the excellence (ἀρετή) of a man consists in surpassing one's friends in beneficence and one's enemies in harm; Xen. *Anab.* I 19.11. More than one modern scholar cites Antiphon IV β 2f. as evidence for a feeling that the aggressor would justly suffer greater damage (which may or may not be greater injustice) than he inflicted.[174] R.A. Gauthier and J.Y. Jolif also cite Pl. *Laws* 843d, 767e, 915a, as envisaging a penalty greater than the original misdeed.[175] But none of these passages, except perhaps the one from Antiphon, offers material certain to be specific to general public opinion in Athens.

Herman, however, has produced passages certainly specific to fourth-century Athens, and redolent of an appeal by a public speaker to public opinion. The speeches containing them suggest general public approval of a certain restraint in retaliation. But there is room for questioning just how much the passages prove. The speeches Herman mentions, four designed for court use and one a sketch of a possible law-court argument, are: Lys. III (a doubtful instance),[176] Lys. IX 4–5, Dem. LIV (*Conon*) 13, and XXI (*Mid.*) 6–19, the last mentioning several hostile acts of Midias before Demosthenes retaliated, and Antiphon *Tetr.* III δ 6. One finds also praise of the amnesty for crimes committed by and under the late fifth-century oligarchy, e.g. Andoc. I (*Myst.*) 140.[177] Herman is clearly right that the society of classical Athens was one in which one did not always exact retribution, immediately or at all, on the first offence against one's honour, person, or property. But there were clearly limits to what a man could tolerate without being the eternal victim, or even a wimp. Further, one should bear in mind that, litigious as fourth-century Athenians were, they did not like in general to appear to be the kind of man that goes to law at the drop of a hat. True, the contrast with Homeric society, drawn by Herman, runs deep: Achilles and Odysseus would not have had a high opinion of vengeance extracted through the courts; but retaliation does not have to take the form of heroic revenge to deserve the name of 'retaliation'. Nor are we entitled to assume that law-court retaliation was invariably just; we do not have, for example, Conon's speech in the case of Dem. LIV *Against Conon*, which might throw a very different light on that particular feud. Retribution postponed is not necessarily retribution either made just or abandoned. Moreover, P. J. Rhodes[178] has cogently stressed 'the extent to which execution of the law-courts' verdicts still depended on self-help'.[179]

It would appear on the evidence and argument thus briefly summarized that in the Greek world at large revenge was not only sweet but admirable; that the limits of extra revenge over and above strict requital were elastic; that actions hard to justify in normal circumstances were acceptable in revenge. In Athens in and around the fourth century BC people thought it sensible and proper to retaliate through the courts, but not necessarily to be so litigious as to go to law at the first sign of insulting or hostile behaviour. But prosecutors could and did, after all, demand the death penalty for many offences. In Athens, further, the limits of retaliation were not set at an eye for an eye. Indeed, in many cases of insult, damage, or injury it would have been impossible to measure the damage etc. done by aggressor or by retaliator to honour, property or person. It would have been at least equally impossible to measure to everyone's satisfaction the degree of injustice exhibited by the relevant actions, viewed in or out of context.

In our present context we must return to the absoluteness of the principles Socrates and Crito accept.[180] It should give us pause. Let us suppose that out of the blue one had asked a fourth-century Greek, Athenian or other, whether he would, in deliberating on his course of action, allow no exception at all ever under any circumstances to a rule such as (R1), (R2), (R3), or (R4). It is then open to question whether in practice more than a very few would have assented in terms as absolute as, despite their varying strictness, these principles all are. What is more, it is very possible that those who would have accepted such absolute principles as determinants of actual practical deliberation,[181] and those who would not, would feel and, if prompted, express hearty mutual contempt. Nothing in the evidence we have examined shows that Plato's Socrates in our passage of the *Crito* is asking Crito to agree to anything implausible in suggesting a low incidence of *absolute* moral integrity under provocation. It might of course be the case that Plato in composing this part of the *Crito* misjudged his own society. He would not be the only intellectual ever to have done so. But it is not necessary on the present reading of the dialogue to suppose that he has.

So why, and with what justification, does Plato allow Crito to accept in his practical deliberation an absoluteness which on his own showing few men of his day would have accepted? We have dealt with that question already. Crito cannot allow any exceptions to the rule enjoining just behaviour – whatever that may be – without destroying the validity of his own argument. The argument runs that it would be unjust for Socrates to remain and die; therefore he must escape.

Here we have to remind ourselves once again of the differing responses of different sorts of readers that Plato could and perhaps should have envisaged as he wrote. The ordinarily unphilosophical and not specially alert reader, understanding Socrates to have labelled all harm done to another person as unjust, and being duly startled by this understanding, would find no difficulty, as scholars too have found no difficulty, in supposing Socrates to mean that this label would be hotly disputed. Indeed, for them Socrates may well mean that. But it would be open to those interested in and capable of more exact and philosophical understanding to ask the question what kind of vengeance falls under the heading of the prohibited injustice: they should readily spot the strong emphasis in the text on the absoluteness of the prohibition. If puzzled to know why Crito accepts such absoluteness without demur, they should be capable of seeing that not to accept it could undermine his argument.

(e) **Premisses agreed**

But how does all this kerfuffle about the meaning of one short passage help with wider issues? How does it help the rest of the dialogue to make better sense?[182] It does so by removing certain inconsistencies detected by recent scholarship, and noticeable only to practised and sophisticated readers, between Socrates' argument against Crito as developed up to the entry of the personified Laws of Athens and the argument put by Socrates into the mouth of the Laws. To show how this works in detail, it is necessary to go through the argument which follows in Plato's text. That argument starts by assembling two explicit premisses. The first premiss is the already agreed hypothesis that one ought never under any circumstances to treat people badly, i.e. wickedly or unjustly, even in revenge for their own unjust or wicked behaviour towards oneself. The second is the agreement at 49e5–8 that one ought not to break an agreement, provided the agreement does not involve one in any unjust action.

(e1) *Some linguistic points*

My readers will observe that in my previous sentence the word 'agreement' occurs in two different senses. In the first, one agrees on an opinion; in the second, one agrees to do something. 'Cognitive' and 'performative' are the expressions adopted for these by L. Brown.[183] The presence of the two senses – or applications – in the one passage is confusing. It is also confusing in Plato's Greek. Whether Plato himself was in any way confused on this point is more doubtful. One of the merits of R. Weiss' interpretation of Socrates' lead-up to the Laws of Athens lies in her having raised implicitly the questions to what extent and why Plato hereabouts uses the word ὁμολογῶ, *homologō*, and its relatives, meaning 'agree', in more than one sense. For argument in favour of the sense 'agree [to do something]' in both the occurrences of the word at 49e6–50a3, the normal interpretation, and against Weiss' different understanding of the sentences involved, my readers are referred to L. Brown (2002) and to my Appendix.[184] But the linguistic and stylistic awkwardness of the double usage in the whole context, together with the similar awkwardness and double usage of the Greek verb meaning roughly 'abide by', ἐμμένω, *emmenō*, deserves discussion here. Furthermore, the discussion will have to encompass the issue of the tense of the verb ἐμμένω. For in the first person singular (among other grammatical persons and forms) the difference between the present and future tenses is purely accentual, and Plato did not write accents, which were introduced into the written language after his time.

Let us tackle ἐμμένω, *emmenō*, (etymologically 'remain in') first. Parts of this verb occur in five places in the dialogue, four of them in the short passage 49e2–50c6, one in a clear reference back to that passsage at 53a6. We may distinguish the senses of the word as 'stand by' [an opinion], meaning 'continue to hold' the opinion, and 'abide by' [a decision or a promise], meaning in effect 'carry out' or 'put into practice'. Let us be clear: 'stand by' and 'abide by' are the phrases we shall use to separate the two senses just mapped out.

At 49e3, then, on its first appearance in the *Crito*, the verb clearly means 'stand by'. 'If you stand by the previous things [sc. remarks, principles or admissions], listen to what comes next.' Here no decision or promise is yet in sight. The tense is *likely* to be present, in parallel with 49d5–6, 'consider then, you too, very well whether you share [sc. 'these sentiments' or 'these principles'] and you concur with them and…;' Parallelism also favours the present tense in Crito's reply (49e4), 'But I stand by [them] and I concur', in which again the sense 'stand by' is the only possible one. So far, so good and clear. But Plato has muddied the waters by making Socrates ask at 50a2–3, '[In escaping] are we abiding by our agreements [i.e. promises], them being just, or not?' Here, for reasons given in the Appendix, I adopt the usual view that ἐμμένω, *emmenō*, certainly present tense here, means 'abide by'. Plato is able to get away with this only because, again on the usual view defended in the Appendix below, he has inserted in between, at 49e6–7, a question about the obligation to perform, or 'do', 'what one agrees', which most naturally refers to 'abiding by' promises. Uses later in the *Crito*, in the course of the Laws' harangue, have the sense 'abide by', at 50c6 ('abide by whatever judicial decisions the city hands down'), and 53a6 ('And now will you not abide by the things [you have] agreed [to do]?') All is plain sailing, *except for* the at least potentially awkward shift at 49e–50a from 'stand by' to 'abide by'.

There is a similar shift in the meaning of the verb ὁμολογῶ (*homologō*) and its relatives at about the same place. The verb may mean 'agree' in the sense of 'assent to [an assertion]', or 'agree' in the sense of 'commit oneself' or 'promise' [to do something]. The noun from the stem means, on its first appearance at 49a8, 'agreements upon' or 'joint assents to' [assertions]. Early appearances of the verb in the *Crito*, at 48b10, 49a7 and, in company with a compound of the verb, at 49d1–2, all bear the sense 'assent to [an assertion]'. But not far on in the text, at 49e6, we find, again as argued below in the Appendix, 'Ought one to do what one promises [*vel sim.*], or deceive [i.e. break one's word]?' At its next occurrence, 50a2–3, the verb means again 'promise': 'Are we abiding by the things we have promised, them being just, or not?' From there on, at 50c6, 51e4, 51e7, 52a8, 52c2, 52d3, 52d5, 52e1, 52e2, 52e5, 53a6 (with ἐμμένω, *emmenō*, again), and 54c3, at least there is no readily visible objection to the sense 'promise' for either verb or noun, *with one exception.* The exception is 52d7, where Socrates puts to Crito a 'deliberative' question, 'Shall we not agree?' evidently in the sense 'Shall we not assent to the Laws' assertions?' The context makes it crystal clear that the question cannot mean 'Shall we promise...?' – for the Laws *have* argued that Socrates and others *have* made a promise. With this one perspicuous exception, then, the words from the stem ὁμολογ- (*homolog-*) mean 'agree' in the sense 'promise' (*vel sim.*) from 49e6 to the end of the dialogue, having not meant that before 49e6.

This is very nearly the same situation as with ἐμμένω (*emmenō*) – and the single perspicuous exception does not seem likely to be significant. Admittedly ὁμολογ- (*homolog-*) words appear rather earlier in the dialogue than ἐμμένω (*emmenō*), but that is likely to be a function of the much greater frequency of the ὁμολογ- (*homolog-*) words in Platonic conversation than of ἐμμένω (*emmenō*).[185] So *why* do we find this simultaneous shift of sense both for the ὁμολογ- (*homolog-*) words and for ἐμμένω (*emmenō*) at the same place in the *Crito*? Weiss might want to suggest that the explanation lies in Socrates' complete change of tack after Crito has failed to understand a simple Socratic argument. But those who, like me, reject that theory might like to consider an alternative explanation. The explanation is not of course Platonic carelessness, since Plato was an astonishingly careful and exact writer. The suggestion is rather that Plato desires to make Socrates' pair of surprising questions to Crito even harder to follow than their unexpected subject-matter would have made them anyhow. If that is right, then we have detected Plato in the act of making Socrates' point(s) *doubly* difficult for Crito to understand. One interesting consequence of this could be that Plato is making doubly sure that his first-time readers are sufficiently baffled themselves *not* to suppose that Crito's bafflement is without good reason. Plato would then be pulling out all the stops in order, among other things, to prevent us, his readers, from supposing that Crito is a mere fool. In addition, if Crito has as good an excuse for giving up as this affords him, then Socrates (and his author) have a good excuse for bringing on the Laws of Athens to clarify matters. But, as Pindar might have said at such a juncture, we must shorten sail, and not voyage further on a sea of conjecture. We should be all the more cautious, in that Plato likes to give his Socrates unexpected and paradoxical-sounding utterances which he then has to explain. The result, and no doubt the intention, is to enliven the conversation and keep readers on their toes. A couple of examples: *Phaedo* 64a4 ff., where the unexpected element lies in the word ὀρθῶς, rightly, picked up at 67e5 when the explanation is complete; *Theaetetus* 149a4 ff., where Socrates' suggestion that he is a midwife and son of a midwife is a well-known dramatic coup.

(e2) *Two difficult questions from Socrates; the continuity of the argument*

We may now return to the two premisses from which this linguistic discussion started out. Premiss (1) One must not treat people wickedly or unjustly (or, for some readers, 'One must not harm people'); premiss (2) One must keep promises if one can do so justly. Insofar as we may presume these to be relevant to Socrates' proposed escape, they give rise to two questions broached by Socrates at 49e9–50a5. Let us call these Q1 and Q2. Q1 is: in escaping, are we treating some people wickedly, and at that those we ought least of all to treat wickedly? Q2 is: are we abiding by an agreement which requires no unjust action of us, or are we not? Weiss has recently made much of Crito's bewilderment at these questions; but that bewilderment seems perfectly natural. First, one can imagine him thinking, 'Whom is Socrates treating wickedly by escaping? His nearest and dearest? I've already pointed out that he'll treat them unjustly by staying.' If Crito can at this stage foresee the line the argument against him is going to take, then he is vastly more intelligent than most scholars, including me, are prepared to admit. The city is not normally a single person, as Gabriel Danzig reminds me, and still less so are the Laws. How should Crito divine that they are about to be treated as such? Indeed, even the cleverest first-time reader cannot be expected to guess at what is coming. Secondly, as for agreements to do something, neither Crito nor the first-time reader, however intellectually gifted, can at this point in the dialogue have the faintest idea what Socrates is talking about.[186] It seems a strong objection to discontinuity hereabouts in the dialogue's argument, that is to the view that totally separates Socrates from the Laws, that these two questions, in themselves, make no sense. They demand explanation. What kind of self-contained dialectical or other argument would it be which ends on so unintelligible a note? Weiss' view that this is where Socrates' argument ends seems on the face of it highly unlikely; it receives further attention in my Appendix.[187]

It cannot be coincidental that two major paragraphs of the speech which Socrates next puts into the mouth of the Laws of Athens explain these two questions. They explain who or what is going to be treated wickedly by the escaping Socrates and also what agreement, requiring at this time no unjust action of him, Socrates has entered into. Indeed, this matching of perplexity and explanation, long ago pointed out in essence by A.D. Woozley,[188] forms a major argument for the continuity of Socrates' whole discussion with

Crito from 46b to the end of the dialogue. It lends coherence to the text to believe that if Socrates bewilders Crito, and the Laws explain the questions which bewilder him, the Laws in some sense represent Socrates. The Laws further, as Socrates is wont to do, question and harangue Crito on the basis of propositions he has advanced. That implies indeed a continuity, tighter or looser, between the sections into which scholars divide the dialogue. The Laws continue a typical Socratic line of thought. That the dialogue in some sense takes a new departure at their entry is evident to any reader. But I can see no reason in the text yet why any reader, practised or unpractised, should suppose that Socrates differs in any important respect with these new entrants he introduces to the scene. The Laws furnish a continuation of the Socratic argument by other means.

Nor is this the only structural argument for continuity.[189] References by the Laws to Crito's previous contributions, mentioned by Weiss,[190] show at least that the Laws are arguing with Crito. That much is common ground. But, further, I have argued above that Socrates in his own person secures Crito's agreement to the proposition that one ought not to commit injustice, but does not show even to Crito that escape will be an injustice. The Laws secure agreement that escape will be an injustice, but do not attempt to show, or to extract from Crito, that one ought not to commit injustice. The two sections are thus clearly complementary parts of a single whole.[191]

But it is important here to make clear the limits to what I am arguing. The claim is not that one can read every word the Laws say as utterable also by Socrates in his own person. Obviously some of the things the Laws of Athens say they do Socrates cannot say he does. He cannot without degenerating towards farce say that he procreated, reared and educated himself. The Laws speak in character here, and do not simply act as a megaphone or as a ventriloquist's dummy for the voice of Socrates. One particular pronouncement of the Laws' cannot possibly be attributed to Socrates. That is, their implied statement that they thought they were acting justly in condemning Socrates (51a). It is axiomatic in this dialogue that Socrates was unjustly condemned. If Crito did not believe this, his attitude would surely be very different. In case anyone had any doubts on Socrates' own opinion, which is not likely, the Laws' apparent admission that the judges had wronged Socrates (54b8–c2) suggests with belated explicitness that Socrates, and even up to a point the Laws, shared Crito's view. It is very hard to believe that the Laws are not speaking in character on their own behalf when they stress their good faith in the matter by saying they were trying to destroy him in the belief that it was just to do so. The claim made here must therefore restrict itself: it must assert merely that the Laws put forward no argument which contradicts what Socrates and Crito have agreed earlier in the dialogue or violates Socrates' dialectical practice. In other words, if the person of Socrates were – *mirabile dictu* – to be transmuted into that of the Laws, he would not find himself giving voice to arguments whose force *in the present context* he would have flatly denied in his own person. That is to say, the arguments he would find himself developing are adequate dialectically against Crito, given the positions Crito has taken up in this dialogue. To accommodate what one may call accidental differences between the Laws and Socrates it is not necessary to separate the two parties completely, as some have recently tried to do. Somewhat similarly it is not necessary completely to separate Diotima in Plato's *Symposium* from Socrates just because she is a woman.

If thus an essential continuity links the two sections of Socrates' argument in the *Crito*, then why does Plato have Socrates introduce the Laws of Athens at all? Certain literary reasons could possibly have influenced Plato here. One is Socratic urbanity. Socrates is fairly harsh to his old friend at the outset in 46b1–3. I shouldn't myself like to be told that my ardour would be of great value *if only* I had got anything right, though critics have my full permission to tell me so. But at least Socrates' harshness is conditional, and he proposes an investigation of it as a question. Socrates has now, at 50a, to attack Crito, and to decline his personally brave and generous offer; it softens the blow somewhat to do so through an adopted persona. It is also a kindness to associate himself, albeit a hypothetical self, with his friend on the defensive. This he achieves by imagining the Laws confronting the pair of them as he is escaping.[192] Crito might have expected a sympathetic hearing from Socrates; he would not be so shocked to receive an unsympathetic hearing from the Laws.

There is also, since Plato may well have produced the *Crito* early in his writing career, a second possible motive. This concerns the deployment against Crito of what amounts to a prolonged rhetorical harangue. Though the Laws include in their long speeches questions, and at a number of points speak in a questioning tone, the whole is still a rhetorical piece such as would arouse the suspicions and perhaps elicit the rebuke of the Socrates of the *Protagoras* at 334c7–d5 and 336b1–3. In my view it is unnecessary to go into the complicated question of a philosophical rhetoric in Plato. Socrates' rhetorical tone may be justified dialectically, for readers sufficiently grounded in Plato's Socrates' dialectic to need any justification, by Crito's. Crito spoke earlier in the dialogue in sizable chunks of polished rhetorically-styled prose. If Socrates is entitled to use his interlocutors' methods as well as their propositional assumptions,[193] then Socrates is entitled here to argue in rhetorical style against Crito. Indeed he has already done so at 46b–47a, as we have seen, so that for him to launch into rhetoric now is not a new policy.

If we ask how to account for Crito's original use of rhetorical devices, without protest from Socrates, we do not have to fall back on the idea that Crito is a mere patsy set up for Socrates. Crito is trying to persuade Socrates, but is not a philosopher, and hence falls back on the most natural non-philosophical vehicle of persuasion, rhetoric. Within the fictional context Socrates may be showing kindness to his friend by not pulling him up short (as he does Protagoras in his dialogue). But though a rhetorical tone may be justified, a whole succession of long speeches such as we have in the final section of the *Crito* was still perhaps alien at the time of writing, or in the refutatory form of dialogue, to Plato's Socrates. It would lessen the resulting awkwardness to have Socrates fictionally 'reporting' someone else's harangue(s). If the harangue starts more dialectically, with more question-and-answer, than it finishes, that too is a feature it shares with Diotima's series of lessons for Socrates in Plato's *Symposium*.

(f) Opening shots

The Laws start, anyway, with arguments on the themes of Qs 1 and 2. Q1, my reader will recall, was about the treating badly of those whom (a generalizing masculine in the Greek, οὕς) we ought least to treat badly, and Q2 concerned the obligation to keep or 'abide by' a just agreement. I will abbreviate to (1) 'treating people badly' and (2) 'keeping agreements'. The opening salvos of the Laws' bombardment mix these two different types of ammunition: it is not necessarily clear either to Crito or to Plato's first-time reader what ammunition is in use on which part of the battle-front. Some first-time readers may have noticed that they are kept waiting for the explanation of our Qs 1 and 2. However, some may have spotted that (a) Socrates has personified the Laws, made them into people (masculine in Greek), who can then be 'treated badly' as in Q1; (b) the hypothetically escaping Socrates, with Crito, stands accused by the Laws at the outset of setting about their destruction, which could in certain circumstances be a case of treating them wickedly or badly – and is certainly a case of harming them. But the argument will not yet have succeeded in convincing Plato's intelligent readers that Socrates in escaping will be harming or treating wickedly those he least ought, let alone that he is breaking an agreement.

We may proceed, as Socrates is about to, from the general to the particular. Socrates lays before Crito a description of the action he has embarked on. This description has assuredly not entered Crito's head or even a normally intelligent first-time reader's head. But that is not because

Crito is a fool or because Plato was writing for stupid readers; it is because men of the world without philosophical inclinations would simply never have thought about it. If Crito had thought about it, it is reasonable to suppose that he would either have suppressed the thought in the interests of rescuing Socrates or found arguments to convince himself that the description did not of itself decide the question at issue. But this point surely does not force itself on Plato's reader's attention, and may safely be left aside. However that may be, the description the Laws volunteer is, as we shall see, couched in terms that Crito in particular, against the background of his previous arguments and positions, will find it hard to refute.

The description, then, of Socrates' hypothetical escape is that he is setting about 'to destroy' the Laws and the whole city 'so far as you are concerned', 'so far as in you lies', or, as T. Irwin renders,[194] 'so far as it is up to [you]'. If one were to destroy a city's laws, or, if you will, subvert them, one would indeed in effect be destroying or subverting the whole city.[195] At least this last is not a position repugnant to common sense. If it is not repugnant to common sense there is no reason why it should be repugnant to Crito or to sensible readers. The Laws' argument, however, is – by no means to its discredit – a trifle more specific. They appear to justify the addition of 'the whole city' by asking whether a city would not be destroyed as such if judgments in it were to have no force, and were to be invalidated and ruined by private individuals. So far, especially in a city as politically and privately litigious as classical Athens, the argument might sound plausible. If the argument persuaded some readers, who was Plato to complain? But the argument that 'if everybody did this it would be disastrous, and so nobody should do it', is open to criticisms, some obvious. Some have indeed treated this passage of the *Crito* as that kind of generalizing argument, and condemned it as such.[196]

Thoughtful or studious readers might have thought there was something fishy here. But scholars have not always been clear, as I suspect Plato wanted his readers to be, about the force here of 'as far as you are concerned'. The Laws do not say exactly that if everybody escaped from prison, or otherwise nullified the penalty arrived at by due process, the city and its laws would be destroyed, and that for this reason Socrates should not escape. They suggest only, by dint of a rhetorical question, that Socrates in escaping is *setting about* the city's destruction as far as he is concerned. The justification they offer concerns neither the total result of his actions nor the effect of everyone's following his example, but what he will be setting about by his act. Now at this point Socrates, the critics will say, could reply to the Laws that it is simply not the case that every single person who escapes from prison is setting about to destroy the city or state, and that is not what Socrates is setting about either. This much, even less practised ancient readers could easily see. The Laws would perhaps retort, though they do not actually say in the text, that any and every escapee is setting about, if he thinks about it as Socrates has, to do what in him lies to undermine that law, vital to the state, which insists on the finality of court decisions.

But what if 'what in him lies' is for practical purposes negligible? Are not the Laws still, in effect, assuming the cogency of the argument, 'If everybody did this it would be disastrous; therefore nobody ought to do it'? The answer to this is 'No: this is rather a case of Platonic dialectic.'[197] A philosopher arguing in the abstract might or (less probably) might not be able to press a successful objection to the Laws' point here; Crito certainly cannot, as we have seen, without cutting the ground from under a substantial piece of his own argument. We can see now that the description the Laws offer of the action Crito has urged and Socrates has hypothetically undertaken is not one that Crito can immediately refute or easily escape. That part of it which appears to be out of line with common sense is bound up with Crito's own previous language in argument, which he cannot abandon. The Laws may speak in rhetorical questions, but their rhetoric has dialectical force.

(g) Rhetoric: a programmatic statement?

Highly relevant here is the phrase at 50b7 'especially an orator' (ἄλλως τε καὶ ῥήτωρ), which has struck many as programmatic, as a warning that what follows will be a rhetorical harangue.[198] The phrase appears in the middle of the following sentence:

> Τί ἐροῦμεν, ὦ Κρίτων, πρὸς ταῦτα καὶ ἄλλα τοιαῦτα; πολλὰ γὰρ ἄν τις ἔχοι, ἄλλως τε καὶ ῥήτωρ, εἰπεῖν ὑπὲρ τούτου τοῦ νόμου ἀπολλυμένου ὃς τὰς δίκας τὰς δικασθείσας προστάττει κυρίας εἶναι. ἢ ἐροῦμεν πρὸς αὐτοὺς ὅτι κτλ.
>
> What shall we say, Crito, in reply to these and other similar remarks? For a man, especially an orator, could find many things to say in defence of this law as it is being destroyed, the one which ordains that judgments handed down should be final. Or shall we say in reply to them…?'

The fact that after some question-and-answer the Laws do indulge in pretty continuous rhetoric reinforces the 'programmatic' interpretation. The position of the phrase, at or near the beginning of a clearly distinct section of the dialogue, strengthens the interpretation further. Greek literature abounds in opening programmatic statements or hints; germane to readers of the *Crito* is Plato's programmatic opening to the *Apology*.[199] R. Weiss' reading of the present sentence of the *Crito* is extreme but not otherwise unusual. She supposes that in calling the remarks rhetorical Socrates 'decisively dissociates' himself from the speeches of the Laws. Socrates, she points out, says at *Apology* 17a–b that he is no orator, even though that statement was itself a rhetorical commonplace. Socrates there contrasts his own skill, that of speaking the unadorned truth, with his opponents' lies. Our sentence at 50b in the *Crito*, on Weiss' interpretation, puts Plato's readers 'on guard'. The reader's first thoughts would not be of a true, philosophic rhetoric, as apparently envisaged in passing in the *Gorgias*, from which Weiss cites 503a–b,[200] and in the doubtless later *Phaedrus.* The programmatic reading of 'especially an orator' may thus lend support to a sceptical attitude regarding Socrates' endorsement of the Laws' arguments.

If the whole sentence is indeed programmatic, then another observation by Weiss comes into play. Noticing that the phrase 'especially an orator' stands in the middle of a clause saying 'someone would find many things to say…' she points out that when Socrates uses such a clause he is not normally – nor would we expect him to be – about to endorse what the 'someone' would say. Like the previous point, this line of argument depends for its force on the common understanding of our sentence as setting out a programme for what follows. If the sentence is not after all programmatic, it becomes much easier to read the Laws' whole argument as a continuation and in part an explanation of Socrates' earlier dialectical reasoning.

Is it rash to challenge the simple assumption that Plato wrote this significant sentence to inform his readers of the sort of thing to come? Perhaps it is; but there is available an alternative interpretation which embeds the sentence firmly in its immediate context, and simply leaves no room for the programmatic reading. The case for this alternative, not to my knowledge made before, needs airing, and may open with a plain statement of what the alternative is. Socrates on the alternative view is saying that the importance of abiding by court decisions is a rhetorical commonplace on which 'someone', especially someone with the gift of the gab, could expatiate at length. Socrates, however, does not intend to go on at length on the vital significance of the particular law enjoining obedience to the courts; instead, he proceeds with a question to Crito. This concerns the proper reply to the Laws' suggestion that if private individuals are allowed to destroy the force of decisions handed down under the law the city will be turned upside down. On this reading the vital sentence turns into a relatively unimportant parenthesis.

A parenthesis, indeed, is what the shape of Socrates' speech suggests it is. Socrates first, at 50b5–6, puts to Crito the question what reply they are to offer the Laws, 'What shall we say, Crito, in answer to these and other such [remarks]?' At 50c1 he offers Crito, by way of a question, an answer to his own previous question: 'Shall we say that…?' What lies between a question and the answer would seem on the face of it to be parenthetical; the particle γάρ ('for') introducing our vital sentence certainly presents no obstacle to this.

But even a casual-looking parenthesis might have had a certain importance and a wider reference. What then is the reference of this parenthesis? It is not far to seek: Socrates, as we have just seen, has added to the obvious question, 'What shall we say in answer to these [remarks]?' the phrase 'and other such [remarks].' He goes on to explain the addition by remarking that there are on offer variations on the theme of this particular law's importance to the system, and that someone, especially an orator, could produce a large number of them. Scholars at least up to and including Weiss have noted indeed that the significance of court decisions for the constitution of Athens was a commonplace of the orators.[201] True, the specific points of their authority and finality tend in the orators to escape actual discussion unless the orator has an axe to grind. But many variations on the general theme were in fact available to the practised orator. But of course Socrates has no intention of supplying them; in the event he does not. He dissociates himself, with the phrase 'someone would find to say', from any such intention. The particular law at issue, though indeed it remains at issue throughout, receives no further amplification of its importance. All that Socrates is doing here is indicating in passing the potentially commonplace nature of the Laws' point. Since the point's commonplace nature and its rhetorical provenience need not make it false in Socrates' eyes, and would not even tend to make it false in Crito's eyes, an answer from Crito, such as Socrates immediately suggests, is clearly called for. The purpose of the addition 'and other such [remarks]' and of its explanation may have been to show Crito to the reader as impelled, being a normal Athenian, not to scoff at the question but to answer it.

A further consideration obtrudes itself. Greek authors' normal practice, after such a prefatory and programmatic statement, if 'especially an orator' is that, would be to begin to fulfil the programme at once. That is not quite what happens here. Instead, we have at 50c1–2 a question from Socrates and Crito about a possible reply to any defence of the law concerned. When the reply is forthcoming we have another question in retort. Oratory has not got under way yet. What comes next, too, far from being a matter of oratory, has for introduction the Laws offering something sounding distinctly like a Socratic 'programme'. At 50c8 they say, 'Socrates, do not be surprised at what we say, but answer, since you are accustomed to asking and answering questions.' For a while at least, the Laws do follow a Socratic pattern of question and answer. If the questions become steadily more rhetorical in manner and content, that too is not necessarily un-Socratic. Plato's Socrates does not always eschew rhetoric in presenting his questions, and some of them are fairly lengthy: see e.g. the questions put to Cephalus at *Republic* 331c, and to Protagoras at *Protagoras* 318b4ff. So in our *Crito*-passage there is nothing obviously unusual for Socratic-Platonic dialectic down to the end of this particular speech by the Laws at 51c4. One observes, however, that from 51c6 to 52d6 the Laws ask no questions, offering instead continuous oratory. After this questions reappear, but they are rhetorical questions: the Laws do not at this stage wait for Socrates' answers, but either leave the questions unanswered or give the answer themselves. If, then, the phrase at 50b7, 'especially an orator', is programmatic, the Laws postpone the implementation of the programme for a page or so; they insert, as we have seen, a quite different programme in that intervening passage. This is a strikingly unusual, if not unique, pattern in classical Greek literature. To say the least, the supposed rhetorical programme would have come in better at 51c–d than it does at 50b. If readers wish to take Socrates' suggested retort to the Laws at 50c1–2 not as anticipating, but as cutting short any rhetorical expatiation in defence of the particular law in question, it would seem rather hard to refute them. Such readers might remind us that Socrates does not equate this 'orator' with the personified Laws, nor do the Laws or he refer to this orator again. They might also point out that the reply Crito accepts from Socrates at 50c1–3 is a reply not to the orator who is singular, but to 'them', the Laws, in the plural. It is presumably a reply to the Laws' essential point here, that if individual citizens were to obey or disobey jury decisions at their whim, this would undermine Athenian society.

9

THE ARGUMENTS OF THE LAWS

(a) Introduction: a notorious passage

At all events, to the Laws' defence of the particular law validating court decisions Socrates offers Crito a possible answer, to the effect that the city had treated him unjustly (50c1–4), and Crito accepts it with apparent avidity. Socrates himself says nothing, at least for the moment, to indicate whether he would himself offer this reply to this defence.[202] Socrates certainly comes across as believing the truth of the proposition that he was unjustly condemned. But to believe a proposition true and to deem it an appropriate answer to a specific argument are two very different things. Crito accepts the conjunction of two statements, namely, with numbers attached, 'The city (1) did us an injustice and (2) adjudged the case wrongly.' Put thus as a possible reply in a question addressed to Crito which receives only Crito's affirmative answer and not Socrates', this pair of questions constitutes no commitment of Socrates. So we have to think what purpose, other than committing Socrates, Socrates' remarks here might fulfil.

This is, to Platonists, a notorious passage. The reason for its notoriety is that it has appeared to make nonsense of what, on older interpretations, was the only thing going on at 49b–e. According to these interpretations of 49b–e, all harming of the laws or harming of anybody else was forbidden. In particular harming in return was forbidden. Some moderns simply accepted, if they noticed it, that Crito comes perilously close to self-contradiction on this reading of the dialogue. Plato may not have minded, may even have foreseen, such readers. He does not, however, portray Crito elsewhere as stupid to the point of self-contradiction, and the plot as such readers see it is not likely to be the whole story. If we are to exercise interpretative charity we should take up again the present, more complicated reading of 49b–e. We would thus suppose Plato to have meant his more experienced and perhaps more thoughtful readers to have seen possibilities other than mere self-contradiction in our notorious passage. Such possibilities arise from readers' perception that 49b–e is vague, being open to more than one interpretation depending on what counted as unjust retaliation.

In view of that openness or vagueness, after Crito's expression of bewilderment at 50a4–5 and before proceeding with a refutation of Crito along the lines of the two bewildering questions which we labelled Q1 and Q2, Socrates would be well advised to attempt some further elucidation of Crito's views. Crito has ruled out unjust or wicked retaliation even by someone wickedly or unjustly harmed. But neither we nor Socrates know what counts for Crito as unjust or wicked retaliation. Experienced readers, and Socrates, need to know which, if any, of (R1)–(R4) Crito accepts. The right question for them to ask here is not so much what proposition(s) Socrates may be relying on, but rather what proposition(s) Crito is to be construed by such readers or by Socrates as accepting. Of course, Crito and even Plato's Socrates are unlikely to have thought of (R1)–(R4) in their modern shape. But 'What counts as unjust in retaliation?' is a question intelligible even for a non-philosopher, and certainly to Plato's Socrates. The relevance of the question in this context, too, should be graspable by Plato's Socrates, even if not fully by Crito.

So, after 49b–e and before asking the question at 50c1–2, Socrates does not yet know precisely what Crito's views are. He does not know whether what counts for Crito as unjust retaliation is what counts for (R1), (R2), (R3) or even (R4). He has as yet no clear premiss on which to base any subsequent argument; and he needs to know Crito's views with some clarity in order to use them to persuade or confute him according to his usual Platonic custom. Indeed, Crito's views on retaliation are not the only views of his which Socrates does not know, though on several of them he might entertain conjectures. Since the question at issue is to concern retaliation, and in particular to concern what counts in the present case as unjust retaliation, the discussion requires a reasonably clear idea of (1) the nature of the initial injustice; (2) the nature of the proposed retaliation; (3) the moral status of the proposed act of retaliation, both in normal (unvictimized) circumstances and in relation to the initial injustice. For all these the arguments Socrates is about to put into the mouth of the Laws and City of Athens, together with a few questions of Socrates' own, supply the necessary foundation.

(b) Nature and moral status of the proposed retaliation

(b1) *General*

The nature of the original injustice, (1) above, is not far to seek: obviously it is the city's apparent guilt of Socrates' unjust killing, in the eyes of Crito and many Athenians his unjust destruction.[203] It should accordingly come as no surprise when the Laws of Athens, appearing before Crito and the hypothetically escaping Socrates, begin at 50a8–9 with a question related not to the relatively easy (1) but to (2) (above), the nature of the proposed retaliation, and ask: 'What, Socrates, do you intend to do?' Socrates allows the Laws, by means of a question or two, somewhat rhetorically phrased, to suggest an answer. He and they give Crito an opportunity of a sort to protest, to give the unexpected and unwanted answer. But, as we have seen,[204] Crito's ability to protest and/or to provide clarification is limited, after the normal fashion of Socratic dialectic, by what he has said previously, and by his whole position.

As for the moral status of the proposed retaliation,[205] question (3) above, that depends on whether or not Crito accepts the excuse for escape which Socrates offers himself and Crito at 50c1–4. The city's initial injustice is relevant only under certain conditions. If Crito intended earlier to agree to (R1), the excuse is irrelevant, and he should refuse it; he does not refuse, but eagerly adopts it. Sophisticated ancient readers, therefore, will charitably have supposed that Crito never intended to accept anything like our (R1). If Crito intended to accept (R2), matters are a little more complicated. If Socrates' alleged attempt to destroy the Laws, so far as in him lies, would under normal circumstances be an injustice, then the proposition that the Laws have treated Socrates unjustly will not justify Socrates in making his unjust attempt. The attempt (i.e. the escape) will be forbidden *unless* there are other reasons to justify it. Now Crito has advanced other reasons to justify it; on most of these Socrates has already cast doubt, at 48c with the preceding arguments. It remains to be seen how much the remainder amount to. If Crito means to stick with (R2), he will have to work hard.

Crito may have meant to endorse only (R3); to stick with that would give him an easier time. On (R3) the city's prior injustice provides a possible line of defence, but with a proviso attached. The proviso is that the injustice done to Socrates is equivalent to or greater than the injustice Socrates' attempt at the Laws' destruction would do to the Laws in circumstances where Socrates had not been a victim. If Crito is taking this line, that is (R3), Socrates will have to do more than refute Crito's arguments for the justice of the escape. In this case he or his creatures the Laws will have to show that the escape would be in normal circumstances a greater injustice even than the Laws' proposed destruction of Socrates. If Crito meant to agree with (R4), the Laws will have to show in addition that no other point that Crito has made justifies Socrates in escaping.

Crito, if we have read him exactly, has accepted a veto not on doing harm, but only on returning injustice for injustice or wickedness for wickedness. Socrates and the Laws have given him as yet no reason to suppose that Socrates' projected escape is a piece of injustice or wickedness, let alone a greater piece of wickedness than the Laws' unjust attempt to kill Socrates. The Laws' immediate response at 50c4 to Crito's implicit disavowal of at least (R1), their response that Socrates has an agreement with them, is a preliminary sketch of a part of their coming fuller reply to that very point. As we shall see, the wickedness or injustice of what Socrates is doing to the Laws lies partly in its involvement of him in a supposed breach of agreement. But of course that is not merely unknown to Crito; it is extremely surprising to any first-time reader.

The Laws, however, have a prior consideration to dispose of, namely, the *moral status* of the escaping Socrates' and Crito's complaint of the city's injustice. In disposing of this, the Laws argue that Socrates' attempted destruction of them is a greater injustice than their attempted destruction of him. They also show, after their lights, that they are the very last entities, indeed (in a sense) the very last people, that Socrates should treat wickedly or unjustly. They thus, in sum, explain both Q1 and Q2. More importantly, they are on the way to showing that the hypothetically escaping Socrates is, even *by Crito's lights*, as revealed by his answer to Socrates' exploratory question at 50c1–2, committing an unjust act of retaliation. That is to say, they are on the way to showing that even under the relatively relaxed (R3) or the still more relaxed (R4) Socrates' escape will count as unjust.

Hypothetically, then, Socrates and Crito defend the escape by complaining about the city's initial injustice to Socrates in condemning him. We find in what follows a set of surprises for Crito and the reader. The mention of an *agreement* to abide by court decisions is only the first of the set. The Laws' words, 'Don't be surprised, Socrates,' indicate how surprising that remains, even after the mention of agreements in the lead-up to the Laws. Next, instead of explaining the 'agreement', the Laws start on another tack: what complaint does Socrates have against the city? The freshness of the tack is itself surprising, but the question is even more so. Surely, most readers want to ask in return, Crito has just answered this question, with reference to the injustice of the trial? Obviously one ought to expect surprises from a dramatist of Plato's calibre. Here, as elsewhere in Plato, a surprising remark becomes gradually clearer as the dialogue develops, until the reader can see it as, for Plato, inevitable. The Laws have indeed on the present occasion a few further surprising questions up their sleeve. What makes some of these remarkable is their seeming irrelevance to the question at issue. But this is a habit of the Platonic Socrates, as scholars have often observed, in beginning an elenchus or confutation: his questions are ambushes. They cause the respondent, here as elsewhere, to give away too much without realizing at the time that he is doing so.

Here Socrates appears to expect, and in fact receives, no protest from Crito when the hypothetical Socrates answers the Laws' questions with helpful politeness. The Laws proceed, by means of such questions, to controvert Socrates' claim of injustice done to him by the city. Essentially they show their own special status; the argument thus makes them out to be 'those whom [he] ought least to treat wickedly'. The designation 'special status argument' accorded to this passage by S. Panagiotou thus fits what it actually says better than A.D. Woozley's 'benefits argument',[206] popular though the latter has remained.[207]

Socrates' answers to the Laws' seemingly irrelevant questions affirm simply his agreement that: (a) he finds no fault with the laws of marriage under which his parents were married and procreated him, and (b) he finds no fault with the laws of nurture and education under which he was educated, the laws having ordered his training in 'music and gymnastic'.[208] Under (a) Socrates agrees, presumably but inexplicitly on the principle *Qui facit per alium facit per se*, that the laws of marriage had procreated him. This admission, or acceptance without protest, turns out to be disastrous for Crito, however plausible it may seem as one reads or listens in the order of Plato's exposition. It leads directly to a further admission: Socrates is – he means he is *in effect* – the child of the Laws. Having, on Crito's behalf, failed to protest earlier, Socrates cannot protest on Crito's behalf now. Nor does there seem to be any apparent reason why Crito himself should leap up in rage. There is nothing *as yet* in the Laws' claim to parenthood that might alarm Crito, however dubious or even outrageous the claim may seem. Experienced readers of dialectic could recall that Crito has pressed the claims of children on Socrates at 45c10–d9. As a child of the Laws, from Crito's present point of view, Socrates has an added claim on their fairness and even their generosity. The special obligations of parents did not go unrecognized in classical Athens: for example, Sophocles' character Antigone at *Oedipus Coloneus* 1189–91 brings them out. Less experienced readers would doubtless be swept up in the powerful dramatic effect of the Laws' questions.

But, though nothing so far directly menaces Crito's plans, he ought to have heard alarm-bells ringing in his mind at (b) above, when Socrates' imaginative creation, the Laws, add casually at 50e3–4 that Socrates, and his ancestors into the bargain, are their slaves. Slaves do not have quite the claims on masters that children have on parents. This anxiety could have lasted at least till 50e8–9, where again Socrates is liable to the disadvantages of slavehood. But that particular set of disadvantages is not likely to cause Crito anxiety for long. There are two reasons for that. First, in any case the slave-image virtually disappears after these two brief forays into the argument, to reappear only once in passing, so that Crito might almost as well forget it. Secondly, this fleeting reappearance, at 52d2, a mere allusion in a flight of rhetoric, is its only appearance independently of the child-image, so that it has little separate *argumentative* force. In the argument the dominant image is that of the father-child relationship, not that of master and slave.

Socrates' status as slave to the Laws is in some ways easier for them to put across than that of their child: masters could and did encourage slaves to breed, without necessarily breeding them in fleshly fact themselves. A few no doubt arranged for slaves to have such education as would fit them for whatever tasks they were eventually to be assigned. Certainly at least basic literacy and numeracy would often have been useful. The Laws do up to a point behave like masters. So this metaphor is at least in part more plausible as an image than the one of parenthood. The two images complement each other: masters bred slaves in a manner more like the Laws' than actual parents; parents did more by way of education than masters. Those Laws that are set over upbringing and education exhorted (παραγγέλλοντες 50d8) Socrates' father to teach him the arts and gymnastic, doubtless more education than a normal slave received. In consequence the Laws make bold to ask 'Could you say that you were not both our offspring and our slave?' It would be easy for Crito, if he were given the chance, to deny that the Laws were his parents or his masters: they are not literally either. But Plato and his Socrates do not give him the chance. Unfair? Well, yes; but there are extenuating circumstances for this procedure of the fictional Socrates. In Crito's earlier argument, at 44c2–3, 44e2–6, and 45a8–b1 Crito himself asks rhetorical questions. The first and third of these Socrates does not answer, and the middle one he protests only mildly against, without stopping Crito's flow of rhetoric. Both parties in this dialogue from time to time expect their opponent to view and answer their argument as a whole, rather than pick nits. Plato's fairness or unfairness is another matter. But in giving us a rhetorical, un-dialectical Crito, he has at least created a common enough type of man, perhaps the type of man he wanted in the first instance to convince.

Socrates need feel no embarrassment at the Laws' method of debate. Still less need he feel embarrassed at their use on occasion of his language. 'Do not be surprised', they say to the hypothetically escaping Socrates, and, though only the most observant of Plato's ancient readers will have recognized the fact, and probably none of the *Crito*'s initial readers, this language is found in Plato, with the present imperative, only in the mouth of Socrates or of other characters who in some measure represent or replace him: Socrates at *Euthd.* 277d4 and *Grg.* 482a3, Diotima at *Smp.* 205b4,

207c–d, and the Athenian Stranger at *Laws* 637c6. It was part of Plato's normal literary technique to have his principal character propound views or questions hard to understand and calculated to surprise, label them as surprising, and dispel the surprise by explanation. Another Socratic trait here in the Laws' address is the request to answer. This is less exclusively Socratic; but the exceptions in Plato are: Dionysodorus and Euthydemus who are sufficiently like Socrates – superficially speaking – to need distinguishing from him; people speaking on Socrates' behalf, e.g. Gorgias at *Grg.* 497b4, Chaerephon at 448b–2, Socrates' 'friend' at *Hipp. Ma.* 288e5 and 291b2. The only 'odd one out' that I have found is in a probably *late* dialogue, at *Phileb.* 18a5, where Protarchus asks Socrates to answer Philebus. The reader may want to argue that Socrates and his congeners give the instruction to 'answer' because in the early dialogues it is Socrates who normally does all the questioning, who adopts a questioning stance. Quite so. The Laws in the *Crito* are therefore adopting that Socratic stance together with the appropriate Socratic language. The use here of ἀποκρίνου, 'Answer!', deepens the Socratic tinge of the Laws' speeches. Their manner is less un-Socratic than one might at first glance suppose.

The 'father'-metaphor presented by the Laws in this paragraph has a particular point. It helps to establish the Laws' credentials not only as quasi-people, but also as extra-special people. This Plato achieves by means of a pun. At 51c1–3 the Laws assert by way of climax that it is not pious to offer violence to either one's mother or one's father, far less to one's fatherland. This pun on πατήρ, *pater*, and πατρίς, *patris*, father and fatherland, is prepared by the contrast at 50e7 and 51a2 πρὸς μὲν ἄρα σοι τὸν πατέρα...πρὸς δὲ τὴν πατρίδα ἄρα..., 'in relation to your father...and in relation to your fatherland' (and see also 51b3–4). The pun causes the laws and the state to seem, rhetorically, closely related to parents. This, in a context where the state acts as master to parents and offspring, reinforces the state's position in the same hierarchy of sacredness as parents, but on a higher level. The Laws' appearance here as specially sacred people, indeed in this respect the whole paragraph 50c10–51c5, exhibits so close a correspondence with Q1, at 50a1–2, 'Are we treating some people badly, and, at that, those we least ought to?', as to show that Plato wrote the question, and imagined his Socrates asking it, with the later paragraph already in mind.

This special point, the pun, is absent from the 'slave'-metaphor. This is one place where the slave-metaphor does not help. But that does not completely explain why it disappears so quickly. That may be because, since Athenians and indeed Greeks in general did not like to think of themselves as slaves, the image has much less emotional power, and carries a higher rhetorical risk, than the father-son metaphor. 'More sacred even than a father' was a far more highly charged description than 'more sacred even than a master' to a free Athenian citizen, even if he owned one or more slaves. But Plato's temporary fusion of the two normally incompatible images, one powerful, the other in certain respects more plausible, shows high persuasive, rhetorical cunning.

It is insufficient to treat these images as *mere* metaphors, without dialectical value. Modern analytical philosophers, quarrying this and other Platonic dialogues for arguments to build into edifices of their own, will find little of direct use in this paragraph of the Crito. This remains true, though the analogy of Law and citizen, or of state and citizen, with father and son still appears, not always with disrespect, in modern philosophical argument.[209] But of Socrates' dialectical argument with Crito the metaphors form a part neither insignificant nor wholly reprehensible. At the point and in the context where Crito faces them, Crito has no reason to stamp on them. Metaphorical they may be, but Crito has no special reason at the time to object. Even before the argument which follows in the text, there is no reason to doubt that one's city did have a special claim on one, a claim analogous to the claims of a parent. Crito is not being stupid in not bringing up the obligations of parents to children. Rather he has no present dialectical reason to interrupt Socrates in mid-flow by bringing up this point. Provided Crito is prepared to admit that one's country has a special claim on one, as many ordinary people would to-day as in classical Athens, any objection he might raise to the metaphors expressing that claim would be peripheral.

(b2) *Unequal justice*

In any case, this paragraph in the dialogue contains more than mere metaphor. It contains also an argument, for which indeed in the larger scheme of the dialogue the metaphors may supply merely rhetorical embellishment or reinforcement. We may call this the argument from Unequal Justice. It runs from 50e1 to 51a7, with ramifications beyond. Its shape is something like this:

	(p) Socrates is the Laws' child (and slave).
Therefore	(q) Justice is not on an equal footing between Socrates and the Laws.
Therefore	(r) (i) It is not just for Socrates to do to the Laws whatever they try to do to him.
And	(r) (ii) In particular, if the Laws *thinking it just* (δίκαιον ἡγούμενοι 51a4) try to destroy Socrates, it is not just

for Socrates to try to the extent of his ability to destroy them.

(s) Socrates is his father's child (and might have been a slave).

Therefore (t) Justice was not on an equal footing between Socrates and his father (or hypothetical master).

Therefore (u) (i) It was not just for Socrates to do to his father (or hypothetical master) what his father (or hypothetical master) did (or might do) to him.

And (u) (ii) In particular it was not just for Socrates to return his father verbal insult for verbal insult or blow for blow, etc.

One notices here that (p)–(r) correspond pretty well with (s)–(u). The argument is mainly an analogy. But, first, the Laws argue (51a7 ff.) that (r) (i) and (r) (ii) have more force than (u) (i) and (u) (ii), since (q) has more force than (t), because the Laws are more sacred than a father. The analogy has an admixture of *a fortiori*. Secondly, (u) (ii) comes with no equivalent of the phrase italicized above 'thinking it just' found in (r) (ii) at 51a4. This second point will receive attention shortly.

That then is the general structure of this argument. Now, on the older interpretation of 49b–e, the present argument contains a dark place discovered, to her lasting credit, by V. Harte.[210] If κακουργεῖν (*kakourgein*) means 'harm' rather than 'wrongfully harm', and if 49b–e accordingly rules out *all* retaliation, then, if Plato realized just what the Laws' sentence implied, he has made the Laws' argument contradict Crito's earlier agreement. We are then driven to divorce the Laws' argument from the line of argument Socrates was developing earlier. Plato could pretty safely have banked on many readers missing the contradiction. But such a contradiction seems an unlikely thing for Plato to have constructed in the awareness that his most sensitive and intelligent readers would notice it.

It is time therefore to apply our earlier results concerning what Crito may have agreed to accept from Socrates at 49b–e to what we find in this argument of the Laws. We established that on (R3) or (R4), neither of which Crito has ruled out, the Laws have to minimize (or abolish) their injustice to Socrates in condemning him, and maximize his injustice to them in hypothetically escaping. The Laws' aim should be to emerge with a view of Socrates' hypothetical criminal escape which presents it as, in ordinary circumstances, a greater injustice than Socrates' condemnation and forthcoming execution. If they fail to do this and if Crito embraces (R3) or (R4), they will have lost or endangered their case, and Crito will, or at least should, have plenty to say at the end of the dialogue, instead of, as is the fact, nothing.

It does not seem likely to take us too far afield if we settle an awkward question first: *in what way* are we to suppose that justice is not equal between parent and child or between master and slave? In what respect is the playing field not level? Imagine, for example, a father catching his teenage son stealing apples from the orchard. The father, in his forties, is still sufficiently stronger than his son to administer a beating, and does so not from spite or other disreputable motive, but rather to teach him a moral lesson, in addition to giving him what seems to the father a just punishment for stealing. There is then no way that any normal society would tolerate (say) a 13-year-old turning round and striking his father. Nor would any normal society suppose that if the 13-year-old caught his father stealing from an orchard he would be justified in going beyond protest by striking his father, however sound his motives for doing so.[211] But, if the father were to extend the beating unreasonably and unfairly, then the son would be justified in turning on him. Though society might not exactly like that either, the son would at least have an arguable case in morals if not in law. *Mutatis mutandis* no doubt the same would hold of a master and slave. In that sense justice is not equal, is not on an equal footing, between either father and son or master and slave. In that sense it would be true that, whereas between adults of the same status one would have a right to take a just revenge on some definitions of 'just revenge', the same does not always hold good between father and son or between master and slave. If the person taking revenge is of lesser standing in a relevant respect than the person doing the original injustice, the line between just and unjust revenge is drawn differently. Even such revenge as is merely equal in *prima facie* injustice to the original injustice done may, on such a sloping playing field, be ruled out. Crito may, quite consistently with what he has rather vaguely agreed, accept that:

(a) if a father, e.g., beats his son unjustly, the son may not, within the rules, beat his father in return, and

(b) if an adult of normal status beats another adult of normal status unjustly, the beaten adult may, within the rules, beat the beater in return.

If we apply this, by the analogy the Laws clearly intend, to their quarrel with the hypothetically escaping Socrates, we find that Crito may, by the same token, accept that:

(a*) if the Laws try to destroy a citizen, the citizen may not, within the rules, try to destroy the Laws in return;

(b*) if the citizen is of equal status with the Laws and the Laws try to destroy him, the citizen may, within the rules, try to destroy the Laws.

But, with respect to (b*), the Laws argue that the citizen is not of equal status with them. If they are right in that, the operative proposition is (a*).

This reasoning appears to work, provided always that one accepts the application of the analogy between Laws and parent, if Crito accepts the proposition (R3). It would not suffice by itself if Crito accepted only the less austere (R4). For (R4) would, with the same proviso, entail that, although the Laws' attempt to destroy Socrates would not justify his attempt to destroy them, some other justification might nevertheless be found for Socrates' attempt. If Socrates is allowing Crito (R4), then Socrates must refute other justifications which Crito has advanced or might advance. Though some such refutation may occur later, it has not yet been announced. At the present stage of the argument, therefore, it remains still unclear, for those readers capable of making the necessary distinctions, whether Socrates has understood Crito as having accepted (R3) or (R4).

One further point in the analogy requires a close look here. We ought to inspect a query raised by P. Unruh.[212] If parents set about the actual destruction of their children, were the children permitted no retaliation in kind? In certain circumstances this could prevent the children from defending themselves. The question whether self-defence is licit is one Plato's readers might want to ask. But Plato has skated over it at 50c–51a. There children are committing injustice if they strike back against parents who strike them. The extreme case of a parent attempting murder receives no attention. The only case of actual destruction the Laws mention here is their own attempted destruction of Socrates, mentioned indeed a couple of sentences later. In the case of parents, blow for blow: in the case of the Laws, attempted destruction for attempted destruction. There is a gap in the Laws' argument here, a gap still yawning when the argument ends at 52c. There the Laws compare *violence* against parents with violence done to the Laws: again no mention of parents attempting to kill a child. Naturally child murder was a rare thing – granted that exposure of infants did not count.[213] This makes it more intelligible that Plato should not have thought about it. Exposed infants, however, were not normally in a position to retaliate. But the Laws' analogy is at this rather central point flawed. Plato may possibly have spotted the flaw himself, but thought that someone like Crito would not see it through Socrates' rhetorical smokescreen. Alternatively, Plato may have been carried away by his own rhetoric. In this particular instance it is hard to produce a decisive argument for either possibility.

In the above account of a crucial argument there is an element of what one may loosely call good faith. That means: if the father is to claim the benefit of a father's superior status, he must, minimally, believe honestly that the punishment he is administering is just. His motives, at least his conscious reasons, must not be disreputable. He must be punishing in good faith. Socrates does not, so far as I can see, mention this point at all in connection with his own father. The Laws, and Socrates with them, are prepared to assume, without directly saying, that Socrates' father was a loving and benevolent one. The nearest approach to explicitness about this is Socrates' admitted lack of complaint (50d1–e1) about the laws concerning his parents' marriage and his upbringing: Socrates might have had a complaint if his father had been other than loving and benevolent. The Laws have to be more explicit than this when they speak of their own relationship to Socrates, in view of Crito's attitude of blame for their injustice to Socrates. They must exonerate themselves from the possible charge of malice. This they do quite sufficiently at 51a4 when they mention that they are setting about Socrates' destruction δίκαιον ἡγούμενοι εἶναι, in the belief that it is just. Crito does not dispute that they believe this, and indeed it would be hard to do so: the legal system has to assume the lack of malice in final legal decisions. In these circumstances, and if the foregoing exposition is right, the Laws are justified in asking sarcastically whether Socrates will say that in setting about their destruction he is acting justly (51a6–7). It does not matter, on their not entirely unreasonable view, that they may be, *prima facie* unjustly, trying to destroy Socrates. That would only be relevant on a level playing field, and the field in their view slopes. If their motives include an honest belief that they are acting justly, and exclude malice, then Socrates may not justly retaliate in kind, or at least may not so retaliate without further justification.

(b3) *The requirement of obedience*

What I have called this crucial paragraph of the *Crito* contains another thing needing discussion. That is the requirement of obedience to the Laws. This is not the place to launch into a full analysis of the extensive literature on the consistency of the *Crito* on this point with the *Apology*. That consistency in any case depends in the first instance on what will be discussed here, namely, the consistency of the Laws' claim to obedience here with earlier agreements in this dialogue between Crito and Socrates. On this subject J. DeFilippo, in *Ancient Philosophy* 11 (1991), in my view did everything necessary but dot a few 'i's and cross a few 't's; and some of his points are repeated unconsciously by D. Gallop in *Ancient Philosophy* 18 (1998). But R. Weiss' reply to DeFilippo deserves some retort, and has called forth the discussion which follows.

Plato's first and fullest exposition of the citizen's duty in this respect comes at 51b2:

> ...καὶ σέβεσθαι δεῖ καὶ μᾶλλον ὑπείκειν καὶ θωπεύειν πατρίδα χαλεπαίνουσαν ἢ πατέρα, καὶ ἢ πείθειν ἢ ποιεῖν ἃ ἂν κελεύῃ, καὶ πάσχειν ἐάν τι προστάττει παθεῖν ἡσυχίαν ἄγοντα, ἐάντε τύπτεσθαι ἐάντε δεῖσθαι ἐάντε εἰς πόλεμον ἄγῃ τρωθησόμενον ἢ ἀποθανούμενον, ποιητέον ταῦτα, καὶ τὸ δίκαιον οὕτως ἔχει, καὶ οὐχὶ ὑπεικτέον οὐδὲ ἀναχωρητέον οὐδὲ λειπτέον τὴν τάξιν, ἀλλὰ καὶ ἐν πολέμῳ καὶ ἐν δικαστηρίῳ καὶ πανταχοῦ ποιητέον ἃ ἂν κελεύῃ ἡ πόλις καὶ ἡ πατρίς, ἢ πείθειν αὐτὴν ᾗ τὸ δίκαιον πέφυκε·
>
> And one ought to reverence and be subservient to and give way to a fatherland when it is angry more than to a father, and either persuade it or do whatever it bids, and suffer quietly anything it may order, whether a beating or an imprisonment, or if it drive you to war to be wounded or killed, you must do these things, and that is how justice stands, and you ought not to yield, to retreat, or desert the ranks, but both in war and in the courts and everywhere you ought to do whatever the city and the fatherland bid, or persuade it, as is just.[214]

First, effectively, ποιεῖν, 'do [whatever the city bids]', is 'glossed' here (as DeFilippo put it[215]) by πάσχειν, 'suffer [whatever the city bids]'. If this sounds at first far-fetched, then my readers are asked to exercise some patience. The Laws mention no example of a citizen *doing* anything active;[216] and when we have at 51b7 ποιητέον ταῦτα, 'you must do these things', the obvious answer to the question what one must do is, in the context, to *be* wound*ed* or kill*ed*. There would indeed normally be certain things of a more active nature that one must *not* do, such as to run away in the face of the enemy, but no positive action makes any appearance among the things enjoined by the Laws here. True, one could describe the suffering(s) concerned in active terms, such as 'endure wounds' or 'face death'. But the Laws do not so describe them. There is no reason to suggest that the absence of such a description is merely coincidental. Secondly, the immediate context limits the Laws' meaning: the first injunction to persuade or obey is predicated on a state of affairs in which the fatherland is angry with you ('when it is angry', χαλεπαίνουσαν b3–4). It is *then* that you must either persuade or obey, in court and not, initially, in any other circumstances.[217] The addition of the obligation to suffer wounds or death in war is merely an addition of another kind of suffering one ought to undergo. In this addition, the city is of course no longer angry with the citizen, and its anger with the enemy is irrelevant, but that does not negate the limitation of obedience at its first appearance to the case of the city's anger. Nor does it change the meaning of 'doing whatever the city bids', which continues to refer to suffering whatever the city metes out to you. The city may mete out suffering in war as well as in court, and perhaps in other spheres as well; everywhere (πανταχοῦ b10) [sc. that it does so] one must persuade or obey, that is persuade or take one's medicine. Presumably one must persuade the city either in court of one's innocence or in the assembly that to go to war is wrong. After that it is too late.[218]

DeFilippo's view of the verb 'do' in 'do whatever [the city] bids', that it is glossed by 'suffer', raises a question: why should Plato arrange for the Laws to use words in this peculiar way? Why bring in 'do' at all when 'suffer' is effectively what one means? Indeed without a convincing answer to this question one can see why scholars might be reluctant to take DeFilippo's interpretation on board. DeFilippo's answer simply makes Plato and his Socrates use language loosely, as (in DeFilippo's comparison) a modern employer might in certain contexts do to a subordinate employee. It is far from clear why Plato should give Socrates loose language at so important a stage in the argument. The answer offered here in any case arises out of, and has a certain effect on, our understanding of the dialogue's structure. It takes us accordingly some way back. It starts with Socrates' question at 49e5–7: 'Should one do the things one agrees [to do] if they are just?' The answer next points to 52d9–e5, where, as will be argued below, the Laws contend that Socrates thought the agreement he had made with the Laws just, in the sense that it did not require him to do anything unjust. This contention is necessary in order to complete the Laws' point that in running away Socrates would be breaking an agreement which required him to do nothing which he thought unjust. It is the breaking of an agreement requiring one to do nothing unjust which Socrates gets Crito to rule out by his question at 49e5–7. So: one must not break an agreement which requires one to do no injustice; the citizen promises to do whatever the Laws, in certain circumstances, order; to do what the Laws in those circumstances order is not to do any injustice. To preserve the logic of this, once the initial question has used the word 'do', the succeeding steps in the argument, if they use a word for 'do' or 'suffer' at all, must employ, however they gloss it, the word 'do'.

Now evidently this line of thought merely postpones our question. We now have to ask why the word 'do' appears in the original question at 49e, when it is going to look inappropriate later. There is more than one reason available. The first is that, if one is thinking about keeping an agreement in general, one's thoughts turn most naturally to doing, rather than suffering, and the question at 49e5–7 is inescapably general. The second is that in the argument immediately preceding the question and forming its context the two participants in the conversation have been talking about and in some sense ruling out doing, rather than suffering, injustice. In this context, fulfilling an agreement is clearly a particular kind of avoidance of doing, rather than suffering, injustice; the proviso attached to the agreement must accordingly itself be that one must avoid doing injustice by way of fulfilment. The third is that Socrates would be dialectically unwise to ask Crito a question about suffering what one has agreed to suffer, in a context where suffering the death penalty is obviously in the foreground of thought. One might expect Crito, who has shown himself not wholly unwary in dialectic, to see the sort of thing that is likely to come, and object. It results that the word 'do' is so important structurally for this whole argument that Socrates cannot allow the Laws to bypass it; but he can and does allow them to gloss it with 'suffer' as and when appropriate.

There are two further, interrelated reasons why this perhaps surprising reading of what looks like a general requirement of obedience ought not, after all, to surprise. Both draw on the context of 'persuade or obey'. The first draws on the immediate context in the Laws' harangue; the second draws on the wider context of the dialogue as a whole and in its fictional setting.

First, the immediate context: this paragraph of the Laws' argument speaks only of not hitting back *when you suffer.* That is what the model of father and son is about at 50e–51a. We hear what the son must *not* do: he must not strike back when struck, and must not respond equivalently when verbally attacked, nor do other such things. There is no word of what the son must positively do; what is enjoined on him is essentially what the Laws enjoin on Socrates: to suffer ἡσυχίαν ἄγοντα, 'holding his peace', or 'going quietly'. In terms of (R3) and (R4), the son should refrain from any revenge which, given his father's status *as* a father, would, by outweighing or threatening to outweigh the father's injustice to him, endanger the justice of the revenge. In the analogy of the father, and less significantly in the briefly despatched analogy of the master, the Laws say nothing at all of the father or master giving positive orders or having to be obeyed in a positive action.[219]

This is thoroughly consonant with the context of the *Crito* as a whole. The context does not call on Socrates to do anything active at the Laws' behest. It requires him only not to attempt to destroy them when they, in the belief that they are acting justly, set about destroying him. He is required to suffer what the Laws of Athens command, not to do, whether or not the action would be just, whatever positive deed they enjoin. They have assigned to him certain suffering, to wit, the death penalty. So, through the personified Laws he insists on suffering it, in the interests of justice.[220]

R. Weiss has attempted, in my view unsuccessfully, to stand this argument on its head.[221] She believes that though the Laws repeatedly (in her opinion) tell the hypothetically escaping Socrates that he is bound to do positively whatever they command, they nevertheless mention only his suffering what they command, because that is what the dialogue is about. That fails to take into account a significant point. To have the Laws say to Socrates that he must on all occasions *do* whatever they order is to have them make a vast claim which they do not need.[222] The claim, moreover, would stand in need of far more defence than is offered by the analogies of father/son and master/slave as the text presents them. A second and separate point is this: the claim ought to raise Crito's hackles. He and Socrates earlier ruled out injustice; what if the Laws command one to do what is unjust? There are possible answers to that: perhaps the Laws' command confers justice on any action, even if otherwise unjust? Perhaps the Laws cannot admit to ever issuing an order to do an injustice? But the point stands: there is a major question here, and only a Crito (or indeed a reader) who was not following the argument and/or had scant verbal intelligence could fail to raise it.[223] What would Plato's intelligent readers then make of Crito – except that he was a mere patsy? That is what some of the moderns (including Weiss) would indeed like to make of him. But their evidence from other parts of the dialogue is thin, and the theory is surely an insult to Plato's contemporary readers, apparently not expected to perceive the obvious. Why *should* the Laws make such a claim, when they do not need it, and when to make it would be so risky? The scholarly literature I have read canvasses no clear answer to that question.

Weiss does, however, present another argument:[224] 'In the passage immediately following that cited by DeFilippo, the Laws say twice that the citizen must do "whatever we bid" (*Cr.* 51e3–4 and 52a1–2), yet there is no…gloss similar to that by πάσχειν [suffer] brought out by DeFilippo at 51b4–5.' To this it is necessary to reply that once you have glossed a word, especially if you have glossed it in a way which fits the context like a glove, you do not need to gloss it again. It is hard to think of a reason why Crito should have been tempted to suppose that the phrases at 51e and 52a ἃ ἂν κελεύωμεν ποιήσειν ταῦτα, or ποιεῖν ἃ ἂν κελεύωμεν ('to do whatever we bid'), have now changed their reference from 'suffering' to one new to the dialogue and not needed in its argument. Weiss' reasoning fails.

In view of that failure, there is a further question to be asked and answered about the parent/child and master/slave analogies. Just how far does the force extend of the analogy between the Laws' relationship to Socrates and the relationships of parent and child and of master and slave? One point of the analogy, at least, should by now be clear: it rules out, because of the Laws' superior status, any otherwise unjustified tit-for-tat on the part of the citizen. But does it constrain the citizen to universal obedience to the law? What is the argument from analogy, and what is it intended to prove? We may begin by asking yet another question, namely: after the superior-status, sloping-playing-field phase of the argument is over, just what role do the analogies take? The answer to this is, 'Not a very substantial role.' Mother and father (and indeed other forebears) serve as a standard of comparison, in that the fatherland is more august, more holy, and held in higher esteem by gods and men, than they; and the angry fatherland requires more respect, yielding, or subservience, than an angry father.[225] The subservient, yielding behaviour required in each case – by father or fatherland – is taking one's punishment without talking or hitting back; it is, as we saw, glossed by πάσχειν..., 'suffer...'.

The alternative to such subservience is persuasion. It is unclear in the Greek at this point whether or not this alternative applies to the father (and there is not even a suggestion that it applies to a master). If it does so apply, then a son is very naturally allowed, when his father accuses him, to persuade his father, if he can, of his innocence – perhaps, indeed, even to persuade him that the supposed offence is not offensive. The requirement of universal obedience to a parent emerges no more from what the Laws say about parents than from what they say about the city, the fatherland and themselves. Nor should this be a matter for surprise. For parents do not, and did not, and could not, exact universal obedience after childhood, whereas the Laws, *if* they exact such obedience at all, do not stop when the citizen grows up. What the Laws do share, by virtue of their special status, is an immunity from force or violence, which against them ranks as worse sacrilege than violence against parents. The gravamen of the whole of Plato's paragraph remains that for reasons essentially of status one may not hit back at, or try to destroy in return, the Laws, as one may not hit back at, or try to destroy in return, a parent.

This has a consequence for the next paragraph in Plato's text, a consequence it is perhaps best to mention briefly here. When the Laws speak at 52e3–7 of disobedience to them as parents and as up-bringers, they must intend Crito and Socrates to think of cases of the son failing, not to obey any imaginable command of his parents, but rather to take the punishment meted out by his angry father. If this is not their intention, then the ground shifts seismically between one paragraph and the next, and a serious *non sequitur* results. My readers may observe in Plato's text that this point about obedience to the Laws as parents is syntactically separate from the point about agreement which forms the main thrust of that next paragraph.

A word needs to be said here about gradations of justice or injustice. Granted that a son may not return blow for blow to his father, nor return harsh words for harsh words, may not a son, e.g., say harsh words to his father for beating him? Is it so clear that *no* harm of any sort may be done to a father, a master, or a set of Laws in return for attempted destruction? If one takes 49b–e to rule out *all* harm, then verbal abuse in return for attempted destruction is ruled out, along with any other similarly muted response of lesser for larger wrong. Interpreters taking that view of 49b–e might not mind taking on board so absolute a veto; but they have in that case some explaining to do. They have to explain why the personified Laws so explicitly prohibit the return of blow for blow, harsh word for harsh word, etc. (The 'etc.' is Plato's at 51a2.) On my interpretation, under which 49b–e rules out only unjust retaliation, it is easy to see why the Laws speak as they do. They speak in this way for two possible and not mutually incompatible reasons.

The first reason is that, if they mention lesser crimes in retaliation it becomes a matter for possible endless dispute what, given a sloping playing field, outweighs what. Neither we as readers nor Socrates nor Crito would wish to get involved in such a dispute, which would in any case weaken the rhetorical effect of the Laws' sweeping statements.

The second reason is more complex: in Socrates' actual situation his choice lies – according to the Laws – between doing the Laws no wrong at all by obeying them and doing the greatest possible wrong by attempting, despite that sloping playing field, to destroy them just as they are attempting to destroy him. One might argue that also on the interpretation of 49be as ruling out all harm, Socrates' choice remains that between doing the Laws no harm and destroying them. But there is then a further question: why is it that the Laws are so insistent on the destruction of the city that Socrates is alleged to be undertaking? Many readers of the *Crito* must have wondered at the extreme nature of the allegation that Socrates is destroying the Laws (so far as in him lies) by attempting to escape. Why not simply, if all harm is forbidden, make Socrates (or the Laws) say merely that he is doing some harm to the Laws? On the present interpretation of 49b–e, however, the Laws must in logic, whether readers perceive the logic or not, allege that Socrates is doing to them what they are doing to him, 'undertaking their destruction'. They must say this so as to produce a misdeed of Socrates' which, given that sloping playing field, *must* contravene our principle (R3) and risks contravening (R4).

However, that Socrates is doing, or rather, trying to do, the greatest possible *single* harm to the Laws in forgetting the uneven playing field and trying to destroy them in return for their attempt to destroy him does not entail that he can do them no further wrong. What Socrates is doing will outweigh the wrong they are doing to him by all the more if he adds other wrongs to his attempt to destroy them. In view of this, though the subsequent development of the argument that Socrates has broken an agreement with the Laws is not strictly necessary to the Laws' argument as a whole, nevertheless it is not illogical and not entirely otiose. In addition, it is rhetorically effective in that it piles one argument on another. It may be possible to say the same of it under other interpretations; but it is not my present task to defend other interpretations.

(b4) *An argument from gratitude?*

In the foregoing account of the superior-status argument my readers will find no place for Socrates' duty of gratitude. But the scholars who have construed the argument as one from the benefits conferred by the Laws are numerous and not of the kind to make up an argument out of whole cloth. They deserve more consideration.[226] The exact position in this part of the *Crito* of benefits, return, debts and gratitude repays inspection. The star passage, though scholars do not always refer directly to it, is undoubtedly the transition between the paragraph on the Laws' special status and the succeeding argument about contract or agreement. At 51c6 the Laws ask Socrates to consider, on the basis that their preceding paragraph is true, the injustice of what he is hypothetically attempting. 'For', they say, 'we, having procreated, nurtured, and educated you, and having given a share of all the admirable things we could to you and all other citizens, nevertheless claim to have permitted any Athenian who wishes…' – and they launch into their argument leading to the conclusion that Socrates has made an agreement or contract with them. So far, the most careful of readers might be tempted to think that the Laws' reason for the accusation of injustice in the first sentence of this paragraph (51c6–8) is that he has received καλά, 'fine things' or 'admirable things' from them. If one were, further, to construe 'admirable things' as ἀγαθά, 'good things' or 'benefits', a construal not always difficult in Platonic Greek, one would then have arrived at the conclusion that the Laws' claim on Socrates is one of gratitude for benefits received. The Laws are in that case telling Socrates that he is not doing justly by them in implicitly, by his actions, rejecting that claim. One can understand very well why many scholars have thought that the point, or at least an important point, of the preceding paragraph of the *Crito* is that Socrates ought to show more gratitude.

But the matter, as so often in this dialogue, is less straightforward than that, whatever even intelligent, experienced readers may at first suppose. What is going on in the sentences from 51c6 to 52a3 is something rather different. The passage reaches a climax at 51e5 with a threefold indictment of the disobedient by the Laws, an indictment subsequently directed specifically against the hypothetically escaping Socrates. The indictment contains three clauses: (1) Socrates does not obey the Laws as parents, (2) Socrates does not obey the Laws as nurturers, and (3) Socrates has broken an agreement with the Laws. (1) and (2) derive presumably straight from Plato's preceding paragraph, and should be read in the light of that paragraph, which said nothing at all about gratitude. (3), however, makes an assertion relevant to the earlier implied accusation of breaking an agreement (50c5–7), an accusation receiving no attention from 50c7 to 51c5. The sentences from 51c6 to 51e5 *must* therefore contain the primary justification for the assertion that Socrates has broken an agreement; they *need not* contain anything relevant to the argument for (1) and (2), which shows no sign of incompleteness when concluded at 51c3–4. Within this justificatory argument for an agreement the statement that the Laws have procreated, nurtured and educated Socrates, and given him and his fellows a share in all fine things, has a clear and definite function. It (51c7–d1) serves as a *foil* for what follows it: witness the word ὁμῶς, 'nevertheless', at 51d2. The point the Laws are making is that *despite* their gifts and their quasi-parental authority they *nevertheless* offer any adult Athenian who wishes the freedom to leave if he does not like them. This freedom lies at the root of the argument that Socrates has made an agreement with the Laws. This foil-passage serves as a transition: it sums up some points from Plato's previous paragraph, but puts them to new and independent use. Since the new argument concerns every Athenian, the foil-passage mentions all Socrates' fellow-citizens. The topic of gratitude for benefits is conspicuous only by its complete absence from the text. One can only suspect that the scholars who have found it there have been influenced by later political philosophy, inaccessible to Plato's original readers.

The absence of gratitude from the Laws' harangue is significant for the argument vis à vis Crito. Crito might well, if asked, agree that the Laws have, in procreating, nurturing and educating Socrates and himself, afforded the two citizens real benefits. He might, as a normal Greek, even insist that benefits conferred create a debt of gratitude. He might also agree readily that such a debt would be ill repaid by an attempt to destroy the benefactors. The argument from benefits and gratitude would have suited Socrates' and the Laws' confutatory purpose very well. This merely renders all the more conspicuous the failure of the text even to mention gratitude. But it also raises the question why Plato's Socrates does not have the Laws put the relevant questions to Crito and to the hypothetically escaping Socrates. No certain answer to this is obvious to me. Evidently, however, either Plato did not see the possibility of such an argument or he thought he did not need it. If he failed, despite his enormous fertility in argument, to spot this one, there ought to be an explanation.

A possible explanation lies in Plato's Socrates' own strict conception of what is unqualifiedly and unambivalently good. Plato may perhaps – it is only a conjecture – have been blinded to the possibility of arguing for citizenly gratitude to the Laws by his own doubts whether the 'admirable' things they do are truly beneficial. I have argued elsewhere that, at least in the *Apology*, the only unqualified good according to Plato's Socrates is virtue, or goodness.[227] The gifts from one's parents of life itself, and of nurture in childhood, do not constitute either goodness or a sufficient condition of goodness, though for many purposes each is a necessary condition. The gift of education, if that includes moral education, is a different matter. On the face of it, if Socrates' parents raised him in goodness, then that would have been a gift and a good beyond price. It is indeed true that Socrates regards himself as in some sense a just man;[228] it does not follow that he owes this to the education he received under the law from his parents. Still less does it follow that he says or implies specifically here in the *Crito* that he owes what degree of justice he possesses to his parents' teachings. We should look at a verbal signpost to the structure of the argument, a signpost characteristic of Plato: at 51d1, as we saw, the Laws do not describe their shared gifts as 'good things' (ἀγαθά) but as 'admirable things' (καλά). Why do the Laws choose the word 'admirable'? The immediate answer is, one must suppose, that the Laws are referring back verbally to the previous paragraph. There they asked Socrates whether he blamed the laws of marriage as not being 'admirable' (50d4–5) and whether the laws concerning nurture and education were not 'admirable'. If they or their puppet-master had had true benefits in mind, 'good' would have been a better choice. The hypothetically escaping Socrates, having agreed that these laws were admirable, naturally does not protest at the Laws' shared gifts being pronounced admirable at 51d1. The signpost informs careful readers that the education pronounced admirable at 51c–d is the same education that was agreed to be admirable at 50d–e. But this last was, quite explicitly at 50d–e, the traditional education in 'gymnastic and music' – the latter covering poetry and other 'humanities' as we should call them. But it is most implausible to suppose that the traditional education of this kind was in the Platonic Socrates' view a successful training in what he would have regarded as virtue or goodness. If it had been, his search for a teacher wise in matters of conduct and morality would have been pointless, and in this dialogue the search for a moral expert could have begun and ended with the person of Socrates himself. There is nothing here to cause Plato or his Socrates to think of gratitude for unqualified benefits.

Nor do I think one can restore unqualified benefits to the text or to its author's intentions by the suggestion that 'fine' or 'admirable' (both καλά) are synonyms in the *Crito* of 'good' (ἀγαθά). One might want to argue this on the basis of Crito's agreement at 48b that 'well' (εὖ) and 'admirably' (καλῶς) and 'justly' are the same thing. So indeed, in some types of context, they are. But in other types of Platonic context they are not. For this linguistic point compare *Ap.* 22d, where Socrates in describing the handcraftsmen's knowledge as admirable certainly does not intend to imply that it is truly good and makes for virtue or goodness. Socrates in the *Crito* can accordingly treat 'admirable' and 'good' as synonymous when applied to actions without necessarily treating them as synonymous when applied to things – of whatever other sort. Gratitude for benefits received cannot slip in by this back door.

(c) Some difficulties

(c1)

Here a point raised by D. Bostock requires examination.[229] Distinguishing the superior-status argument and the agreement argument as Arguments A and B, Bostock puts, in effect, a stark choice to the interpreter. Either Argument B is part of Argument A – or part of one argument with Argument A – or Argument B is independent of Argument A. Now B cannot be fitted into A; yet if B is an independent argument, it fails as such. Bostock writes:

> According to this interpretation, the proviso on keeping agreements, that what is agreed should not be wrong, is to be taken as applying to the whole argument. But in that case the Laws must show, somewhere during this argument, that it is not wrong for Socrates to do what the laws now require of him (namely to remain in prison until he is executed). It is clear that they make no attempt to show any such thing – the topic is simply never mentioned – and their argument therefore contains a very notable gap. Nor are we permitted, on this interpretation, to repair the gap by referring back to Argument A (e.g. by claiming that argument A has already shown that escaping would be wrong, and hence inferring once more, by argument B, that Socrates is obliged not to escape).

The point is well taken. But perhaps the choice thus laid before us is *too* stark. There is perhaps a middle way here. The place occupied by Bostock's argument B, the agreement argument, could be, and I think it is, a halfway house. That is to say, B functions as a makeweight, rather than as a fully independent argument. B adds to the injustice Socrates is, according to argument A, already doing if he escapes; and the question of Socrates *doing* an injustice by *suffering* the death penalty does not arise in the Laws' harangue until they come to answer Crito's own specific arguments later. If Crito has a valid objection to the agreement argument, on the grounds that Socrates has not refuted his claim that to stay and die would be unjust, then he has to wait for an answer. But there is no reason why the Laws should not make him wait for it.

One reason why Bostock has landed himself in this apparent – but only apparent – difficulty lies in his view that the Laws' arguments buttress a generalizing authoritarian conclusion, with the Laws demanding total obedience to any command, whether to do or suffer. As separate arguments for such a conclusion, both Bostock's Argument A and his Argument B do indeed fail. But, as we have seen, that is not the conclusion the arguments are designed to buttress; the Laws' argument, taken as a whole, has a tighter relevance to Socrates' actual situation in this dialogue than many scholars credit it with.

(c2)

We turn to the Laws' following argument, which concludes that Socrates has made a valid contract or agreement with them. R. Martin objects that a contract or formal agreement cannot be legally made between master and slave, and that in general the slope of the playing field between two parties of unequal status and power forbids in law or in equity a binding contract.[230] From this there would result the possibility that the argument of the Laws contains within itself what amounts to a contradiction. The Laws, one could then argue, cannot have it both ways: they cannot *both* claim superior status and high, sacred authority, *and* claim a valid contract between Socrates and themselves. But – and this is a very substantial 'but' – a normal *contract* contains *mutual* promises of service or payment between the parties. Now with respect to the agreement between Socrates and the Laws, neither Socrates nor the Laws ever even mentions the Laws' side of any bargain. The Laws speak at 50c6 of things which 'have been agreed between us and you', but they do not go on to speak of anything they themselves have agreed to do; they speak only of things they have done, or that Socrates has agreed to do. Moreover, if the Laws and Socrates had bound themselves to mutual obligations, one would expect the question to be raised whether or not the Laws had fulfilled their side of the bargain. But Plato raises no such question. Nor, for good measure, does Socrates' question at 49e5–7, with Crito's helpful answer, so much as suggest the existence of mutual obligations. So there is nothing between the Laws and Socrates which can strictly be called a contract.[231]

This, however, merely postpones the difficulty. Granted that Socrates and the Laws have in the strict sense no contract, the Laws do claim that Socrates has made an agreement. If a master, or a father, obtains an agreement to do something from a slave or a son, can we be sure that the agreement was entered into voluntarily? In the case of a master or a dominant father it might be hard, or even impossible, to be sure. But the Laws do not have to persuade Crito, nor Plato to persuade us, about the cases of son or slave. Those were only analogues, and analogies need not be exact in every particular. As the analogy established in any case only the Laws' superior status, and not any supposed claim to universal obedience, the constraints on a potential maker of an agreement with them are rather less than might otherwise be the case. Socrates, or the Laws, must simply persuade Crito that Socrates has an agreement with the Laws, that his escape would constitute a breach of it, and that he entered on that agreement voluntarily.

Now without stilling all possible doubt the Laws' words do offer at least some reassurance in the matter of voluntariness. At 51c8 ff., for example, they in effect deny having exerted undue or unfair pressure on the citizen. Any Athenian may leave if he wants to. He may take his money or other movable property with him; he may go to a colony or elsewhere; the Laws do, and will do, nothing to stop him. Further, the Laws (51e8 ff.) claim not to be despotic in their requirement of obedience; they offer an alternative in the well-known choice: 'persuade or obey' (51b–c, 51e–2a). Furthermore, in the particular case at issue, they point out that Socrates could have proposed exile as his penalty when found guilty at his trial, but he did not (52c). They go on after an interval, at 52d9 ff., to claim that Socrates did not make his 'agreement' under duress, nor as a victim of deceit, nor under compulsion to make a hurried choice. Each one of these claims is open to critical scrutiny. Nevertheless, it is clear that the Laws are defending themselves vigorously against the possible allegation that they have so dominated Socrates as to invalidate the agreement they claim he has made.

(c3)

Another problem concerns the Laws' injunction, 'Persuade or obey'; this is in the narrower context not immediately easy to understand. We may leave on one side the suggestion by R. Kraut that 'persuade' here means 'try to persuade'; sufficient rebuttals have already appeared in print.[232] But who, precisely, and in what type of situation, precisely, is, in the injunction 'Persuade or obey', to be persuaded? And how does 'Persuade!' function as an alternative to 'Obey!'? In general, the most likely subjects for persuasion are (1) the legislators who make, and can un-make, the laws; (2) the executive, whether person, committee, or constitutional body, which gives the actual orders; (3) the courts which decide whether and what someone found guilty shall suffer by way of punishment. In classical Athens the distinction between the legislature and the executive is largely irrelevant. We are left with the Assembly, which functions in many respects as both legislature and executive, and the courts. As the court which condemned Socrates represented the same Athenian People that gathered in the Assembly, the question at issue becomes, almost entirely, the question in what *situation* persuasion or obedience were proper alternatives for Socrates' choice.

Two situations are likely candidates, in the well-known absence from Athenian law of any regular appeal procedure against the verdict or the sentence of the court. One is the opportunity to persuade the Assembly that the law was wrong and should be changed. This opportunity was theoretically available to all citizens at almost any time. It would normally in practice be available only to those with the ear of the Assembly, those engaged in a reasonably successful political career. But the Laws could be speaking theoretically rather than practically, just as Socrates and Protagoras do in the *Protagoras.*[233] So perhaps the Laws are saying to Socrates and Crito that either they should have persuaded the city to change its criminal or its procedural law, or, failing that, they should now obey the law and allow it to take its normal course. The analogy between law-court obedience and military obedience implicitly suggested at 51b would then lead us to suppose that the equivalent choice with regard to the command to go into battle would be that between successfully persuading the Assembly (or possibly the generals) not to mount the war and, failing that, going into battle and enduring loss of life or limb as required.

The second such situation is the opportunity to persuade the legal system, the city as represented by the court, of one's innocence or of one's deserving leniency, or, failing both of these, accepting and undergoing the full rigour of the sentence handed down. The military analogue for this would be the choice between persuading the commander in the field not to join battle in the prevailing circumstances, and, failing that, obeying his order and taking the consequences. Which of these two situations Socrates or Plato has in mind for the Laws' argument is, despite a rumbling scholarly controversy, clear in the context of the present interpretation. It is the city's anger[234] which shows that the law-court type of persuasion is what the Laws have at least primarily in mind.[235] But the question has no great significance for the dialogue. In the context, Socrates has neither persuaded the city beforehand to change its criminal or procedural law, nor persuaded the court to acquit him or to substitute another sentence for that of death. So he is bound – so far as this pronouncement of the Laws is concerned – to obey the law as it stands and undergo the sentence handed down. The matter does not seem likely to have caused any difficulty to any contemporary of Plato's as he read.

This conclusion does not, I think, fall by reason of any expressions Socrates puts into the mouth of the Laws. The phrase 'persuade or obey' appears not as an independent and substantive argument in itself against disobedience to the law, but in the description of a factor exacerbating Socrates' injustice in breaking his agreement to obey the Laws. The Laws are saying at 51e that Socrates is disobeying them despite their special status as parents and nurturers. He is also doing injustice by breaking his agreement to obey them. Despite their mildness in not exacting automatic obedience but in allowing themselves to be persuaded if they are making a mistake (εἰ μὴ καλῶς τι ποιοῦμεν at 51e8), he neither persuades them of any defect or mistake in the present case nor (hypothetically, as ever) obeys them. Socrates has not succeeded in persuading the court that the charge laid against him under the law was mistaken, and he must now obey. The phrase might appear to function also as an element in the argument to the effect that Socrates has agreed to obey, but it is not obvious how it could so function. The phrase enters the discussion only after Socrates is said to have so agreed (after ὁμολογήσας ἡμῖν πείσεσθαι, 'having agreed that he will obey us', 51e7, and cf. e4).

(d) The agreement argument – does it work?

(d1) *Introduction*

Even if the Laws have not exerted undue pressure on Socrates or any other citizen, how can they claim that the citizen, and especially Socrates, has agreed to be obedient at all? The question is of obvious importance for any student of the *Crito*, but it is necessary to emphasize the limits on its importance. The argument leading up to the agreement and then depending on it functions, on the present interpretation, as a makeweight. By returning attempted destruction for attempted destruction when his potential victims are of relevantly superior status Socrates is committing already an injustice, at least according to our principle (R3); on that principle the Laws do not strictly need to prove any more injustice on Socrates' part. But any further injustice they can prove will add more weight to Socrates' injustice, which they have already shown by their lights to outweigh their own in condemning him; hence it will make it even clearer that he is contravening at least (R3), and possibly (depending on subsequent argument) (R4).

It is time to examine the actual course of the argument by which the Laws seek to show Crito that Socrates would be breaking an agreement by escaping. Its opening offers Plato's reader some hints of the sort of thing to be expected. The first-time reader may surmise that the Laws are about to take up the question (50c) whether Socrates had made an agreement with the Laws. But such a reader cannot be sure of that, and it is some time before the Laws make it clear and certain. They begin at 51c6 by asking Socrates to consider whether their previous remarks, the special-status argument, are true, in that he is (hypothetically) undertaking something unjust. This much might refer the reader back to the preceding argument about special status. The participial statements which follow will have reinforced that idea: we have heard about the Laws' 'procreation, nurturing and education' of Socrates in the course of that argument. But with the word ὁμῶς, 'nevertheless', it becomes clear that something new is happening. Instead of having explanatory force for what went before, the participles now have concessive force in relation to the sequel, to be rendered by something like 'although we procreated nurtured and educated you…'. Previously the Laws' procreation etc. of Socrates were advanced as reasons for a point of view. Now they have become factors which might make a point of view surprising. This is something new indeed, despite the allusion to what precedes. The question in what respects, precisely, the new argument diverges from and depends on the old will have to occupy some of our attention as we follow the argument itself.

The topic of agreement still has to wait for a while, even after that 'nevertheless' in the Laws' mouth. Despite the Laws' parental functions, despite their having given Socrates a share in all the fine things they give to their citizens, despite, we may perhaps reasonably add, any claim these give them on Socrates' respect, they nevertheless – what? Claim that he has made an agreement with them? Not yet. They claim only that they have permitted any Athenian who so wishes to leave the city with his property and go wherever he wants, when after being admitted to the adult male citizenry of Athens he inspects what is done in the city, and [the workings of] the laws. They elaborate on this permission, adding significantly that the permission is granted to anyone who wishes to go if he is not satisfied with them and with the city.[236] They now add, at last, that anyone who stays, who does not avail himself of the permission to go, when he sees how the city is run and especially how court cases are conducted, has agreed by his action(s) (ἔργῳ at 51e4[237]) to do, i.e. to suffer, everything they order. By that they mean he has agreed in particular to abide by the sentences of the courts whose workings the adult male has inspected. This particular force of the agreement emerges not only from the mention of the courts in this context, but also from the remarks introducing the notion of agreement at 50c above. Plato could reasonably expect the alert reader, and the Laws can reasonably expect Crito, to recall that at 50c the Laws asked, in effect, whether Socrates had agreed to abide by *all* the city's legal decisions, including those that go unjustly against him, or *only* those that are just or go in his favour.

The conclusion the Laws draw from the argument so far is quite general, applying to all Athenian citizens. It includes the results of the previous argument from special status together with a statement of the wrong done by someone who breaks the claimed agreement. Anyone who does not obey, that is who does not submit to the judgments and sentences of the city's courts, is guilty of injustice on three counts: disobedience to the laws as parents; [disobedience] to [them as] nurturers; and a failure either to obey or to persuade after agreeing to obey them. The hypothetical agreement-breaker has neither obeyed nor succeeded in effecting the alternative to obedience the Laws claim to allow, namely persuasion of them if they do something which is 'not admirable', or wrong. As suggested above, the persuasion is supposed to take place in the law-courts. It follows that the kind of wrong thing that the Laws may do is to bring, or to arrange to be brought, a charge that is unjust or mistaken. When the Laws declare, as they do next, that they propose and do not fiercely order, but allow either persuasion (within the law, of course) or obedience, they are saying that they offer the accused citizen a fair trial in open court. Under the laws of Athens there was indeed scarcely any room for the arbitrary and tyrannical infliction of 'punishment' of a citizen not allowed to mount a defence. This applied to all citizens. The agreement the Laws mention has in their view been made by all who have as adults, knowing the legal system, remained resident in the city, and thereby supposedly expressed satisfaction with it.

(d2) *Difficulties in the agreement argument*

The very real difficulties raised by this account start with this last point, that a citizen who remains at home thereby expresses his satisfaction with his city. At least in informal reasoning, the proposition is relevant here that (51d2–5) the Laws permit all who are not satisfied with them to go, sc. to a colony or into exile. So if a citizen (e.g. Socrates) is not satisfied he has the Laws' standing permission to go. We may charitably carry the argument further. If, given that permission in case of dissatisfaction, the citizen remains in Athens, then he must be remaining because he wishes to. For either (A) he is satisfied, in which case he would wish to remain, or (B) he is not satisfied, in which case he is not compelled to remain, and must be remaining because he wishes to. On the assumption that if not satisfied he would not wish to remain, B results in a contradiction, and must be ruled out. On that assumption, if, given permission to leave if dissatisfied, the citizen remains, then he is satisfied and would wish to remain. Accordingly, every day of his adult life that he remains in Athens he expresses in deed (ἔργῳ) a wish to remain. In effect, the more days he remains in Athens, the more consistently and the more persistently he expresses his wish to remain. But on the assumption mentioned above, that if not satisfied he would not wish to remain, if he wishes to remain he is satisfied. So each day that he remains in Athens he expresses anew his satisfaction with the city and its laws. The Laws specify that the citizen who remains does so in awareness of ('seeing', ὁρῶν, 51e2) the way in which they decide cases. So the satisfaction a citizen expresses with the laws includes his satisfaction with the particular laws which determine how court cases are decided, verdicts, sentences and all, and presumably also with the law (50b6–c1) that court decisions have final authority. Now the Laws at 50c1–7, admittedly speaking of agreement rather than of satisfaction, suggest rather strongly that the relation, whatever it is, that Socrates bears to the Laws he bears to them all, and all the time, and that he is in no position to pick and choose, or to obey court decisions only when it suits him.

The question obviously arises here, why should one assume that if not satisfied the citizen would not wish to remain? There is more than one possible answer. The first is that the assumption derives from a false conversion: in this answer from 'All satisfied citizens wish to remain', the Laws derive surreptitiously 'All citizens who wish to remain are satisfied', which easily gives 'All citizens who are not satisfied do not wish to remain.' In a piece of argument as compressed, as rhetorical, and as sweeping as the Laws' harangue sounds, one could not entirely rule out such an origin for this assumption. But a more charitable theory – and I believe in charity of interpretation – would be that in assuming the inevitability of a citizen leaving if dissatisfied the Laws have been made by Plato and his Socrates deliberately to overlook the drawbacks and difficulties in ancient Greece of going into exile.

How is this view of the matter more charitable? Critics of the Laws' argument have suggested that an ordinary citizen may have many and diverse motives for staying where he is, and often stays, even despite his disapproval of his country's institutions. Such reasons include sheer inertia, the emotional satisfaction of feeling 'at home', or the reluctance to face the economic risks or even physical dangers of exile.[238] Economic risk the Laws might claim to have minimized by stipulating that the departing citizen may take his property with him; but the hard work, the emotional wrench, and (in the Greek world at least) the physical dangers remain. It deserves repetition here, however, that Crito cannot make this point to Socrates in their present situation. Crito is trying to persuade Socrates to go into exile. Accordingly he cannot rebut the Laws' argument at this stage by calling attention to the dangers and unpleasantnesses of exile. Should we believe that Plato did not see the possibility of arguing in the abstract that exiles are disadvantaged? Or should we suppose that the neat fit between the gap in the argument and the plug offered by Crito's situation is fully part of Plato's intention in writing the dialogue? In favour of the dialectical neatness being intentional we can offer not only Plato's evidently acute eye for the possibilities of argument, and not merely the natural familiarity of a Greek of Plato's time with the disadvantages of exile, but also the unflattering portrait of exile painted in Plato's *Apology* (37c4–e2). As for the other disadvantages of choosing exile, Crito could reasonably be expected to realize, by this time, that non-moral considerations such as emotional satisfaction with one's home, or the necessity of some hard work, will not readily sway Socrates. Having once agreed, for his own sound dialectical reasons, to the paramountcy of moral considerations, Crito himself cannot now advance others against them.

So *ad hominem*, or dialectically, the Laws have established, *within this argument with Crito*, the satisfaction with the laws of a permanently resident adult male citizen. Nevertheless they are still a long way from establishing that such a citizen has made an agreement with them, promised to abide by their decisions, or even committed himself to abiding by their decisions. One cannot of course look in this context for an actual verbal ageement, oral or written; the Laws expressly speak of an agreement in deed. Nor, I think, do considerations of game-playing help us to understand the *Crito.* Certainly, if the Laws were to be demanding universal obedience from the citizen, then the analogy of a game, participation in which binds one to obey the rules, would be helpful. As we have seen, however, the Laws do not demand, or need to demand, anything so sweeping. In any case, though the Laws are not frightened of analogy, they do not themselves mention games – though certainly the Greeks had games, even if they did not codify the rules in the modern manner, and they did have a concept of cheating.[239] So how are we to bridge the gap between satisfaction with the Laws and an agreement with them?

The best approach to this question is by way of another. The first question to ask here is what it means, in the Laws' speech, to 'be satisfied' with them and the city. Now in their context, however we decide to render the Greek word ἀρέσκειν here (e.g. 52b2), whether with 'satisfy' or 'please' or whatever, the expression very clearly connotes in this context the approval of the Laws by the person so affected. In theory such approval might be merely selfish: 'I'm alright, Jack' is modern only as an expression, not as a sentiment. But whatever kind of approval the resident citizen evinces it is still approval. One should now consider what a permanently resident citizen is committed to. Since the Laws at no time forbid him to depart, he makes each day, month or year, a choice to remain in the city. That is to say, since *ex hypothesi* he would move elsewhere if he disapproved, each day, month or year he declares in deed his approval of the laws. And that approval encompasses in particular, as we saw, the way in which court cases are conducted and decided. For that, one may add, was an important part of Athenian community life and democracy, and the claim that it was an insignificant detail would not convince. Furthermore, since in any choice of action, according to Crito's earlier agreement with Socrates, moral considerations are paramount, the resident citizen's choice ought to be based on such considerations. Therefore, if the citizen's approval of the laws is not moral approval, its basis is inadequate. It would then be the kind of basis that 'the many' of the early parts of this dialogue would accept. Are the Laws entitled to assume that the citizen concerned is not one of 'the many' in this respect? No, they are not. As applied to the generality of citizens who guide their lives by other than moral principles, their argument fails. But then for such citizens their argument will have no force anyway; for the whole argument is predicated on the paramountcy of justice. The escaping Socrates and Crito might claim that the Laws had not made out an adequate case to prevent the escape of an ordinary citizen in Socrates' kind of position. The two of them could *not* claim that the case was inadequate as against themselves.

Is that the best we can do for the Laws' argument here? Not quite, I think. If the citizen, day after day, month after month, year after year, makes a voluntary choice to remain in the city, the reason for this, since inertia and the problems of exile have been effectively banished from the discussion, must be that he accords the city, warts and all, whatever kind of approval he deems appropriate as a basis for his personal choice. This approval he declares continually in deed. He accepts, obviously, the ups and downs of his life as the fault of his neighbours, the gods, or of whoever it may be. But insofar as he may blame the city, with its laws and workings, he declares all the time that he still approves of the city at least on balance. At the same time he takes advantage, whether voluntarily in adulthood or involuntarily in childhood, of all the fine and admirable things the city offers him a share of. One does not in these circumstances have to think in terms of gratitude or ingratitude in order to find something morally repugnant about his running away the moment the city does anything which might be thought seriously to harm him. If not an agreement in any formal sense, or even a tacit agreement, the citizen has given the city some kind of commitment. Specifically, he has raised in the city an expectation of his continuing obedience if it calls upon him to suffer some penalty. Nor can the average Athenian citizen say, 'Ah, but I didn't reckon on the city commanding me to *die.* That's too much for me to swallow.' He would meet at once with the city's – and its Laws' – retort that he did not have any such objection to being called upon to risk wounds and death on the battlefield, or, if he did so object, that he did not regard his objection as sufficient to make him abandon his commitment to living in the city. The city has indeed a justifiable expectation, rooted in the permanently resident citizen's behaviour, that he will put up with whatever suffering it legally ordains. The difference between raising a justifiable expectation by one's behaviour and agreeing in deed is thin. It is all the thinner because, just as the breaking of an agreement has something morally offensive about it, so also there is something morally offensive in raising an expectation and then reneging on it the moment it looks uncomfortable for oneself. To raise a justifiable expectation in others is, after all, to enter into some sort of commitment to them – as I think the old English law of breach of promise of marriage used in some measure to recognize.[240]

One crack there is in this argument, a crack I can see no easy way to fill.[241] If one were to ask the Athenian in the street whether he meant to raise such an expectation as I have outlined, the answer would certainly have been negative. One does not go through life acting in one's everyday existence with the intention of creating an expectation in one's community that one will suffer whatever it commands through thick and thin. Challenged by the city's Laws with having created and then reneged on such an expectation, any ordinary person would have replied then, as they would today, 'I didn't mean to raise that expectation', or 'I wasn't aware of raising that expectation.' There is something morally offensive about holding someone to a commitment they never meant to enter into, and/or were actually unaware of at the time. Though the *deliberate* raising of an expectation only to go back on it indeed deserves blame, one can blame someone for doing this unawares only insofar as they ought to have been aware. In the present instance awareness is rather too much to expect. As Athenian law could on occasion distinguish voluntary acts from unknowing or involuntary ones, and as Socrates in Plato's *Apology* (26a) shows himself fully cognisant of this fact, it is not easy to see how Plato could have failed to see this crack in the argument. The best one can do is to suppose that a series of actions, each of them deliberate, which together create an expectation, might be confusable with the deliberate creation of the expectation. The confusion is perhaps not so obvious as to rule out Plato's having fallen into it himself. But though the agreement argument has by now diverged from the preceding one on special status, it is to some extent dependent on it. Bostock has observed this.[242] In criticizing the agreement argument as an authoritarian argument, he points out that its 'leading premiss' comes at 49e5–7 with a proviso, namely, that what is agreed is not unjust. Socrates, and any normal Athenian, is obliged by his 'agreement' to abide by the decisions of the city's courts only if they do not force him to do something unjust. But nowhere in the agreement argument we have analysed is there any indication, let alone proof, that the citizen can fulfil his agreement with his city without doing anything unjust. Proof of this point is needed to support the argument; it will not stand up by itself. On the present interpretation, as opposed to the authoritarian understanding of the argument as a whole, this, though entirely correct, presents no difficulty. The necessary support is to be found, in part, in the special-status argument.

This part of the support works like this. The special-status argument makes plain (see above) that the Laws are not requiring Socrates to do anything unjust. They are requiring him *not* to do anything *un*just, in that they demand he refrain from a retaliation which, given their superior status and the resultant sloping playing field, would be unjust. They require him accordingly to suffer the penalty which they in good faith assigned. So far as this whole part of the Laws' argument is concerned, the question of Socrates being called upon to *do* something unjust simply does not arise. If this question did arise, then Plato's reader would be at liberty to suppose that Socrates was doing something unjust, or morally wrong, in going to his death. As things stand, however, the Laws offer no basis whatever for that supposition.

One can, however, smell a large and noisome rat here: there are still Crito's old moral arguments to be dealt with. According to Crito, and he elaborated a case, Socrates is perpetrating an injustice on himself, friends and family in refusing the offer of an escape. Crito's overtly moral case remains, at this stage, unanswered. If it continued unanswered to the end of the dialogue, then Crito, and Plato's more alert readers, would have at the end a complaint to offer against the agreement argument. But it does not remain unanswered. How cogent the answer is, is a genuine question, subject to debate. Clearly, however, the section from 52d to 54b attempts to supply an answer. Once again we see that the Laws' harangue hangs together as a whole in the context for which it was composed. That part of the necessary support for the agreement argument which does not come from the whole nature of the special-status argument comes from the Laws' subsequent specific answer to Crito's original case.

So much, the Laws say in effect, for the generality of Athenians. But Socrates is a special case, and they proceed to explain in what ways he is special. They begin at 52a by describing him as more liable to these charges, or more subject to such blame, than any other Athenian. Now this is a somewhat vague pronouncement, as sentences containing a demonstrative pronoun often are. The most obvious meaning for it, however, is not that Socrates' breach of his commitment was in some way greater than any other Athenian's, but that he had done more than anyone else to raise the expectation of his continuing to obey. Since that expectation was based on actions showing approval, the more Socrates showed his approval of the city's institutions, the firmer the expectations he raised. The Laws ought therefore in the succeeding argument to give reasons for their supposing Socrates to have shown his approval more clearly, and raised stronger expectations, than other citizens. It ought therefore to cause no surprise when they propose at 52b–c to do just that.

The reasons they give, however, are not all as cogent as one could wish, and it is just as well that the whole argument, rather than the subsidiary point the Laws are trying to make, does not depend on them. Their reasons are at least two in number. The first concerns Socrates' unusually continuous presence in the city. He has never (with a single exception) been abroad on a sightseeing trip or on any other expedition except on military service, and he has never desired to know at first hand any other city or its laws. That he has never taken a sightseeing holiday might suggest a home-loving rather than a patriotic citizen, and seem to have little but rhetorical force. But if each day that one spends in the city marks a renewed approval of it and wish to stay in it, the point appears to have somewhat more than rhetorical force. Nevertheless the key point here is that he has never desired to know at first hand about any other city's laws; if he had, he would have gone abroad to see them in action, which he has not done. So he had no such desire. The qualification 'at first hand' might surprise some readers of the Greek, but the verb concerned (εἰδέναι, 'know', at 52b9) is the perfect tense of a root which in the aorist (ἰδεῖν) means 'see'. In this context of the *Crito* the perfect must have the particular meaning 'know at first hand' or 'know from experience'. There are two reasons for that. The first is that later in the dialogue Socrates is faced by the Laws with his own verdicts on Sparta and Crete (52e) and on Thebes and Megara (53b): he says that they are either blessed with good laws or are law-abiding (depending on the rendering of the verb there εὐνομεῖσθαι). On neither rendering could Socrates deliver such a verdict without *some* previous inquiry about the laws of the states concerned. The point must therefore be in our earlier passage that his inquiries had not been at first hand, but based on hearsay. The second, in case someone should accuse us of reading the dialogue for once backwards, is that the context at 52a–c itself requires, for its argumentative force, that the lack of any desire to know other states' laws should be relevant. The lack cannot be relevant to Socrates' stay-at-home habits, which dominate the context, unless first-hand inquiry, or desire to know at first hand, is meant. Now any citizen is, according to the Laws of Athens, free to go wherever and whenever he likes. If Socrates in particular had been dissatisfied with those laws and wanted to go, he most certainly would not, being the man he is in the pages of Plato, have emigrated to any other city without previously inquiring at first hand about the laws of the city which initially attracted him. What is more, there is no good reason why Crito should at this point in the dialogue, when he has admitted moral considerations to be paramount, have supposed Socrates ready to move to another environment without previous inquiry into or consideration of the moral merits of that other environment as a place to live one's life.[243] The absence of such inquiry argues Socrates' commitment to Athens. To sum up, the Laws' argument here has a great deal of force against a hypothetically escaping Socrates. It suggests rather strongly that Socrates' choice in his daily life not to leave the city, except on one trip to the Isthmus of no political relevance, was one more sign of his warmer approval of the laws of Athens than of any other city's, and was for this and other reasons a sign of his commitment to live and die under them. Socrates' exceptionally stay-at-home habits of life and thought suggest his exceptionally strong commitment to and satisfaction with Athens and its laws.

In the next sentence (52c2–3) the Laws advance briefly another reason for believing in Socrates' commitment to the city, namely that he has begotten children in it:

> So strongly did you keep choosing and keep agreeing that you would conduct yourself as a citizen in accordance with us, both in other respects and [in that] you procreated children in it (sc. the city), [an indication] that you were satisfied with the city.

The logic of this argument, if it is meant as evidence for Socrates' *special* commitment to his city, is not beyond reproach. Many others besides Socrates founded families in Athens. So to do so was hardly a sign of *special* personal commitment to the city or its laws.[244] One is left wondering whether Plato intended the Laws here to be mounting another argument for Socrates' stronger commitment than any other Athenian, or whether this point gives merely an additional sign that he was, by his deeds, committed. The beginning of the sentence quoted, 'So strongly', refers back to the previous argument for Socrates' special commitment from his failure to inspect other cities; but that reference could perhaps by this time have faded, and given way to the mere reinforcement of the evidence for his commitment. Some disquiet is in order, but not deep anxiety. One's judgment of the Laws as arguers hardly depends on this one clause whose argumentative aim is unclear; rather one's general judgment of them will influence one's decision on what the clause is arguing for.

The two phases of this argument are distinguished by L. Brown (2002), very handily, as the 'black-and-white' and 'coloured' arguments for an agreement. The 'black-and-white' version runs from 51e2 to 52a3, the 'coloured' one from 52a3 to 52d4. The first or 'black-and-white', applies in the Laws' view to all citizens. The second, or 'coloured' version applies especially or most of all to Socrates. I find, however, no good reason to look for any difference of kind, as opposed to degree, between the two versions. Indeed, the text supplies reason not to look for differences of kind. The Laws expressly say at 52a3, in beginning the second version, 'Of these charges, Socrates, we say that you in particular (καί) are guilty, if you are going to do what you have in mind.' Here 'these charges' must be the ones levelled at all disobedient citizens in the black-and-white version. Brown's distinction is this: she supposes that the second version differs from the first in appealing, as the first version does not, to attitudes (and in particular to Socrates' attitudes). In my opinion this distinction, between appealing or not appealing to attitudes, is a mirage. In the black-and-white version, the Laws allow anyone to leave the city who *is not satisfied* with them when registered as a citizen and after observing their workings. (Note ᾧ ἂν μὴ ἀρέσκωμεν ἡμεῖς at 51d4 ['whomsoever we do not please'] and εἰ μὴ ἀρέσκοιμεν ἡμεῖς ['if we were not to please'] at d7.) It is understood that any citizen who stays is satisfied. In that case, not to leave demonstrates publicly one's satisfaction with the laws. In the black-and-white version no less than in the coloured, the citizen's public demonstration of his satisfaction raises an expectation that he will continue to obey. In both versions it is a matter of the citizen's publicly demonstrated attitude. The 'coloured' version, directed against Socrates personally, is what the Laws in effect say it is – a special case of the 'black-and-white' version.

Brown suggests that agreement *that* something – frequent in Plato's Socrates' discourse – which may be a private attitude, has spilled over into the field of agreement to do something. If she is right, cognitive agreement has infected performative agreement. I see no reason to saddle Plato with any such confusion. It is at least as plausible and on the whole more charitable to suppose that in the interests of rhetorical force Plato used the rather tight word for '[performative] agreement' somewhat loosely, when he ought to have used an expression meaning 'raising a justifiable expectation'. The distinction between cognitive and performative ageement is in practice an easy example in Greek of homonymy; the distinction between the raising of a justifiable expectation and performative agreement is easily blurred in any language.

Here is perhaps a convenient place to meet head on any argument to the effect that Socrates' commitment, like that of any other Athenian, was a matter of a decision taken at once on reaching manhood and being enrolled as a citizen, and then and there seeing how the political and legal system worked. The first and perhaps indecisive evidence against this view lies in some imperfect tenses the Laws use hereabouts: ἠρέσκομεν, 'we were pleasing' (52b2), and at 52c1–2 ᾑροῦ καὶ ὡμολόγεις, 'you kept choosing and agreeing'. One could press this evidence harder if one were satisfied, as I am not, that we are entitled to certainty about the meaning of the Greek tenses in general and the imperfect in particular. The paraphrases given here, tempting and plausible though they are, do not strike me as certain to be right. A further argument I owe to Spiro Panagiotou, who pointed it out to me in discussion (I paraphrase from memory). If Socrates and other citizens were supposed in this context to have taken their decision and made their agreement and commitment once and for all on enrolment as citizens when attaining manhood, the extra days more that the adult Socrates had spent in the city as compared with other citizens would be irredeemably and risibly irrelevant.

The Laws' second main argument in this sub-paragraph aimed at Socrates in particular proceeds at 52c4 by citing what he had said in court – whether he actually did say it, or whether he said it only in the pages of Plato's *Apology*. The Laws are fully entitled to argue thus *ad hominem*, since at 52c3–5 they have openly declared their intention to do just that in this section. Socrates or 'Socrates' had had it open to him to propose for himself after conviction the penalty of exile, and had not done so. Indeed he had explicitly rejected exile as a penalty. The Laws plausibly say that the jury would have accepted such a proposal. In that case, Socrates could, in going into exile, have done with the city's consent what he is now undertaking to do against its wishes. This argument may look as if it lies open to the retort that many individual Athenians might have been willing, even relieved, to see Socrates go after all even now into exile. But that is not the point: the city corporately, and its legal system as an institution, have now expressed their wish through the jury's verdict and sentence, and the sentiments of individual Athenians as individuals, however numerous, are irrelevant. Irrelevant also now is the failure of Socrates to give the city the choice of sending him into exile. The Laws may very reasonably continue by pointing out Socrates' expression in court of preference for death over exile. They do not merely say that he expressed such a preference; they say he put on airs based on his equanimity in the face of death.[245] A mere expression of preference might have left a change of mind in some measure defensible, despite the Platonic Socrates' known hostility to inconsistency. But the abandonment of something he had openly prided himself on is more likely than a mere inconsistency to make Crito, a friend rather than a disciple, sympathize with any shame Socrates might feel. The Laws duly ask the 'escaping' Socrates if he is not ashamed in face of the proud remarks he had made. This perhaps emotional point should not be allowed to obscure what is at least the ostensible purpose of this argument in its present position. That is, presumably, to show Socrates' special level of commitment to staying in Athens through thick and thin, from which one might infer his special satisfaction with the city. Right up to and including the day of his trial Socrates had given evidence of his commitment: he had even chosen to die, rather than to leave the city and live out his life in exile. What is more, he had made that choice, so revealing of his commitment, *after* the court, presided over by the Laws who now hypothetically address him, had convicted him, in his view, falsely. The Laws would appear, on this evidence, to be justified in supposing Socrates' commitment to, and satisfaction with, the city and its institutions to be virtually absolute; it is proof against even a conviction of himself on a false and potentially capital charge. Socrates, as in the first of these *ad hominem* arguments, is simply not interested in living elsewhere than in Athens; so strong is his preference for his own city and in consequence (on grounds we have already seen) its institutions.

(e) An interim conclusion

(e1) *Introduction*

With a neat use of a 'neither…nor' conjunction at 52c8, the Laws tie in Socrates' hypothetical lack of a decent shame in face of his remarks at his trial with other aspects of their case. The first is his lack of respect for the Laws, in his attempt to destroy them. This of course takes us back to 50a–b, to the Laws' initial accusation of trying, so far as in him lies, to destroy them. The phrase 'so far as in [him] lies', having served its dialectical purpose, now drops out, doubtless for reasons of brevity and rhetorical effect. We – and naturally Crito too – must recall also the respect due to the Laws' superior status, as argued from 50c to 51c. The reference next, at 52d1–2, to Socrates' hypothetical behaviour being exactly that of the most rotten slave trying to run away, recalls that one of the images which symbolized the Laws' superiority in status was that of master and slave.[246] And the Laws add, summing up the agreement argument which they have just completed, that he would be running away in contravention of the agreement he made with them, or the signs of commitment he showed them, concerning his future behaviour as a citizen. They include all major aspects of their argument so far in this magisterially summary conclusion.

They do not include quite all these previous arguments in the question they put next to Crito, as the arbiter of truth in the discussion.[247] At 52d4–6 they ask only, 'first', whether they speak truth or not when they say that Socrates had agreed in deed, not word, to conduct his life as a citizen in accordance with them. They do not have to ask the same sort of question here about the special-status argument. To that Crito had already given his own and the hypothetically escaping Socrates' consent at 51c3–5. Socrates and the Laws nowhere require or ask for Crito's open or formal acceptance of the point they make at the outset that Socrates in escaping will be trying to destroy them so far as in him lies. They hardly had any need to do so, in view of the sheer dialectical force against Crito of this accusation qualified and supported as it is.[248] Crito never suggests or agrees to any answer to this accusation except to cast in the Laws' teeth the injustice the city did to Socrates in convicting and condemning him – a throw the Laws evidently at least suppose they have by now successfully repulsed. Crito as arbiter of truth has now either let pass or agreed explicitly to every part of the argument so far.

We may, then, have some sympathy with Crito's feeling, expressed at 52d8, that he is compelled to agree. No further agreement is asked of him until the Laws' intervention comes to an end at 54d2. By that time, at the end of the Laws' and Socrates' detailed reply to his original moral case, Crito is prepared to remark that he has nothing left to say. But that detailed reply does not begin until 53a9. We need to examine what may be called an interim peroration, between 52d9 and 53a8, before concluding our study of the Laws' own substantive argument.

This 'interim peroration' begins with the conclusion already drawn, that the escaping Socrates would be breaking his agreement. It adds at once, in a series of participles, that Socrates has not entered on his commitment to the Laws under any compulsion, nor as the victim of deceit, nor under the necessity to make a quick decision. The absence of compulsion the Laws have already suggested, when they mentioned their standing permission to any Athenian to leave, and their offer of an opportunity to persuade them. The absence of deceit scarcely needs supporting argument: the laws of Athens were at this period open to litigants', and hence to public, knowledge and even inspection.[249] The Laws do however amplify the point about giving him proper time to decide. Socrates had had seventy years in which to make up his mind. His adult years will have numbered at least eighteen fewer, but let that pass for rhetoric's sake. During those years he could at any time have left if he was not satisfied with the Laws and did not think his agreements just. If, that is, his decision had gone against the Laws, he would have had ample time to arrive at it and put it into effect. He would in that case have based his unfavourable decision on his dissatisfaction and on his estimate that the agreement he had made with the Laws involved injustice. 'Involved' here is a vague word – deliberately on my part. 'Just agreements' here in the Greek is an ambiguous expression. Is the justice of the agreements here substantive or procedural? Is the point merely the one of the paragraph we are examining, that Socrates has been neither forced nor deceived nor hurried, or is it that in agreeing to obey the laws and suffer whatever they bid Socrates has not agreed to do anything which he thinks unjust? In trying to decide this question it is necessary to inspect the context with considerable care.

(e2) *'Just agreements'*

Inspection may start with the little word 'and': '...if we had not satisfied you *and* (καί) the agreements did not seem to you to be just'.[250] Unfortunately this word is also ambiguous: it may conjoin either near-synonyms or terms of widely differing meaning or reference. That does not help. But supposing the Laws were saying, 'You are breaking agreements; the agreements were made neither under compulsion nor under deceit nor in a forced hurry. You had seventy years to make up your mind (a) whether we satisfied you and (b) whether the agreement was procedurally correct.' What the Laws would be saying would then be, among other things, that Socrates had had seventy years during which to decide, among other things, whether seventy years was long enough to make an unhurried decision. One sees already here the beginning of an infinite regress: is seventy years (or any other lifespan within reason) long enough to decide whether seventy years is long enough to decide whether seventy years is long enough to decide...? The logical difficulty finds its match in a factual one. The length of time that has been available for Socrates is irrelevant in that it could take no more than a year for anyone with intelligence, awareness and an interest in the subject to make the relevant discoveries: namely, that Athenian law permitted you to take your property and go, that it was open to public knowledge, and that you had a lifetime to make up your mind. Certainly no citizen of sufficient awareness to see that he was committing himself, by raising the corresponding expectation, to obeying the laws could have failed to see very early on the absence of compulsion deceit and haste.

If these considerations incline us to take the view that the hypothetical dissatisfaction with the laws is the same thing as the finding of injustice in the agreements, we may find other considerations supporting the same view. First, we decided earlier that satisfaction with the laws implied, in the context of this dialogue and among other things, moral approval of them. It would follow from this that they do not in this context compel the citizen to *do* any injustice, and hence that one can agree to obey them within the restrictions imposed by the context in the *Crito* without agreeing to do anything unjust. Secondly, the argument requires rather urgently that the Laws should somehow indicate that the agreement they say Socrates has made does not require him to do anything that is in his view unjust. The Laws would be saying such a thing here in pointing out that, if he had thought he had agreed to doing something in his view unjust, he could under the terms of the agreement have left the city whenever he wished. (They do not need to spell out that since he had not left, presumably he had not thought so.) Thirdly, justice and agreements were mentioned together at 49e5–7, where very plainly an agreement, to be binding, must be an agreement to do just things,[251] however that might later be 'glossed'. Normal literary form and structure, let alone logic, would suggest that, now that at 52d we have an agreement, we should read the word 'just' attached to it as having the same force. One completes this third consideration by pointing out that the words 'just' and 'agree[ment]' do not occur together between 49e and 52d; and also that, as we have seen,[252] the use of ποιητέον, 'one must do', at 49e has already influenced the structure of the argument, so that one has no right to be surprised that it makes itself felt here at 52d–e. Altogether the probability is already very high that 'just agreements' at 52e5 means 'agreements the keeping of which will result in the doing of no injustice by the person keeping them'.

The immediate sequel bears this out. The Laws remark that Socrates did not prefer to Athens either Sparta or Crete, both of which he is always saying εὐνομεῖσθαι: the Greek word means either 'to be law-abiding' or 'to have good laws'. Despite G. Vlastos,[253] 'have good laws' is the only sensible rendering here. Whether Spartans and Cretans abide by the laws they have is wholly irrelevant to this context; the question exercising the Laws of Athens is why, if he was not satisfied with *them*, he did not choose to live in Sparta or Crete. This question would have no relevance here if Socrates had merely said that Spartans and Cretans abided by their respective systems. It is relevant only if Socrates showed esteem for the actual systems. In that case clearly, disregarding inertia and emotional factors as ever, he would have left Athens for either Sparta or Crete unless he felt at least equal esteem for the Laws of his native city. The same, *mutatis mutandis*, applies to all other cities, Greek or non-Greek. But instead of thus emigrating Socrates was absent from Athens less than the lame, the blind, and other handicapped people; so little attention did he pay to other cities. What this is all about is the high quality of Athens' laws; it is not about the question whether Athens bullied, deceived or railroaded its citizens into agreeing to obey its laws. The circumstances of Socrates' making of his supposed agreement receive no attention, not even a mention, in the argument of this section from 52e5 onwards. This supplies an additional reason for not believing the circumstances of the agreement's making to be the point of the clause about the agreements seeming just. And when the Laws go on to say at 53a3–5, 'So much more did the city satisfy you than it did other Athenians', the aim of the whole paragraph becomes clear. The aim is to show that Socrates is breaking an agreement fairly entered into, breaking it *despite* his continuing display of moral satisfaction with the Laws of Athens with whom he made the agreement.

(f) A particular law singled out?

We must discuss another difficulty arising rather obviously out of the text on most interpretations. The question is this: at 50a–c, the beginning of their intervention, the Laws accuse the escaping Socrates of destroying them and the whole city by depriving of force the single law enjoining the valid finality (κυρίας εἶναι) of law-court decisions (τὰς δίκας τὰς δικασθείσας). Given this opening accusation, do the Laws rely right through to the end on the relation of this single law to the system as a whole, and on the relation between disobedience to the single law and the destruction of the system? Or do they render nugatory the dependence of the system on the acceptance of court decisions by treating *any* law-breaking as harming the laws and the city? On some extreme interpretations of the Laws as insisting upon total obedience in all circumstances and in all walks of life, their opening gambit seems to pale into insignificance. If the Laws are going to argue that any law-breaking was harmful and therefore unjust to them, then why should they insist on the destructive power of disobedience to one particular law? If any disobedience is harmful, any disobedience is potentially destructive to the system. Plato, however, does not allow the Laws to make that point, though if the Laws were out to impose universal obedience it would be a good point for them to make in view of their own attempt to destroy Socrates.[254]

The theme of obedience to court judgments does not just quietly go away,[255] nor is it drowned out by the Laws' rhetoric. The agreement the Laws immediately suggest at 50c4–6 that Socrates may have made with them is to abide by whatever legal decisions the city hands down.

But at 50c10 there appears to be an abrupt change of tack on this as on other topics. The approval the Laws seek and obtain for their activities as arrangers of marriages, education and nurture would seem to have little to do with the law on acceptance of a court's judgments. We seem not to return to the courts until, at 51b9–10, the Laws say that one ought to do, that is in this passage suffer, whatever the city orders 'in war, in court, and everywhere'. But the gist of the intervening passage, as we have seen, is that it is not just for Socrates to attempt to destroy the city in return for its attempt to destroy him, because between the city and Socrates there is no level playing field: the city is more august, more sacred and more important even than parents and all other forebears – and the questions about the laws of marriage and child-rearing were part of that argument. This paragraph thus developed points relevant to the theme of Socrates' attempted destruction of the city, a theme deriving very clearly from the original suggestion that for an individual to disobey the court was to subvert the whole system. After this development, Socrates asks Crito whether he accepts what the Laws say. Crito's assent ought to depend on his agreement to the proposition that Socrates in escaping would be doing his bit to destroy the state, though the question whether he agrees to that specific proposition is not one that Socrates cares to have the Laws put to Crito.

The Laws' next major argument is the agreement argument. This for the most part does ignore the question of Socrates' disobedience to our single specific law. The agreement Socrates is supposed to have made is made with the laws of Athens as a whole; only the laws as a system could make the initial claim of this section that they allow an Athenian citizen to depart when and where he wishes. But even here one must enter two considerations. First, the Laws return at 52c9–10, near the end of this paragraph, to the accusation that Socrates 'does not yield to us in his attempt to destroy [us]'. Secondly, though in context the attempt to destroy consists in Socrates' running away from his legal penalty, and his agreement is in effect to suffer whatever the laws require, nevertheless the Laws, having once put across the idea that Socrates' escape would tend to invalidate a law whose invalidation would in turn destroy the city and its laws in general, do not have to repeat that whole concatenation every time they accuse Socrates of attempting to destroy the laws. What the Laws emphatically do *not* say is that *any* disobedience to *any* law will tend to destroy the city and its laws as a coherent entity.

These considerations apply also, *mutatis mutandis*, to the arguments at the close of the dialogue which specifically answer Crito's earlier worldly and moral case. Twice here the Laws allude powerfully to Socrates' alleged attempted destruction of the laws. Once, at 53b5–c3, we find them arguing that in other cities those who care for their city will not welcome a destroyer of laws. A second time, in a characteristic piece of ring-composition, the Laws warn that their brothers in Hades will not welcome Socrates, knowing as they hypothetically will do that Socrates tried to destroy the laws of Athens so far as in him lay. Both, the second even verbally, allude to the argument with which the Laws began, that by disobeying the law giving finality to court decisions Socrates was indeed doing what in him lay (note τὸ σὸν μέρος again) to destroy the whole legal system and city. There is no room here for any allusion to a point that has not been made, to the effect that *any* law-breaking is destructive, so far as in the criminal lies, of the system.

If this line of interpretation is right, the *Crito* is not about civil disobedience in general. It is not about the problem of what to do when you feel a *prima facie* obligation to obey the law *qua* law, but feel another *prima facie* obligation to do what the law forbids. The question occupying Socrates and Crito is not whether, believing the Vietnam War unjust, you should, as an American citizen past military age, have refused to pay the relevant taxes. It is doubtful that it is about whether, being an American citizen, you should or should not have dodged the draft, though that perhaps comes nearer to the *Crito.* According to the Laws at 51a7–c3 one should obey one's country so far as to suffer what it commands in war. The above doubt concerns whether the Federal Government's decision to wage war, in the absence of a plebiscite, would have seemed to an Athenian a command of one's country. It is easy to forget that classical democratic Athens was governed quite largely by something like plebiscite. One thing the *Crito is* about is the necessity in civil society of accepting the verdicts and sentences handed down by the courts, once the decisions concerned are legally final. Not only would the Laws' arguments rule out, for example, springing a Great Train Robber from gaol; they rule out even rescuing the innocent victim of a miscarriage of justice. Socrates is of course portrayed as just such an innocent victim.

This might seem a ridiculous mouse to come out of a mountain of moral argument. Not many of us experience a serious temptation to try bribing a friend out of gaol before he can be executed. But we can rescue the dialogue's profundity, or at least its universality, by viewing it as a study in moral heroism, as an expression of a preference for death over injustice, in replacement of what Plato saw as the Homeric ideal of death rather than dishonour. In this, no less than in its story-line, the *Crito* continues the *Apology.*

(g) Back to the text

But we must return to the text: the Laws still have a last word to put in place. Socrates has shown the measure of his approval of the city, but the link between approval of the city and approval of its laws needs emphasis – not so much defence as emphasis. This the Laws provide by saying at 53a3–5 not just 'you were so much more than other Athenians satisfied with the city' but '...the city and us its laws, obviously; for who would be satisfied with a city without [being satisfied with] (*or* 'without [reference to]') [its] laws?' The Greek may help here. Οὕτω σοι διαφερόντως τῶν ἄλλων Ἀθηναίων ἤρεσκεν ἡ πόλις τε καὶ ἡμεῖς οἱ νόμοι δῆλον ὅτι· τίνι γὰρ ἂν πόλις ἀρέσκοι ἄνευ νόμων; Here it may seem more than a little bold to insert in the translation the words placed in square brackets; but on the other hand if one does not insert them then the Laws are guilty of an obvious paralogism. From the premiss that one would not be satisfied with a city without laws or (as A.D. Woozley translated in his *Law and Obedience*) 'that had no laws', it does not follow that if one is satisfied with a city one is satisfied with its laws. Linguistic boldness or clear logical error; which shall we attribute to the Laws? If this kind of linguistic boldness can be paralleled elsewhere, there can be no doubt about the choice. I think it can. The Lexicon cites Plato, *Grg.* 465a, where '...he [the cook] guesses at the pleasant without [reference to] (*or* 'without [guessing at]') the best' is pretty clearly the sense required for τοῦ ἡδέος στοχάζεται ἄνευ τοῦ βελτίστου, since 'the pleasant without the best' is an unlikely object for the cook to aim at.[256] That being so, we need not hesitate to free Plato, his Socrates, or the Laws from the imputation of paralogism in our passage of the *Crito.* No-one would be satisfied with a city, it says, without reference to, or without being satisfied with, its laws. Since Socrates is evidently satisfied with his city he must be satisfied with its laws.[257] As we have seen, Socrates' continuing display of satisfaction with Athens' laws has given rise to an expectation that he will abide by their decisions, and in that sense he has agreed to abide by their decisions. The Laws feel entitled to end with a rhetorical flourish: 'And so now will you not keep your agreements? If you take our advice, Socrates; and so you will not incur ridicule for leaving the city.'

'Ridicule'? That is a strong word not obviously justified by what has preceded it. Explanation is needed. One of the functions of the next and final stage of the Laws' total argument is to supply it. It does so by countering Crito's moral case almost point by point.

(h) The Laws counter Crito's moral arguments

The necessary explanation of 'ridicule' and the counter to Crito open at 53a9 with a sentence containing a combination of particles (γὰρ δή) which can, and here probably does, emphasize the explanatory force of the sentence.[258] Explanation need not be the only function of the passage that follows, but it is certainly *a* function. One reason, then, why the escaping Socrates would incur ridicule, a reason given in the form of a rhetorical question, is that his broken agreement and his wrongdoing will do no good to himself or to his friends. In what follows what would count as 'good' or 'bad' for self or friends turns out to be more what would count as such in Crito's book than in Socrates', as Plato normally portrays the latter. However, on the hypothesis that this is, though in rhetorical clothing, dialectic, aimed at refuting Crito on the basis of his own beliefs and attitudes, this need cause us no disquiet. The rhetoric and the dialectic may have appealed to different classes of reader, but that does not matter here. Socrates' friends, since the Laws deal with them first, will risk exile and disfranchisement or forfeiture of property. Crito had admitted at least this much at 44e. So by leaving at this juncture Socrates would be harming them? In Crito's estimation perhaps so; but he had made light of the risks in the same earlier passage. He had added that to run the risks on Socrates' behalf would be a just act. The Laws do not at 53a ff. even attempt to deny that the friends' proposed action would be just, nor do they take issue in detail with Crito's earlier minimisation of the risks. Nor do they contradict what Socrates says at 48c2 ff., to the effect that considerations of loss of money and so forth are the considerations merely of the many. All that the Laws say or imply in their rhetorical question is that Socrates' escape would do his friends no good, and they instance the kinds of effect that will do the friends no good. It would be difficult to mount any argument for the proposition that these effects in themselves would do them good. One could argue on Socratic lines, if one were well acquainted with Plato's Socrates, that any just action of theirs will do Socrates' friends good, and that Crito asserted the justice of the actions concerned. But on the same Socratic lines, the friends will be abetting an action of Socrates' which the Laws are in process of showing, by their (the Laws') lights and those of dialectic, to be unjust in that it is an excessive retaliation. Indeed by the standards of (R3) the action is already shown to be unjust. We are left with a deliberate unjust action on Socrates' part, escape, which will do no clear good to his friends.

What good, then, will Socrates do for himself by escaping? The Laws in answer to this – and aiming naturally at a negative conclusion – paint a picture of Socrates' prospective life in exile. The picture is formally a diptych, depicting first, from 53b3 on, the life he will lead in nearby cities like Thebes and Megara, and secondly, from 53d1 to 54a2, the prospects in more remote places such as Thessaly. There follows a connected appendix in answer to Crito's earlier argument concerning the upbringing of Socrates' sons. The first half of the diptych closes with a rhetorical flourish by which the Laws answer their own rhetorical question.[259] 'One has to think so', they say (οἴεσθαί γε χρή), a phrase which also closes the above-mentioned appendix. This division cuts across, in the text, a different and morally more relevant distinction, that between cities which have good laws and the most orderly citizens (53b3–c4), and other states in which Socrates will find not good laws, but very great disorder and profligacy. Thessaly, the Laws' example of the second type, is the refuge Crito suggested at 45c2–5, as I think most classical Greek readers would have recalled.

In the foreground of the first picture of this diptych the Laws put three things: Socrates will arrive in a city with good laws as an enemy of the constitution – for having, one immediately supposes, broken his agreement with, and indeed subverted the laws of Athens. The citizens of his refuge will regard him with suspicion as a would-be destroyer of the laws – a clear reference back to the Laws' contentions at 50a9–b5 and 51a2–6. Thirdly – a new point – Socrates will thus be confirming the jurors' finding of 'guilty'. It would be thought that whoever destroys the laws is a destroyer (διαφθορεύς) or, as we should say in English, a corrupter, of the young and foolish. Much of this, if not all, concerns itself with reputation, which Socrates had declared at 48c to be a consideration of the 'many', and implied to be not worth taking into account. Either the Laws here are deploying arguments based on Crito's own fundamental values in a direct refutation of the arguments he advanced before he agreed for his own dialectical reasons to something more nearly Socratic; or they have in mind already the contrast which emerges directly at 53c5–d1 between the actions, in Socrates' case mostly talk, and the reputation both of the same person. This contrast seems to have exercised Plato's Socrates at *Ap.* 34b8–35a9.[260] On neither of these interpretations are the Laws arguing un-Socratically.

The Laws go so far at 53c5 as to ask if Socrates will find his life worth living at all in cities not endowed with good laws or the most orderly citizens. The reason why it may not be worth living appears to be that he will not be able without shame and unseemliness – resulting from the contrast just mentioned between reputation and reality – to talk there as he has in Athens of how the (*or* a) most valuable thing for human beings is goodness and justice, and the legal and the laws. Here one can readily understand from the *Crito* itself, let alone from other 'early' Platonic dialogues, how the Laws could identify the highest human value in Socrates' thought and talk as that of justice. But the addition here of 'the legal and the laws' to the highest value makes a difficulty. D. Bostock has brought out the difficulty well.[261] In effect, if the Laws are representing Socrates this is *prima facie* an odd thing for them to say. It looks as if we must either abandon the view that Socrates speaks through the Laws in the *Crito*, or find a way round the difficulty. There is not, I think, any halfway house here. If, for example, we suppose that the Laws are simply accommodating to the context what they attribute to Socrates, then, on the face of it, we ascribe to the Laws a disingenuousness beyond what most of us would wish to ascribe to a mouthpiece of Plato's Socrates. How should we proceed?

One way at least is barred to us. We cannot fall back on certain expressions in e.g. Plato's *Apology* which closely associate, if indeed they do not identify, the just and the lawful. *Ap.* 32b9, for instance, 'on the side of law and the just', proves nothing to our purpose. In the particular case narrated there of the trial of the generals after Arginusae, Socrates evidently held that the legal and the just coincided, but that is no reason to believe he held that they always coincided. Nor do we find help in *Ap.* 35c2–5, though there with reference to the jurors' oath 'the just' and 'the laws' correspond and probably coincide; that passage is rhetorical dialectic, and there it is suspiciously convenient for the jurors being addressed that the two should indeed coincide.[262] By contrast, it is not at all convenient, on the face of it, that the two should coincide in the *Crito*, where there is nothing obviously illegal, but much that is unjust, about Socrates' conviction by the court. Cases not parallel to the one under discussion in this dialogue offer us no secure escape-route.

As readers, Plato's or mine, may have realized, the superlative without the definite article in Greek is ambiguous, and at 53c8 the Laws' expression (πλείστου ἄξιον) can mean either 'of very high value' or 'of highest value'.[263] It would not be fair of the Laws to attribute to Socrates the thesis that the laws are of the highest value; but it is clear that in Plato he does set great store by them and value them highly. There are places where he regards the law as offering a sufficient reason for doing something. 'One must obey the law', he says of offering a defence at *Ap.* 19a6–7; similarly at *Ap.* 25d2–3; at 26a what Meletus ought to have done is to teach Socrates according to law, not bring him to court for a crime he had no wish to commit. So at *Laches* 199a Socrates takes it for granted that what the law ordains is what should happen. But more significant than any of these passages is one at *Grg.* 504d1–4. There, following a speech in which he says he is giving his own opinion (ἐμοὶ γὰρ δοκεῖ), Socrates declares '[The name given to] orderly arrangements of the soul is lawful and law, the origin of people becoming lawful and orderly; and these are justice and temperance. Do you agree or not?' – and Callicles, for the sake of argument only, lets this pass. This suggests that the laws' importance lies in their educative function: they are the source and origin of people becoming just and temperate. This justice is not the virtue based on or equivalent to knowledge or wisdom of which Socrates sometimes speaks; but it is a kind of virtue, nevertheless. The passage strongly suggests that this lesser kind of virtue originates from, and at least largely consists in, legality of action. Hence the high value placed on law and legality. Readers contemporary with Plato who did not know his Socrates well enough to find this explanation will also not have known him well enough to perceive the difficulty.

The context in the *Crito* itself prepares its readers for the importance of law. The point is not only that the Laws themselves are the speakers; the passage rises in a crescendo towards the statement we are analysing. At 53b–c, giving only what is thought, or opinions which are held, the Laws say that the destroyer or corrupter of the laws would be thought to be a corrupter or destroyer of 'young and foolish people at any rate'. This suggests that laws are at least thought to have their educationally moral uses. A couple of sentences later the Laws speak of 'cities with good laws, and the most orderly of men', as if cities with good laws had the most orderly men; and there is nothing here restricting the implication to what is merely thought. It would seem that laws are important here too for the inculcation of virtues, not necessarily only in the young and foolish. Evidently they do not offer the kind of wisdom-virtue that Plato's Socrates sought in other dialogues; but they do offer a particular kind of virtue, or of justice.

These points taken together supply what we need, without, in my judgment, too much special pleading. It is well known that καί, 'and', often means 'and in particular'.[264] So, since in Socrates' view legality is a kind of justice, and justice is of very high value, the Laws are not stretching the point too far if they attribute to him the statement that he attaches very high value to 'goodness and justice, and in particular legality and laws'. Such an attribution would be the less surprising in that Socrates appears to attach high value also to the laws as educators – even if they did not and could not educate their citizens in full and perfect goodness. What is more, Crito is not the man to distinguish between the ordinary man's justice and full 'Socratic', knowledge-based justice. The Laws can get away with speaking merely of justice when they mean that legality is only *a kind of* justice, no less than Socrates in our *Gorgias* passage above (501d) got away with speaking in similar vein to Callicles. What we needed for present purposes was an interpretation giving the Laws an argument not alien to the Socrates of the earlier part of the *Crito*, or indeed to the Socrates of the 'early' dialogues in general. Here, then, it is.

But should Crito have intervened on hearing this tricky sentence, and asked Socrates why he was making the Laws claim to represent a kind of justice, any kind of justice at all, when it was under these same laws that the court had unjustly found Socrates guilty? Perhaps; but, if so, the Laws have given themselves, a few paragraphs further on, at 54b–c, a let-out: it was not they who had wronged Socrates, but men – presumably the jurymen who voted for 'Guilty' and for the death penalty. Whether those are merely weasel words,[265] or whether they offer in context a valid defence of the Laws' apparent behaviour to Socrates, remains a question to be argued below. In the meantime one notices that the characters in this dialogue have from the start been allowing each other to finish a long speech, and close off a substantial stretch of argument, without interruption. This makes the *Crito* unusual among the 'early' Platonic dialogues, but it is a fact. Taking the fact into account, we need not worry that the question Crito might have raised at 53b–c finds an answer only at 54b–c. The interval of one Stephanus page is not long. Plato's more intelligent readers can carry the question in their heads that far. There is no need to feel that Plato is asking them to read the dialogue backwards. Less intelligent or less experienced readers would not have been expected to see the problem.

It is time now to pass to the second picture in the Laws' diptych. This colours Thessaly, a remoter place and Crito's chosen refuge for Socrates, in black. The picture is one of very great disorder and dissoluteness, and a willingness to make a joke of Socrates' escape in disguise from the prison and from Athens. No-one there will say how short a time, being old, he bought by transgressing against the greatest laws, not just those of Athens – until he offends someone; then he will be subjected to remarks 'unworthy of him'. To avoid these, he will have to flatter everyone, and be a slave to them. His life will be a perpetual banquet, as if he had left Athens for Thessaly to go to a dinner party. Not all escapees would have objected to such a life, but it is not for Socrates. It contrasts too strongly – we have seen this motif before – with those remarks or arguments of his about justice and other good qualities. Where, the Laws say, will those arguments be? The question as phrased seems ambiguous. Does it mean that it will be impossible to sustain conversations of Socratic type in such a milieu? Or does it mean that all Socrates' fine words will go for nothing, if that is how he actually lives? In this flight of rhetoric it seems impossible to tell, and in either case the future Crito envisaged for Socrates looks black indeed. It looks no less black because Crito himself had at 45d7–9 made sharp use of the need for Socrates to show the good quality of courage, when he had claimed all his life to be caring about goodness. It was Crito who brought up the question of a contrast between Socrates' words and deeds.

An appendix now, beginning from 54a2, answers Crito's argument of 45c10–d7 concerning Socrates' sons. Crito had accused Socrates of letting them down, of abandoning their nurture and education. He had, further, charged him with choosing the laziest course, in that he had brought them into the world but was not prepared to work right through to the end of the task of raising them. In that context Crito imputed unmanliness to Socrates. Already, in the portrayal of life in Thessaly, Socrates through the Laws had dropped remarks seemingly relevant to these charges, and unlikely to be so by coincidence. The first is that the Thessalians might, if Socrates displeased them, say that he was an old man with not long in any case to live – which puts his failure to see his sons through to adulthood in a proper perspective. The second, in the same sentence, says his hosts might accuse him of excessive desire for continued life – and though not used here, φιλοψυχία, love of life, together with its relatives, has what the Lexicon calls (s.v. φιλοψυχέω) a 'collateral sense of cowardice' or unmanliness. In more direct answer to Crito on his sons, Socrates has the Laws point out that if he goes off to Thessaly, either his sons will go too, or they will stay behind. If they go, they will be foreigners, with all the disadvantages which that entailed in the ancient Greek world, and with the added disadvantage, from the moral point of view, that they cannot be brought up to be good citizens, since they will not be citizens at all. If they stay behind Socrates will not be able to raise them anyway, and his friends will naturally take as good care of them as if he were dead. Crito is in no position to deny this last point; how could he? The Laws make no explicit mention of the moral aspect of the first of the above two points, the one about his sons, but some such moral aspect must be present, as we shall see shortly, if the Laws' subsequent remarks are not to seem unfair. With this supplement, the arguments of this appendix are strong; without it, the Laws will, as we shall see, stand convicted here of clear unfairness in argument.

Taken together, the stretch of speech and its arguments between 53a9 and 54b2 offer a decent, even a strong case that Socrates will be doing no injustice to his children or to his friends by staying to die. He will be doing them no injustice, one gathers, because his escape would do them no good. He will not be letting them down or 'betraying' them. Nor, for good measure, will his willingness to die be unmanly cowardice; on the contrary, to escape would be a coward's choice. What he is choosing to do in fact will be the action not of an unjust and unmanly man, but of a good and brave one, contrary to Crito's imputations at 45d–e.

Crito's imputations and arguments had of course to receive an answer, to complete the dialogue as an argument and as a work of literary art. The answer, however, has other functions as well. We have seen that it is vital to the argument from agreement that the agreement should not entail the doing of any injustice. And here in this answer to Crito we find that the injustices he had attributed to Socrates if he stayed to die do not constitute wrongdoing after all. Further, it was not clear from Crito's earlier responses which principle of non-retaliation he was accepting, whether it was the one we have labelled (R3) or (R4).[266] If it was (R4), then, if Socrates had been doing injustices by staying to die, Crito could have claimed that these constituted adequate moral reasons for escaping death even though the injustice he was doing to the Laws would under normal circumstances have been a greater injustice than the one they were doing to him. The aim is not now to clarify Crito's, by Socrates' standards, somewhat confused ethics; that is no doubt hopeless in the time available, and is in any case unnecessary; the aim is rather to leave Crito with no possible leg to stand on in the argument. By confuting even a Crito who holds to the laxest principle of non-retaliation, namely (R4), Socrates has done all that can be required of him.

(i) The Laws' peroration

The peroration that follows, from 54b3 to 54d2, is not a *mere* peroration; it offers some new points. It continues and develops the superb rhetoric of the Laws' last argument, and it pulls together verbally much of the preceding argument. The Laws remind Socrates that they brought him up – always, of course, in a manner of speaking. They say, '…take our advice who nurtured you'. They then add, 'do not set a greater value on your sons or on your life or on anything else than justice…'. A reader could be forgiven for finding this addition puzzling. Crito raised in his earlier argument, at 45c5–d6, a question about the sons which was not only one of morals, a question of betrayal, but one pretty explicitly of justice, since this betrayal is contextually parallel to the betrayal of himself which was actually labelled 'not just'. In dismissing Socrates' sons now as of no account compared to the moral issue of Socrates' justice in behaviour, the Laws have to presuppose that by now there is no longer any moral issue at stake concerning them. That is to say, they must regard the argument of their immediately previous paragraph as conclusive. Exile for the sons – presumably preventing their training in citizenship – outweighs Socrates' own paternal nurture and education of them; if they stay in Athens Socrates' friends will look after them no better if he is in Thessaly than if he is in the next world. Why will Socrates' paternal education count for so little? Because Socrates does not in the *Crito* any more than in the other 'early' dialogues claim any special gifts as a moral teacher. Socrates' 'irony' here is indirect, but still perceptible, though it would certainly help first-time readers here if they had read the *Apology*. There are good reasons why Socrates has the Laws here mention both nurturing and education:[267] in neither will he benefit his sons by escaping to Thessaly; so he is doing them no injustice by staying to die. In the moral ledger Socrates' sons can be left out of account. Once again, Plato's more subtle and/or more experienced readers will have been expected to spot a possible way out of the difficulty, whereas the less subtle and/or experienced will not have been expected to spot the difficulty at all.

One role played by the reference to sons is, one supposes, to link this peroration verbally and thematically with the immediately preceding sentences. Plato forges other such links. He has just at 54a8–10 planted a reference to Socrates' being 'away' in Hades, away from the city and from his sons, as if the world of the dead were a simple alternative to Thessaly. He has thus prepared the reader in some measure for subsequent references to the rulers and laws of Hades, treating Hades as if it were just another country. The motive the Laws give to Socrates for just values and behaviour is to create a comprehensive defence for him when he appears before the rulers and the laws of Hades. Readers might be inclined to suppose that the Laws of Athens, in speaking of punishments for ordinary folk in the next world, are talking out of character, and voicing Platonic or Socratic sentiments. If Crito meekly accepts such sentiments, this *could* be construed as an example of his accepting Socrates' views whenever it is convenient for Socrates or for Plato as author that he should. In his character as an ordinary Athenian distinguished only by wealth and by long personal knowledge – though hardly discipleship – of Socrates, would Crito have naturally been inclined to take the view that one had to face a judgment in the world to come? Without quite asking this question in this form, M. Miller describes the reference to the laws of Hades and their likely reception of Socrates as 'in provoking inquiry into the relation of the immortality of the soul and living virtuously…proleptic for the *Phaedo*' – and, presumably, 'proleptic' also for other dialogues in which Socrates constructs arguments for the soul's immortality.[268] It may be so, in whatever reasonable sense one attaches to the word 'proleptic'.

Some caveats and distinctions, however, will not come amiss. First, no 'otherworldly flourishing' (Miller), which may encourage Crito, receives direct mention. We have in the text of the Laws' speech only a warning of an unfriendly, even angry, reception in the next world for destroyers of earthly laws. We find in the text an equivalent of Hell, but no equivalent of Heaven. Secondly, though the Laws speak thus of a regime of punishment in the next world, they say nothing of strict immortality such as the *Phaedo* and other dialogues attempt to prove. Thirdly, whatever Plato's own beliefs when he was writing the *Crito*, the Laws of Athens say little or nothing here which would have been unacceptable, though much that would have seemed doubtful, to contemporary Athenians; and what they say will have chimed in harmony with common fears.

Clearly this third point needs some elaboration. The evidence leaves room for controversy. As J.D. Mikalson pointed out, mounting a powerful argument from silence, orators attacking villains do not in Athens threaten them with punishments for their misdeeds in any afterlife.[269] He adds, 'there is no indication in the epitaphs or in the other sources for popular religion that rewards for virtues were expected in the afterlife'. This silence would militate strongly against a common belief among Athenians in rewards and punishments after death. K.J. Dover in 1974 had already pointed to a few exceptions to the second of Mikalson's generalizations, and some passages in the orators which suggest that the evil and impious were somehow segregated in the next world.[270] Dover continued in his edition of Aristophanes' *Frogs* to cite these and say accordingly that '…a belief in judgment of the individual's moral record as determining his fate after death was widespread'.[271] The three fourth-century epitaphs Dover cites are a very small proportion of the extant Attic epitaphs of that period; references in the orators are notably indirect, and in one case ([Demosthenes] XXV) suspect of Platonic influence. As evidence for widespread *belief*, all this remains thin. But there does exist literary evidence for reasonably common *feelings* of hope or, especially, fear. Adeimantus at Plato *Rep.* 363c–e remarks on tales told by Musaeus and either Orpheus or Eumolpus.[272] These indicate that one could escape, by means of rites and purifications, from filth and other punishing circumstances in the afterlife to the delights of eternal drunkenness 'enjoyed by the righteous', i.e. those with virtue, ἀρετή, here equivalent to justice, to their credit. Naturally this raises a question, how many people in Plato's day read, or were influenced by those who read, Musaeus and the rest. But of one thing we can be reasonably sure: the priests who used such poetry to proselytize would have made a scant living if no more than three Athenians a century had experienced fear of a punishment after death for their sins. Hence the aged Cephalus of *Rep.*I cannot have been outrageously untypical in finding cause for anxiety in the 'stories that are told' of punishments after death for wrongdoing in this life. Cephalus, one observes, speaks not only of his own emotions, his own bad dreams; he speaks in generalizing terms: 'When a man (τις) comes near to thinking he is going to die…' (330d). Cephalus, admittedly, had laughed at such stories when young; but, again, did the priests batten only on the old? The Attic orators' indirect remarks and conditional references to rewards and punishments in the afterlife may constitute weak evidence for anything so firm as common belief, but they suggest a set of hopes and fears that they expected audiences to recognize. In the fifth century too, if we treat the existence of reward-and-punishment stories as evidence for feelings, we possess sufficient. Omitting Pindar *Olympian* II as dubious evidence for Athenian attitudes, and the *Homeric Hymn to Demeter* 367–9 as uncertain in meaning, we still have Aeschylus *Suppliants* 230–1, where King Danaus tells his daughters that 'another Zeus' in Hades judges men's transgressions in this world, ὡς λόγος, 'as the story goes'; we deduce that the story was known to Athenians of the first half of the century. By the end of the century, Herakles in the *Frogs* (145–51) can give us a mixture of serious and comic sins which will lead to an unpleasant, not to say sticky, end in the underworld. At least a substantial part of the audience must, to follow the joke, have heard of serious speculation concerning such punishment for certain sins. The Athenians had no universally revered gospel or church to tell them what to believe, and their religion did not in general treat faith, that is belief, as necessary for salvation; in their circumstances not many would have claimed certainty about the next world, whether in oratory or in epitaphs. That forms no obstacle to the supposition that quite a number of classical Athenians experienced deeply felt hopes and fears for their afterlife in relation to their moral record.

This discussion, all too brief though it is, may have seemed a digression from our main theme; it has, however, cleared the decks for a point about the *Crito.* It is open to Plato's readers to suppose that Plato either remembered or imagined his Crito as sharing the hopes and the fears of so many Athenians. We notice that Crito himself is an old man, like Cephalus in the *Republic.* Certainly nothing in the eventual prospectively unkind reception of the escaped Socrates by the rulers and laws of Hades will have struck an intellectually ordinary citizen like Crito as outrageous or absurd. Nor will Crito, as an admirer and friend of Socrates, have wanted tactlessly to rise up and deny that Socrates' general moral record as he (Crito) sees it will stand him in good stead in the afterlife. In a city where the expression of such hopes and fears was permissible in public and in private, the Laws of Athens may be permitted to express them. Further, Plato has helped to overcome any doubts Crito, or his readers, might feel on that score by the rhetorically brilliant device of treating the personified Laws of Hades as on a par with, even as the brothers of, the personified Laws of Athens. This makes it natural for the Laws of Athens to refer to them.

The rhetoric of the whole passage leads up to the reception of Socrates in Hades, as examination of its structure shows. The structure of the argument at 53a–54c follows the form of a well-known theme of the Epic, of Tragedy, and possibly already of part of Gorgias' prose composition, the *Defence of Palamedes*.[273] The theme is that of the Hero(ine)'s Choice. Significant tragic examples appear in Sophocles' *Ajax*, and Euripides' *Hercules Furens*, *Hecuba*, *Heraclidae* and *Medea*. One should not forget Plato's own *Apology* here. The form dictates the posing of a series of deliberative questions, asking what the Hero(ine) should do, or where (s)he should go, or to whom (s)he should turn. In general the answers given by the Hero(ine) to each possibility are unfavourable. The point is to exclude all alternatives but one. The unfavourableness of each answer depends on the hostility or awkwardness of the Hero(ine)'s likely reception in each case. Of this structure the Laws of Athens in the *Crito* offer what we might call an indirect example: the Laws are not deliberating on their own future. They put instead questions to Socrates about his future if he escapes, and supply the usual kind of negative response to each alternative given. They do not have to put the question to Socrates, whether he will in any case eventually die and go to Hades, simply because we all die. The Laws of Athens may naturally harp, as they do, on the reception of Socrates by and in relation to the laws of the various alternative communities to which Socrates might, if he follows Crito's urgings, escape. At 53b the sound *constitutions* of Thebes and Megara will treat him as an enemy and view him with suspicion as a destroyer of laws. The less well-governed cities of 53c presumably have no right to do that, but will make him ashamed to talk of goodness and justice, and of *laws and what is legal*. His reception in Thessaly will eventually include a taunt that he disobeyed *'the greatest laws'* out of mere cowardice (53d–54a). When Socrates eventually arrives, as he must even if he now escapes, in Hades, we expect his hypothetical reception as an escapee to be unfavourable and to include a climactic reference to laws. We duly find that, in the form of hostility of the rulers and also of the *laws* of Hades.

Individual details in which this final prospective reception continues the traditional theme include the hostile reaction to his arrival 54c7–8, with which one should compare the hostile reactions of people in different cities in Eur. *HF* 1281–98 and Gorgias *Pal.* 20. There is also the mention of prospective shame (αἰσχρῶς 54c2), to be compared with Gorgias *Pal.* 21, Eur. *Hecuba* 374, and *Heraclidae* 516 ff. The question at 54b6–9 of what will be better, or not, recalls Eur. *Heraclidae* 525 f., 'Isn't death better…?' These might look like trifles of no significance, but Plato has prepared the ground for these too, with a series of stock items from the theme. This whole section of the *Crito* begins with the question (53a10) 'What good will you do yourself…?', resembling *HF* 1301, 'Why indeed ought I to live? What shall I gain?' (and compare *Hecuba* 349 'Why ought I to live?'). The prospective enmity of the

Theban and Megarian constitutions at 53b4–6 echoes the hostility of the expected reception at Eur. *Medea* 506–7, and in the interpolated lines at *HF* 1291–3 and 1299–1300. The suspicious looks at 53b7 reproduce verbally (as G.W. Bond pointed out) those at *HF* 1287.[274] The mention of laughter at Socrates' hypothetical actions (53d4) is in a way parallel to the less sympathetic laughter at *Heraclidae* 507. Socrates' apparent excessive love of life at 53e1 is a common motif: see *Heraclidae* 518 and 533, *Hecuba* 348, Pl. *Ap.* 37b5 ff. The unworthy names Socrates will be called at *Crito* 53e3–4 recall the prospective name-calling at *Hecuba* 357 and the unworthy consequences at *Heraclidae* 525. When the Laws more than once contrast Socrates' previous talk with what he can say in his prospective refuges they exemplify the commonplace motif in this type of context of contrast between the Hero(ine)'s past and his or her future life: see *Hecuba* 349–66, *Heraclidae* 513, Gorgias *Pal.* 20. Plato has satisfyingly prepared his readers to regard the laws of Hades as continuing this traditional theme, as being appropriate 'persons' to do so, and as uttering fully appropriate sentiments – appropriate, that is, to the situation and to themselves. Any ancient reader conversant with previous literature will have been capable of following what Plato is up to here.

We may now return to the Laws of Athens. They explain at 54b5 ff. that it will not be better for Socrates in this world, nor more just in him, nor more pious, if he escapes; nor will it be so for any of his friends or relatives; nor will it be better for him in the next world. Their explanation why it will be the worse for Socrates in the next world takes up a whole fairly long sentence, and falls into several sections:

(1) Socrates has been wronged not by the Laws but by human beings. This appears, since city and Laws have been practically interchangeable throughout, flatly to contradict the assertion on which Crito was prepared to rely back at 50c1–3, that the city had treated Socrates and Crito unjustly. It runs also counter to the Laws' assertion that Socrates had agreed to abide by the judgments *the city* hands down (50c5–7). It seems to abandon the principle inherent in the Laws' questions at 50c10–e4, *qui facit per alium facit per se*; the Laws might find it difficult to take the credit for procreating and rearing and educating Socrates if they now disclaim the responsibility for condemning him unjustly. But nevertheless the distinction made at 54b9–c2 is no quibble, nor (in the vernacular) a cop-out. It makes a perfectly valid point. Yes, as said at 50c, an injustice was done. Inasmuch as citizens in a properly and legally constituted court condemned Socrates, the Laws condemned him. The Laws, however, which governed the setting up and sitting of the court to try Socrates, and under which

he was condemned, can argue – and have argued – that because of their special status they may in good faith, believing it just, attempt to destroy him. On the other hand, those of his fellow-citizens who voted unjustly to condemn and sentence him can mount no such defence for their action, because between him and them the playing-field is level, and they have no special status in relation to him. Their action is unjust; in the Laws' action there is no injustice. The special status argument as interpreted above seems thus to offer a particularly clear-cut explanation of this sentence in the final peroration.

(2) Socrates has shamefully returned injustice for injustice and wrong for wrong. This raises the immediate problem that the Laws have in the very last clause denied that they had treated Socrates unjustly. So what is this about committing injustice and wrong 'in return'? Should we think of the retaliation as being transferred to Socrates' fellow-citizens, and of Socrates as wronging them more than they have wronged him? That would, controversially or even implausibly, make out the wrongful effect of Socrates' escape on the jurors as being greater, in normal circumstances, than the wrong they have done him. This is implausible because it is, after all, the Laws that the escaping Socrates has arguably set about destroying, not his fellow-citizens. It seems more plausible, though hardly palatable, to suppose that the Laws here accuse Socrates of returning injustice for imagined injustice and wrong for imagined wrong. Why would Plato in that case put the notion of 'returning' into the Laws' mouth at all? Was Plato *merely* rounding off the discussion, since so many earlier motifs are revived hereabouts, with one last reference to 'returning injustice for injustice and wrong for wrong', as mentioned at 49b9–10 and 49c4? Did Plato imagine his characters as thinking that injustice 'returned' to the wrong party is doubly 'shameful'? Or, since the verbs ἀνταδικήσας καὶ ἀντικακουργήσας, 'treating unjustly and wickedly in return', govern in this sentence no explicit object, are the Laws talking vaguely of injustice and wrong done by the escaping Socrates in return for the wrong and injustice he has suffered, without thought for the actual person(s) at whose hands he has suffered? Unpractised readers, if they saw the problem, might have accepted one or more of these dusty answers. But Plato's motives vis à vis his more experienced readers are surely less shoddy than these. The difficulty how, if the Laws have not wronged him, Socrates can wrong them 'in return', if they are indeed the specific objects of his retaliation, confronts most reasonable interpretations of the dialogue as a whole, and not just the present one.

In tackling this difficulty we need to keep in mind, as with so many other difficulties, what Crito has or has not assented to. The personified

Laws have just distanced themselves from the actual jury's decision. But Crito has not yet assented to this 'distancing'. He has, however, agreed that the city and its laws have treated Socrates unjustly. So the Laws may still legitimately rely on his earlier assent to the proposition that they treated Socrates unjustly, and use accordingly the expressions 'treat unjustly in return' and 'treat wickedly in return'. Crito never does assent explicitly to the proposition that the jurors and not the laws are responsible for treating Socrates unjustly. But if he takes this proposition on board at all he should perceive that it cuts the ground from under his feet. In the light of it, even his plea back at 50c that the city treated Socrates unjustly will not stand up. Crito really is left with nothing to say.

In this passage Plato is clearly both eating his cake and having it. But there is nothing dishonest about his procedure. The Laws keep this bombshell for the end. They thus avoid putting it as a question to Crito. Once again the choice and ordering of questions matters in dialectic. The interrogation of Crito is complete, all the necessary questions to that end are asked, before this Parthian shot from the Laws. Plato's Socrates confutes Crito on Crito's own ground before cutting that ground from under him. My readers may observe that, on an interpretation of Socrates' question at 50c1–2 which makes it effectively an assertion that the city condemned Socrates unjustly, the Laws' later distinction between themselves and the jurors makes, on present assumptions, no sense at all. Theoretically, the Laws might here be contradicting Socrates, and thus sharpening the distinction between Socrates and them. But we have abandoned, with reason, that line of interpretation. So, in order to make sense of 50c1–2 together with the Laws' distinction at 54b–c, we must necessarily treat Socrates' question at 50c1–2 as a genuine question exploring Crito's views. This in itself compels us to take seriously the dialectical interpretation of the whole Laws-passage.

There are difficulties here. If the Laws can at the end of their harangues undermine the initial point that Crito agrees to, why could they not undermine it right at the start, without any of the elaborate argument we have been following? The answer to this is that the 'Parthian shot' itself depends in large measure on the 'elaborate argument'. Without the argument that the Laws stand in a special relationship to citizens in general and Socrates in particular, the distinction between the jurors and the city would not work. It is because the playing field as between Socrates and the Laws slopes, whereas the playing field between Socrates and his fellow-citizens is level, that the Laws can make the distinction they do between the jurors as treating Socrates unjustly and themselves as not having treated him unjustly. The same consideration renders inoperative here the principle implicitly invoked by the Laws earlier, à propos of Socrates' procreation, namely, *qui facit per alium facit per se.* The act performed by the citizens on the jury is quite distinct from the act perfomed by the Laws under which the court was convened: the one act is unjust, the other is not. The Laws have not performed an unjust act through the jurors: they (the Laws) have not performed an unjust act at all.

(3) The Laws expand on the notions of injustice and wrong treatment, mentioning, evidently in parallel with that pair, the breaking of his agreement with them and his wrongful treatment of 'those he ought least' to have treated wrongfully (54c4–5). Earlier, they had argued that they themselves were those Socrates 'ought least' to treat wickedly. They now include Socrates himself, and his friends, in addition to his fatherland and themselves. They do not say here directly how they would justify this addition: they are summarizing, and this part of their summary corresponds neatly with the mention of Socrates' self and intimates at 53a9–10. There they put to Socrates the question, 'What good will you do yourself or your own intimates (ἐπιτηδείους)...?' They follow this up by pointing out that his intimates as well will, obviously, risk exile and also deprivation of citizen rights or loss of property. Will this harm them wrongfully, rather than merely doing them no good? In the purest Socratic terms, I believe not.[275] But the Laws are aiming to convince Crito, together with a Socrates who has hypothetically been persuaded by Crito, a Socrates who has decided to put life before the justice of keeping his agreement with the Laws of his country. Crito and such a Socrates have to stand by the values they have espoused. So they cannot now take refuge from the Laws' argument in the purest true Socratic values. The Laws are required to answer Crito's arguments, in terms which Crito (and a Socrates hypothetically sharing his values for the nonce) would be ready to take on board. Now those whom one ought least to treat wrongfully are, in common Athenian parlance, one's family.[276] But close friends could perhaps be included, and the Laws in the special-status argument have set themselves above even family. As for wrong done to the hypothetically exiled Socrates, the Laws have cast reasonable doubt on whether his life would be worth living, at 53c5. They have also at 53e4–5 described it as one of a kind of slavery, that is, as one without freedom of speech because he cannot afford to annoy anyone. 'Slavery' and 'a life not worth living' are terms calculated to bring 'wrongful treatment' or 'harm' to the mind of either the normal Platonic Socrates or his hypothetical counterpart in the *Crito.* Further, such a contrast with his previous talk about goodness and

justice would be acceptable neither to the hypothetical nor to the normal Platonic Socrates. Certainly a Socrates who chose this would be treating himself wrongfully, indeed damaging his apparently blameless life. The Laws have already shown dialectically that Socrates' action in running away will be unjust to them. That, however, is perhaps not clear evidence that the harm he will do himself and his friends is also in itself wrongful. But that harm will be unprovoked and deliberate; in most people's book that would surely make it wrongful and wicked treatment.

These then are the grounds justifying the Laws' anger with Socrates in this world, and indeed their brothers' prospective hostile reception of Socrates in the next, when he arrives there. Specifically, the hostile reception there will be due to the Laws in Hades knowing that Socrates has tried to destroy the laws of Athens, so far as in him lay. This last phrase takes Plato's readers back to the very starting-place of the Laws' harangue, to their initial accusation of attempted destruction, so far as in him lay, at 50a–c – a fine and effective example of 'ring-composition', or rounding off. Indeed, in this peroration Plato takes up a number of themes from earlier in the dialogue and brings them back to our and to Crito's attention. The Laws are Socrates' nurturers (cf. 50d5–e1); justice must be paramount (48b10–d6); what is just and what is good coincide (48b7–9); an escape will be impious (cf. 51c1–3); the insufficiency of the claim that the city had wronged Socrates (for the claim cf. 50c1–4); the shamefulness of, or the rightness of avoiding, returning injustice and wrongdoing (cf. 49b9–10); the agreement broken (cf. 49e5–50a3 and 51c6–52e5); the ill-treatment of those whom one ought least to treat so (cf. 49e9–50a2); and not least the reaction of another country's constitution or citizens or rulers to Socrates' arrival there (cf. 53b5–8) in the capacity of a destroyer of laws so far as in him lies (cf. 50a6–b2). Plato here deploys a matchless eloquence; he deploys it, as at times in his *Apology of Socrates*, in the service of hard dialectical argument. He planned, and largely contrived, to leave Crito, at least, with nothing to say. His personified Laws can now finish with a simple warning to Socrates to take their advice and not Crito's.

It is worth singling out in the present context one feature of the Laws' arguments, attacks, and sneers. At no point in the whole harangue does the argument depend for its effectiveness on the proposition that any harm to anyone or anything is automatically an injustice. The Laws fall back on the assertion that to harm them is unjust because they stand *in loco parentis* or higher, and to harm a parent in particular is unjust on the principle of unequal justice. They mount a further argument, specifically for the injustice of Socrates' action in escaping, *videlicet* that he has broken an agreement which required of him no unjust action. The supposed principle that any harm is forbidden because any harm is an injustice thus not only contradicts one passage in the special-status argument, as we saw, but also fails conspicuously to put in any other appearance in the Laws' harangue. The most plausible reason for this is that neither Socrates nor Crito subscribes to the supposed principle. The odds are that Plato did not intend his more experienced or alert readers to imagine that Socrates or Crito has subscribed to it. Those who interpreted 49b–e as subscribing to the principle Plato might have thought unlikely to notice its complete absence from the subsequent argument, and if they did notice it, likely to start thinking again.

10

THE DIALOGUE'S CONCLUSION

Socrates reacts briefly, but again eloquently, to the Laws' series of speeches. His reaction raises a number of questions. At 54d3 Socrates turns in his own person to Crito, and says:

> Ταῦτα, ὦ φίλε ἑταῖρε Κρίτων, εὖ ἴσθι ὅτι ἐγὼ δοκῶ ἀκούειν, ὥσπερ οἱ κορυβαντιῶντες τῶν αὐλῶν δοκοῦσιν ἀκούειν, καὶ ἐν ἐμοὶ αὕτη ἡ ἠχὴ τούτων τῶν λόγων βομβεῖ καὶ ποιεῖ μὴ δύνασθαι τῶν ἄλλων ἀκούειν· ἀλλὰ ἴσθι, ὅσα γε τὰ νῦν ἐμοὶ δοκοῦντα, ἐὰν λέγῃς παρὰ ταῦτα, μάτην ἐρεῖς. ὅμως μέντοι, εἴ τι οἴει πλέον ποιήσειν, λέγε.

> These sayings, my dear companion Crito, are assuredly what I think I hear, just as the corybants think they hear the flutes, and within me the sound of these arguments buzzes, and makes me incapable of hearing the other arguments. But rest assured, so far as my present opinions are concerned, if you speak to the contrary you will speak in vain; nevertheless, if you think you will gain any advantage, speak!

But Crito has nothing further to say, and a single enigmatic reference to 'the god' closes the dialogue.[277]

Crito, then, acknowledges defeat. Acknowledgment of defeat surely is, in dialectic, defeat. We have seen that it is the combined arguments of Socrates and Socrates' creation, the personified Laws of Athens, that have defeated him. We have found the Laws to be arguing not infallibly but on the whole Socratically. Socrates seems on the face of the text to be persuaded himself; he does what the Laws argue for. But there is a scholarly view, more popular than it used to be,[278] that because Socrates compares the Laws' speech to the Corybants, and because any reference to Corybants in Plato is derogatory, therefore this particular reference to Corybants is derogatory, and Plato did not mean his readers to take the Laws' arguments seriously as a counter or part of a counter to Crito's. We have to examine this interpretation, and may start with some brief general considerations.

In interpreting the end of the *Crito*, one must first inspect the dramatic situation. The practical decision cannot be postponed (as indeed Crito says at 46a4–7). Provisionality is no longer an option. This runs clean counter to Socrates' normal practice in the 'early' dialogues (with the possible exception of the *Gorgias*). But Socrates must now make up his mind, finally. The prospect of drinking hemlock to-morrow or the day after no doubt sharpens the powers of decision wonderfully. Discussion must end. Socrates must somehow indicate to Crito that it has ended. But also, somehow, the *convenances* of the Platonic confutation or elenchus, including its generally provisional nature, must be observed.

It is hard to imagine any more skilful handling of these apparently contradictory requirements than Plato offers. The Laws' arguments, by sounding in Socrates' mind's ear, prevent him from hearing the other, that is to say Crito's,[279] arguments. Further persuasion will be vain, so far as Socrates can tell now. But Crito is welcome to try, and it is only when Crito confesses he has nothing more to say that Socrates pronounces the solemn end. If – and it is a big 'if' – Socrates at the beginning of his penultimate speech uses expressions not consistent with full endorsement of the Laws' arguments, or even expressions ambiguous in this regard, that could easily be due to the need both to leave the question Socratically open and, for contextually practical reasons, to close it. Whatever the upshot of discussion about the connotations of the language Socrates uses in this speech, Plato's high skill as a dramatist remains unimpaired.

More specifically, two recent attacks on the Socratic credentials of the Laws' speech, attacks relying largely on the image of the Corybants, need detailed consideration. But first, before the attacks, let us look at the simile itself. It is not clear from the text whether Socrates is like Corybants in hearing sounds persisting (1) after they have actually ceased (so Burnet), or, (2) since Corybants are devotees, in the intervals between one ritual occasion and another, and indeed generally (so Linforth).[280] But whichever of these is right, there are perhaps two main points to the comparison. (a) Socrates hears, even when no longer himself giving voice to them, the arguments he puts into the mouth of the Laws; the Corybants hear flutes even when the flutes are not actually playing. (b) Though nothing more is said of the Corybants in this connection, the continuing sound of the Laws' argument in Socrates' mind's ear drowns out Crito's earlier arguments. It is not clear in the text whether the Corybants are to be thought of as hearing nothing but the flutes.

People want in various ways to make these points out to be pejorative. At least two recent interpreters, R. Weiss and V. Harte, suppose the image to shed doubt on Socrates' acceptance of the Laws' arguments. They suppose that this conclusion prevents us from regarding those arguments as simply continuing Socrates' earlier dialectic against Crito and as forming with it a whole that is dialectically valid. Their arguments deserve inspection.

Weiss' argument is rather hard to summarize. But

(i) She contends that those who hear Corybantic sounds even when the latter are not physically extant are still in frenzy. Such frenzy includes elements of phobia and anxiety, to be cured by the music of the flutes. Perhaps the music induces the disturbance it cures? In the *Euthydemus* it is a prelude to initiation.

(ii) Answering the question what it means for Socrates to compare the effect of the Laws' speech to the effect of Corybantic flutes, she supposes that the Laws provide a cure on homeopathic lines for Crito's earlier distracted grief.

But there is at least one conclusive argument to be made against this view. The text lacks even the least suggestion that anyone but Socrates is affected by the Laws' speech(es) in the way the Corybants are by their music. The transfer of the effect to Crito is wholly unwarranted.[281] If the Corybantic flute-music is curing anyone here, it must be Socrates. But a beneficial effect of the music on Socrates would deeply undermine Weiss' interpretation.

Weiss adds:

(iii) The Corybantic sounds are for Socrates, who is not ill, 'painfully overwhelming, excruciatingly loud, deafeningly so'.[282]

Of these, 'painfully' and 'excruciatingly' are not in the text at all, and the words 'overwhelming' and 'deafeningly' are Weiss' own gloss on the simple fact in the text that the sound is loud enough to prevent Socrates from hearing the other arguments. It is not clear that Socrates on this occasion regrets that. There need be nothing pejorative about it. Some word for a relatively loud noise had to be used, and most such words can be used pejoratively; Weiss offers no good reason to see any pejorative force here in βομβεῖν, 'buzz' or 'boom', unless one is convinced beforehand of its presence. She seeks a reason for such conviction in the well-known passage of the *Protagoras* (316a1–2) in which Prodicus' voice 'booms' and prevents his words being heard; on the strength of this she declares 'sophists boom'. This is a rather large conclusion from a rather slight piece of evidence.

There follows:

(iv) 'Philosophy, too, is described in Plato as having corybantic effects.'[283]

This statement derives from the speech of Alcibiades in the *Symposium*. Weiss says that 'it is quite specifically the unphilosophical, more corrupt interlocutors who have strong, even violent reactions to Socrates and his plain conversation'.[284] She later infers that if the Laws strike Socrates as the music strikes the Corybants, then the Laws are unphilosophical:

> Socratic philosophy has a corybantic effect on the unphilosophical.
> Therefore, what has a corybantic effect on Socrates must be unphilosophical.

One may doubt if this inference is sound.

Even if the inference were in itself sound, the generalization in the premiss is founded only on Alcibiades when drunk, in the *Symposium.* Meno's simile of the sting-ray, dragged in by Weiss as a parallel instance – her only one – is surely irrelevant. For if Meno's simile of the sting-ray represents a strong, even violent, reaction of an unphilosophical character to Socrates, in a way Socrates would reject, then its strength and violence have escaped the commentators, and even Socrates, who cheerfully applies the simile to himself. We have again a rather large conclusion from slight evidence.

Harte's arguments deserve closer study.[285] She starts from a piece in the *Phaedrus,* of which she argues only that 'the frenzy which Lysias' speech induces is not an indication that Socrates believes it to be true'.[286] This negative statement we can accept with equanimity: it could amount to a concession that the effect of the Corybant-image may be neutral. But there may be more. In context, at the opening of the dialogue, Phaedrus has heard a speech by Lysias, as he tells Socrates. Socrates desires to hear it from Phaedrus as they walk, suspecting Phaedrus of having it by heart or to hand. As Socrates puts it, Phaedrus, 'having met a man sick with passion for hearing speeches (λόγοι)...was glad to be going to have a companion in his Corybantry and...'. Here a metaphorical Corybant must resemble to some extent a man metaphorically sick with passion. It is difficult, even if the metaphor of 'sickness' is a dead one, to rule out all pejorative force here. The context is playful: Harte says 'not straightforward in tone', but that only means that the pejorative force is playfully applied, not that it is not there. Plato and his Socrates do not entirely approve of Corybants. However, though Socrates eventually turns out to reject the content of the speech of Lysias, there is no reason at all to suppose that that rejection is the reason why he uses the Corybant metaphor. Socrates does not apply the relevant verbs to the particular speech, but to speeches in general. Socrates is expressing his and Phaedrus' overmastering desire for speeches (λόγοι), and if a compelling desire outran reason, Plato's Socrates would be unlikely to approve. But it is hard to see any reason why one should suppose that Socrates is, by use of the Corybant metaphor, signalling in advance his rejection of the intellectual content of the speeches which follow, or that Plato's readers would take him to be so signalling. The most one can say on that is what Harte says: 'It should be clear that the frenzy which Lysias' speech induces is not an indication that Socrates believes it to be true.' Somewhat similarly, Socrates' statement after Phaedrus' recitation of Lysias' speech, that he shared Phaedrus' 'Bacchic' feelings as he followed the speech, does not necessarily indicate Socrates' belief that the content of the speech was untrue. General enthusiasm is consistent with belief and with disbelief alike.

But, as Aristotle has it, one swallow does not make a spring. So we may pass to the next passage where Plato uses the Corybant figure, in the Alcibiades episode of the *Symposium.* Here (at 215e1–4), to quote Harte, 'Alcibiades compares the effect which Socrates' conversation has on him to the madness of those who take part in Corybantic rites: his heart leaps and the tears flow.'[287] This paraphrase however, is slightly tendentious: the word 'madness' and its relatives make no appearance in the Greek text. What Alcibiades says is that hearing Socrates' 'speeches' (again λόγοι) makes his heart leap far more than the hearts of people engaged in Corybantic rites, and makes the tears flow too. It is not clear that this mention of Corybants is any more than a casual passing reference; but if it is, and indeed it may be, then its import needs a close look. Since Alcibiades is the speaker, what needs to be looked at is Alcibiades' attitude to the effect Socrates has on him. No-one else, he says, not even the great orators, has so disturbing and annoying an effect on his soul. Alcibiades compares Socrates' effect to that of the satyr Marsyas, who in mythology was the inventor or finder of the αὐλός, the flute or oboe, but came to an unfortunate end. So what effect did Socrates have on Alcibiades? Alcibiades tells us, in brief, that Socrates convinced him that his whole life was on the wrong track, and that he was looking after Athens at the expense of looking after himself. He had to block his ears and run away, to avoid spending his life at Socrates' feet. He could find no answer to Socrates' arguments, and he was ashamed not to be able to do what they implied should be done. The upshot of this is that for Alcibiades what he compares to one bodily effect of the Corybantic rites is intellectually convincing, though emotionally disturbing. That Socrates or Plato may have disapproved of Alcibiades' ultimate course of conduct is, *pace* Harte, neither here nor there. This passage, at least, does nothing to persuade us that a Corybantic reference shows Socrates to be intellectually unconvinced by the Laws' arguments in the *Crito.*

One can top up the above arguments by reference to the *Laws*, the dialogue of Plato so called, not of course to be confused with the Laws (unitalicized) in the *Crito.* In Book VII of the *Laws*, the Athenian Stranger at 790c5 ff. elaborates a comparison between the sounds and movements of the Corybants and the movements and melodious sounds by which mothers put their babies to sleep. He attributes both infant sleeplessness and Corybantic frenzy to fear, which the relevant sounds and movements serve to calm. An explanation follows, to the effect that the fears thus calmed are potentially harmful, in the case of the infant, to moral development. Now no-one should lightly, or indeed at all, read back into the *Crito* the doctrine or argument of the *Laws.* But we may legitimately extract from this passage of Book VII the possibility of the Corybants' sounds and movements being used as an analogue for something actively helpful. If this is a literary possibility in the *Laws,* then there is at least no obvious reason why it should not equally be a literary possibility for the Laws of the *Crito.*

The Corybant-image thus, over our three passages, turns out to be at least ambivalent, if not actually neutral, in its effect on the reader's evaluation of that which is so imaged. We have found one passage in which it could have pejorative associations, one in which it serves as analogue to something intellectually convincing but emotionally disturbing, and one passage in which intellect has nothing to do with it but the emotional effect of the Corybants is calming. In the face of this evidence no sweeping statement as to the favourable or unfavourable implications for a passage of a mention of the Corybants or their rites is advisable. There is no decisive evidence that Plato would have expected *any* set of readers to see in a bare mention of Corybants any signal whatever.

If we ask for further evidence Harte gives us a much more sophisticated discussion than Weiss of the word βομβεῖ.[288] Noting its common sense of 'buzzing', she insists that 'In Greek things that buzz are not good things at all. Things that literally buzz are bees, wasps, mosquitoes, etc.' Citing examples, including one of Plato's, at *Republic* 564d–e, she argues that 'A bee buzzing round you is irritating, dangerous and not to be welcomed.' But her passage of Aristophanes' *Plutus* (537–9) does not refer either to bees or explicitly to anything more dangerous than annoyance; clearly there is nothing immediately harmful or even annoying about the buzzing bee of Theocritus III 13, to which Harte does not refer; the *Republic* passage refers again to buzzing as a loud noise drowning out speech – but there is no reason why Plato's dislike and disapproval of the buzzers there should rub off on other uses of the verb. The buzzing of the sophist Prodicus' deep voice at *Protagoras* 316a again prevents Socrates from hearing what Prodicus has to say, much though he would like to hear it; but that is not otherwise annoying, is certainly not dangerous, and gives an engaging comic effect. If readers notice that all these examples are of X drowning out Y when Y would be nice to hear, then that is natural enough: one much more often talks of a sound being drowned that one wants to hear than of a sound being drowned which one does not want to hear anyway.

So should we suppose, then, that Socrates in the *Crito* wants actively to disown the arguments of the Laws which are buzzing within him, in favour of 'the other arguments' which he endorses? There is no need to suppose so. It is a no less plausible interpretation of the image to suppose Socrates to be saying that the Laws have succeeded in drowning out the other, that is to say Crito's arguments – that being a courteous, urbane, indirect and self-deprecating way of saying that he and they have confuted Crito. Plato's Socrates would normally like to hear any arguments on any moral topic; he is, as he says in the *Phaedrus*, a lover of speeches or arguments. On this occasion, however, he cannot. But he gives Crito leave to try to find some more, presumably some he can hear, that is to say some stronger (to change the metaphor) than those Crito has advanced up to now, and capable indeed of disarming the Laws. As we saw at the outset of this discussion, Plato and his Socrates must provide the discussion in the *Crito* with both finality and provisionality. The occasion is exceptional. Socrates accordingly deals with it in a way not paralleled elsewhere.

But the immediately above paragraph assumed, perhaps illegitimately, the answer to another question. M. Miller, in another article designed to destroy the Socratic credentials of the personified Laws of Athens,[289] begins by asking about the expression 'the other arguments' (τῶν ἄλλων λόγων): 'Is it possible... that Socrates, even as he closes the conversation, alludes to a *third* set of λόγοι [arguments], neither Crito's nor the Laws', which the Laws' speech leaves unvoiced?' [emphasis Miller's].

In answer to this it is hard to rule out altogether anything by way of Platonic allusion. But to allude to such a third way is certainly not the primary purpose of the expression mentioned.[290] The sequel at 54d5 makes this clear. '... if you speak against these things, you will speak in vain'. Here normal coherence of speech and writing would suggest most strongly that the things against which Crito will speak in vain are the things which prevent Socrates from hearing the other arguments, and that their noise is the reason why it will be vain for Crito to speak. In that case the Laws' arguments are the things against which Crito will speak in vain. To put the point another way, the two demonstrative pronouns in 'the sound of these arguments' and 'if you speak against these things' should refer to the same antecedent, the arguments of the Laws, and 'the others' in between must mean 'those other [than the Laws' arguments]'. The only candidates, in the context, for these other arguments than the Laws' are the arguments of Crito which have just been refuted. Plato could not in this context have expected his readers, whether casual or thorough, to think of any further, third, set of arguments of which nothing has hitherto been seen or heard. So whatever degree of finality attaches to this close of the discussion attaches to the Laws' arguments, and not to some other arguments, un-mentioned, which Socrates may have in mind. And, if that is right, then the Laws' arguments must be at least part of what Socrates finds a conclusive reply to Crito's original arguments for escape. And – one more step – what Socrates cannot now hear must therefore be Crito's original arguments. Reference to any third set of views or arguments is entirely superfluous; if it is entirely superfluous Plato will not have expected any normal reader to think of it. Miller's theory looks like a clear example of the 'documentary fallacy'.

Now of course, one has to add, Crito might have other arguments up his sleeve. But as things are he has none: he put forth his best effort in his earlier attempt to persuade Socrates to escape. It would be extremely surprising if Crito had not done his best in real life, and in literature it would have been truly astonishing if he had come up with extra arguments at the end of the Laws' harangue. Though judgments on such questions are somewhat subjective, Crito does seem to have put forward a full practical and moral case early in the dialogue, so far as the situation allowed him to. Of course, someone else might have put a different case. Plato's Socrates would then doubtless have used a different set of questions to probe and ultimately demolish the different case and the different person. If Crito's defeat owes something to the nature of the case he put forward, that is not in any way unfair unless the case was skewed. But neither the expression 'so far as in you lies' nor the appeal to 'justice' nor the failure, due to futility, to paint death in harsh colours nor any other point in his original case seemed in context forced or unnatural, let alone skewed. Crito could not complain that his author did not on the whole give him a fair crack of the whip. Crito, at least, can find nothing to say. So far as he is able to think, his arguments have been defeated.

EPILOGUE

This may seem to some a disappointing conclusion, and the dialogue as here interpreted a philosophical disappointment. But what other sort of dialogue did Plato in refutative mood or period construct? The views and/or arguments in such dialogues are put forward by people whom Socrates confutes, taking into account their characters, their words, their weaknesses. Normally he does this in close dialectical questioning. In the Crito he turns, after a bout of close dialectic, to rhetoric. But the rhetoric too is aimed at a particular person built as Plato has formed Crito for us: that is, a plain Athenian gentleman, not skilled in philosophy but capable in general of keeping the thread of an argument. This gentleman is much more susceptible to rhetoric than Socrates is, but not outrageously or improbably so. Crito has no professional presuppositions that I can see for Socrates to make use of. But his character, his situation and his commitments in the dialogue play their part. His lack of skill in dialectical in-fighting – though he can see the outline of a position as well as most – is important: in the early part of Socrates' argument he has trouble with ambiguities, he misses a false dichotomy, he has difficulties in general with linguistic sleights of hand. However, he is no fool and no patsy. We have to remember from time to time that Plato did not write entirely for scholarly or for philosophically mature readers. Most of the faults in Socrates' line of argument that Crito misses could reasonably be called technical. Since Plato pretty certainly knew about some of them, he was presumably writing at least in part for readers who were no better equipped technically than Crito. Should Plato rather have written for his Socrates a public lecture laying down his arguments from his own premisses? If so, he would have convinced very few, as indeed Socrates implies at 49d2–5. And Plato, having done that, would effectively have abandoned the way of writing that he had adopted in all seriousness.

Plato has faced his readers with two main pieces of dialectical argument. The first is essentially protreptic, drawing Crito and any reader unfamiliar with philosophical argument and/or sceptical of its benefits into a piece of dialectic they might otherwise neither listen to nor read. Those of Plato's contemporaries who enjoyed and were familiar with his Socrates and the kind of shenanigans he gets up to will have looked over this first argument with a perhaps critical but not malevolent eye, and waited for the meatier dialectic to follow. The second argument presents on one level a sweeping, elegantly crafted rhetorical harangue serving to persuade the casual, uninitiated reader who has read this far that Socrates' ethic, with its emphasis on justice above all, gave him no choice but to remain in prison to die. The *Crito* even at this level would impress readers with the pathos of its drama and the heroism of its central figure. On a somewhat higher intellectual level Plato could hope to convince alert but unsubtle readers that, given the paramountcy of justice even in retaliation, the proper citizen would not, even if he could, evade the city's judgments as handed down by the courts. As for the fully-fledged dialectician, well versed in the kind of argument Plato's Socrates conducts, Plato could hope that such would realize the ambiguities involved, work his way through the dialogue's concluding argument, pick up the thread which makes dialectical sense, and come to an understanding of the whole. Moreover, since justice formed an essential element in the moral education which normal Athenian and doubtless other Greek parents gave their children, almost all Plato's readers would find an uplifting moral lesson in Socrates' use of the paramountcy of justice and his persistence in it even at the cost of his life. Plato's Socrates is firm and persistent in his preference for death over injustice. At all levels Plato is writing for honourable Athenian or indeed Greek gentlemen, promoting a similar firm persistence in them.

Furthermore, whatever one may think of individual sections of the argument, the general strategy of the argument against escape is scrupulously fair. Plato first allows Crito to rule out unjust retaliation as being a species of injustice, injustice itself being ruled out for reasons natural to a presentably intelligent Crito. Socrates then puts a question (50c1–3) which Crito again very naturally answers in a way establishing that Socrates' escape is to be considered under the head of retaliation. His answer also, contrary to (R1) above, commits Crito by implication to the view that the escape's status as a retaliation is relevant to its evaluation as just or unjust. That left Socrates in ignorance whether Crito embraced (R2) (R3) or (R4). It might appear dubious conduct in argument for Socrates not to inquire which of these three different principles Crito actually meant to accept. But when the Laws have completely unfolded their argument that the escape would be unjust, we find that they have conducted the case in such a way as to confute a Crito who adhered to (R4). Any arbitrariness attaching to this choice vanishes when we consider that in confuting a Crito believing in (R4) Socrates has performed a harder task than would be set by a Crito believing in (R2) or (R3). Indeed the task of refuting a Crito believing in (R4) *includes* the tasks of refuting a Crito who believes in (R3) or (R4).

This should make clear what is meant by saying that the strategy pursued by Socrates and the Laws is scrupulously fair.

Whether the tactics are as fair as the strategy remains open to debate. There are one or two places where the Laws, even read dialectically, may seem to readers to be stretching a point. But the points stretched are minor ones. In general, granted a licence to argue *ad hominem*, Socrates and the Laws argue the moral case *ad hominem* fairly, or at least more fairly than many interpreters have thought. The same cannot be said of the earlier tortuous argument which persuades Crito to argue carefully without over-reliance on common opinions or judgments. But a person not yet interested in careful and detailed argumentative in-fighting is not the person to detect the flaws in the reasoning thereabouts. Plato accordingly does not have to be so scrupulous in his dialectic as he becomes when he and his Socrates confront the central moral issue of the dialogue.

This study has not shown, and did not set out to show, that Socrates would have accepted every proposition or inference in the Laws' argument. The object was rather to show that, rhetorical garb apart, the status of the argument is the same as that of many another 'early', 'Group I', or 'refutatory' dialogue. It is the kind of argument that Plato's 'early' Socrates uses. It plays a vital part in refuting or, as one should perhaps rather say, 'confuting', Crito and his arguments, in the form in which Plato makes him present them, with very few dubieties of reasoning. In that sense it offers, as Socrates desiderates at 46b5–6, τῷ λόγῳ ὃς ἄν μοι λογιζομένῳ βέλτιστος φαίνηται, 'the argument which seems to me as I reflect the best', better, that is, than any other which is presented to him. If that is right, it follows that there is no reason to see any radical philosophical discontinuity in the *Crito*, no reason for dissociating Socrates from that part of the argument against Crito which he puts into the mouth of the Laws of Athens. One can thus give the Laws their rightful place at the climax of a continuous and dialectically coherent argument. In so doing one is saving not only the dialectical, but also the artistic coherence of the dialogue.

This whole line of thought places the present interpretation in a kind of scholarly limbo. There are those who think that the Platonic Socrates' reasons for staying to die appear straight and undiluted in the final argument of the *Crito*. There are those who find the Laws' share of the final argument to be in conflict with Socratic principles or with Socratic methods of argument. The version of the argument offered here rejects the second view, but does not altogether agree with the first. Socrates' methods, on my view, do not reveal his own private and personal opinions or inferences or justifications for his decisions. In the 'early' dialogues, at least, Plato does not give us his Socrates' private and personal thoughts:

he normally gives us only the arguments Socrates develops in clashes with and confutations of others. By asking rather than answering questions Socrates avoids the responsibility, as we saw in the Prologue above, for the premisses and inferences which lead to the conclusion.[291] There is nothing un-Platonic, and nothing untypical of Socrates in a range of dialogues, in *ad hominem* argument.

After the analysis of the course of the argument we have carried out, is there room left for a more 'doctrinal' interpretation of Socrates' questioning of Crito? Take for example the response Socrates offers to Crito through the Laws at 50c1–2: 'The city treated us unjustly…' Certainly, as we saw, Socrates believes this. Furthermore, if we take in one particular sense Socrates' earlier questions about the moral necessity of avoiding injustice, it makes sense for Socrates to put forward this as a defence for his hypothetical escaping self, just as much as it makes sense for Crito to accept it as a defence if we take his assent to Socrates' earlier questions in the required sense. But Socrates is about to demolish the defence. Does he put it forward as his own defence in the knowledge that he is going to demolish it? Of course he knows his intention, as we readers, all of us, know it; of course he is not putting up a mere Aunt Sally. Difficulties of this kind are inseparable from the doctrinal method of interpretation. On the interpretation offered in this book the situation is the same as it often is elsewhere: we do not know whether Socrates would accept the arguments or not. We do not have to know, so long as the respondent is at the end confuted.

Nor is that all that can be mustered against 'doctrinal' interpretations of the *Crito*. At 47a–e Socrates, if his questions are merely suggestions, in effect assertoric, is himself in his own person guilty of contradicting himself within the space of a few lines. He first (virtually) asserts that there is only one man who knows; he then (virtually) asserts that the knowers are more than one. On the dialectical reading of the passage, it is Crito who, bemused by the subtlety of Socrates' series of questions, and being inexperienced in this kind of logic-chopping, is prepared to accept a contradiction. Would readers prefer a self-contradicting Socrates or a bemused and self-contradicting Crito, with or without Socrates joining in the contradiction? The choice is easy: it is Crito, and not Socrates at all, who here contradicts himself. To arrive securely at that obvious choice all we have to do is to take Socrates' questions as questions, requiring an answer, and expecting an external commitment from Crito that will further his confutation. Socrates himself avoids any commitment that he does not *explicitly* take on; for the course of the argument he does not explicitly take on any responsibility.

But nevertheless he is to some extent responsible, as intelligent readers normally acknowledge. He bears ultimately the responsibility for deciding to stay and die. That responsibility is his alone. He bears also the responsibility for the general shape of the argument.[292] Crito is lured into certain responses early in the argument, responses he might not have given so readily at a later stage. The admission that there are no exceptions to the rule against injustice is a case in point. It is pretty clear that Socrates knows where he wants the argument to go, and is, by selection and timing of his questions, making as sure as he can that it gets there. He also – equally clearly – believes before starting the confutation that Crito is wrong, and that his case will not stand up to examination of a Socratic kind. He says at 46b1–2, 'Your zeal, Crito, would be most precious, *if it were to be* accompanied (εἰ μετά τινος ὀρθότητος εἴη) by the getting of anything right.' The 'remote' condition, as grammarians call it, implied in the Greek grammar of the words I have italicized and cited, is a giveaway. Why does Socrates believe he will win the argument? That is by no means clear; and in any case the question smells of the documentary fallacy. Perhaps he has positive arguments of his own, and in the light of what seems to him their solidity cannot conceive of the contradictory conclusion being successfully maintained.[293] Perhaps we must suppose him to have successfully encountered during his month in prison so many arguments for escape that by now he is confident of defeating any that anyone can produce. A particularly plausible explanation is that he can see in advance a line of argument, at least in general outline, with which he can drive Crito to surrender his position. One is reminded of his fairly confident assertion that Gorgias has contradicted himself, made when there is still a good deal of dialectic to be gone through before Gorgias finds himself compelled to admit it.[294]

So Socrates bears, but does not openly take, the responsibility for the outline of the argument, for the path which the conversation as a whole follows. He does not bear, and does not take, the responsibility for any individual response of Crito's in which he does not expressly join. He bears the responsibility for his decision to die; but Plato and his characters do not expressly say so. It is clearly axiomatic that Socrates will do whatever the argument concludes he ought to do. It is indeed axiomatic at 46b, where Socrates stresses his firm habit of doing what the argument that seems to him best enjoins.

What makes this dialogue unusual is the degree to which it is bound up with a particular moral decision. Why, then, did Plato, given all the difficulties presented, choose to write *this* dialogue? No answer to that can pretend to be more than conjectural. We may hazard a couple of guesses, by no means mutually exclusive. One is that Plato wanted to show that the Socratic elenchus he portrayed, with an allied rhetoric, can help not only in abstract discussion but also in deliberation about a single practical decision.[295] The other is that he wanted to illustrate, and illuminate with argument, the essential importance, indeed the paramountcy, of considerations of justice, fair dealing, righteousness, in making such a decision, and the importance also of seeing the full implications of those considerations, even at the risk of one's life. The choice between righteousness and life itself, or between death and injustice, is the ultimate moral choice confronting a human being. In the *Crito* we have Plato suggesting that in one particular such choice any ordinary gentleman with, like Crito, a moral sense, may find it difficult to justify any but the hero's choice, that of death over the betrayal of ideals.

What is more, this understanding of the *Crito* makes it fairly easy to comprehend why Plato never wrote another dialogue about a particular moral choice, why the *Crito* remained the only example of such a deliberation in Plato's work. For, if justice prevails in the moralist's choice over even death itself, then it must prevail in his or her deliberations over anything lesser – lesser, that is, in any ordinary person's scale of values. If, on the other hand, Plato finds a reader who is not a thoroughgoing moralist, who spurns moral argument or will readily admit exceptions to moral principles, then Plato is not interested in arguing particular moral choices with him at all. One cannot equate Plato's Socrates with Plato, but it is rather hard to envisage a Plato who would not have gone along with the words he puts into Socrates' mouth at *Crito* 49d3:

> For those who hold these opinions and those who do not, there is no common deliberation, but they must necessarily despise each other when they see each how the other deliberates.

APPENDIX

A philosophical argument against escape?

R. Weiss, in her *Socrates Dissatisfied*, puts forward the view that in the middle part of the *Crito*, 46b1–50a5, Socrates advances an argument against escape which is complete in itself and needs no completion from the personified Laws of Athens. Evidently this would rule out the present reading of the dialogue as offering a continuous argument from 46b to the end – to say nothing of the other interpretations it would rule out. To deal piecemeal with Weiss' interpretation of that middle section of the dialogue, à propos of smaller stretches of text, would be fair neither to her approach nor to mine. Hence this appendix examining her view of the relevant passage as a whole, with the exception of 49a–e, which has been discussed at adequate length earlier. The choice of extended treatment here rather than either leaving her argument to reviewers or dealing in snippets, pays a compliment to an original and challenging interpretation.[296]

Weiss and I can agree that Socrates insists he will obey the argument which seems to him best (46b5–6). Weiss also points out that the Laws of Athens 'cannot qualify as another authority not "my own" that Socrates would obey'.[297] That too is acceptable. But we have seen earlier that the Laws are not here asking for blind obedience, but are presenting their portion of an argument which turns out better than Crito's, in that it refutes Crito on his own terms. A part of the argument culminating in the Laws' harangue consists of the 'old arguments' (λόγοι 46b6) which Socrates still honours and Crito is constrained, willingly or unwillingly, to honour on this occasion. We do not have to choose, as Weiss thinks, between those 'old arguments' and the Laws' arguments.[298] One cannot kick out of the way, by forcing such a choice on us, the view that it is the total argument from 46b1–end which proves superior to Crito's, and neither just the Laws' harangue nor just the remarks Socrates offers in his own person.

When Weiss adds that Crito and Socrates cannot share, as Socrates would wish, in a common deliberation because they do not share the 'critical view' that 'injustice ought never to be done', she may or may not be right about Crito's moral choices in his everyday life.[299] To Crito's everyday life we as

Plato's readers have no access. We have access only to Crito's remarks and arguments in the dialogue, and in the dialogue Crito argues that Socrates must not stay and die because to do so would be unjust. For the purposes of the deliberation in hand Crito commits himself to the obligation to do what is just and not do what is unjust. The drift of Crito's own argument commits him to rising above the 'many'. He does not abandon his position and revert to the ranks of the 'many' (*pace* Weiss[300]) when he agrees (48a–b) that yes, the 'many' are able to kill us: Socrates has not previously refuted either that simple fact or the belief of the 'many' that to kill is to do the victim the greatest evil (implied at 44d1–5).

Socrates has simply denied this belief. He, not initially Crito, revives the fact of the 'many's' ability to kill at 48b10–11, presumably in order to settle a vital premiss (as he does) by refuting that accompanying belief out of Crito's own admissions now. Those admissions include the judgment that it is more important to live well than merely to live. Such admissions consort well, as we have seen, with the implications of Crito's own earlier arguments.

From these preliminaries, having discussed earlier what the parties agree at 49a–e, we may pass directly to what Weiss calls 'Socrates' Argument against Escape'.[301] It is necessary to recall that she regards that whole argument as complete before the entry of the Laws of Athens. It is necessary also to quote her own summary at some length:[302]

'(1) If Socrates attempts to escape with Crito's help, Socrates will fail to do what he agreed with the Athenians to do – that is, abide by his penalty – even though what he agreed to do is just.

'(2) If Socrates does not do what he agreed upon with the Athenians, Socrates will be involved in the injustices of deceit – that is in stealth and paying money and gratitude to those who would lead Socrates out of prison.

'(3a) Since it is unjust to fail to fulfill one's just agreement and engage instead in deceit, Socrates and Crito, by involving themselves and their friends in the attempt to escape, would be doing bad things to, in the sense of damaging the souls of, those to whom bad things ought least to be done: oneself and one's friends.

'(3b) Since escape will involve Socrates and Crito and their friends in injustice, Socrates and Crito by attempting Socrates' escape will fail to abide by the just principles upon which they have agreed with each other, principles that would forbid such action.'

In examining the texts cited in support of this version of the argument, we must note Weiss' view that the argument 'relies only on old ideas and upon events with which Crito is familiar'. With this in mind, let us begin with (1).

Has Socrates agreed with the Athenians to abide by his penalty? Not in the *Crito*, as Weiss would be the first to admit, not yet at 49e6 when Socrates first mentions a prohibition concerning an agreement. Weiss finds this agreement at Plato, *Ap.* 39b6 '...and I abide by the penalty and so do they [sc. the prosecutors]'. Now here in *Ap.* there is no word of an agreement, no word of a promise; there is just a statement, 'I abide' (*or* 'I will abide'[303]) 'by the penalty'. The two passages, in *Apology* and *Crito*, have in common only the single word (in Greek) ἐμμένω (*emmenō*), in the future ἐμμενῶ (*emmenō* with a different accent) 'abide by'; and that word is differently applied in the two passages. If one is to suppose that Crito recalls this sentence of the *Apology* on the basis of this single word together with the notion of an agreement which is not explicit in the *Apology*, then it is axiomatic that Plato's readers too must recall the relevant words of his *Apology*. If readers do not themselves recall the relevant sentence of the *Apology*, then they are not in a position to suppose Crito to have failed to recall it, or to have ignored it. So on Weiss' view Plato must be relying on readers of his *Crito* remembering at the right time, with only one not uncommon word to prompt them, the drift of a single sentence in the *Apology*. At the same time they will have had to construe that single sentence as constituting in particular an agreement.

Even readers, many readers, who know the *Apology* rather well, have failed to make this connection. This fact of course constitutes Weiss' originality here. But if they so failed, whether as ancient Greek or as modern readers, they have, on her view, quite mistaken the whole drift of a major portion of the dialogue, if not of the dialogue's argument as a whole. If this is right, then Plato was running – to put it mildly – a serious risk of being seriously misunderstood. Perhaps he chose to run that risk; one should, however, accept that view only with caution, in the absence of any examples elsewhere of his running similar risks. This point does not depend on the somewhat controversial principle (which I should in general accept) that one should not interpret one dialogue out of another without specific and open cross-reference in the text. The difficulty in Weiss' view here, even for those who would not accept that principle, lies in the microscopic thinness of the thread supposedly connecting the passages in the two works. If Plato had meant his readers in the *Crito* to be fully aware at this stage, before the Laws' appearance, that Socrates has *promised* in court to abide by his penalty, it is hard to find a reason why he should not have inserted a reminder. Further, if Plato meant Socrates to want Crito to have his previous 'agreement' in the forefront of his mind at this stage it is hard to find a reason why Socrates in the dialogue should not have reminded him.[304]

This point is already complete in itself. But, for a separate *ad hominem* development of it, does Weiss imagine Plato's Socrates as expecting Crito to be so quick on the uptake without a reminder? After a lifetime's friendship with a man Weiss takes to be a fool? It is hard to find any solid reason to believe that in this part of the *Crito* Socrates is entitled to expect Crito to think at once of Socrates' 'agreement' with the Athenians to abide by his penalty. Weiss attempts to show that Crito is stupidly forgetful in being bewildered by Socrates' questions about an agreement. The attempt is unsuccessful.

Weiss' (2) concerns the second half of Socrates' question at 49e6.[305] Socrates there asks, 'Is there an obligation to do whatever one agrees with someone, so long as it is just, or is there an obligation to deceive?' This Weiss apparently construes, uniquely in the scholarly tradition to my knowledge, as asking whether one ought to act upon the just moral principles one agrees upon in discussion or whether one ought to use deceitful procedures such as being 'stolen' out of prison and paying bribes. That these are not obvious alternatives to each other Weiss is aware; hence her remark that 'Because escape defies the will of the Athenians, the alternative to Socrates' doing what he has agreed upon with the Athenians is for him to engage in deceit.' This justification, however, does not work. It makes the question personal to Socrates in the situation of the dialogue; but there is nothing at all in the question to make it individual or personal to Socrates. It is as general in form as it could be. Observe that 'someone' (τις). We face a similar question here to one faced on Weiss' (1): if Plato's Socrates means what she thinks he means, why does he not say it? No solid explanation is on offer. On the other hand, if the question in the *Crito* here is as general as it certainly looks, and if 'agree' (ὁμολογῶ, *homologō*) means 'make an agreement' or 'promise', then the phrase 'an obligation to deceive' gives a perfectly natural alternative. To make a promise or enter into an agreement and then break it is a deceitful thing to do. The Greek verb concerned, ἐξαπατᾶν, 'deceive', is used of breaking an agreement by Thucydides, at V 42.2; to make it mean something else, in a context concerned with agreeing, can only be special pleading.

Weiss' understanding of her (3a)[306] is equally special pleading. She duly cites the question, 'If we go away from here not having persuaded the city, are we treating badly those who ought least to be so treated?' On this she argues that if Crito is to 'have any chance of following the argument' Socrates must refer to those Crito would acknowledge to be least deserving of bad treatment; they, she insists, must be not the city (singular), but rather Socrates' own self, his family and friends. The trouble with this is that it stands the text on its head. Crito does not follow the drift of Socrates' questions, and says so. That is a good reason for Socrates, through the Laws, to explain his questions. Weiss' objection would convince only if there were not in Plato other examples of Socrates or other dialectical questioners putting questions or statements to their interlocutors whose drift the interlocutors are not yet in a position to follow, for reasons of ambiguity, obscurity or other difficulty. Here one recalls, for example, Socrates' description of himself as a midwife in the *Theaetetus*.

Weiss is of course aware of the existence of parallels.[307] They are not hard to find.[308] Among less striking but still pertinent examples are the following. At *Lysis* 217c–d Socrates baffles Lysis, and has to explain his question. A callow youth quite unpractised in dialectic could certainly not have been expected to give the answer by distinguishing *being* a colour (e.g. 'being yellow') and appearing or looking a colour (e.g. 'looking yellow'). At *Rep.* 382a1 ff. it takes several layers of explanation before Adeimantus grasps a point which Socrates had put obscurely to begin with. Other passages repay attention, such as *Euthphr.* 10a1 ff., *Phaedo* 93a11–b4, *Rep.* 352e, 376e–7a, 392c6 ff., 413b1 ff. (where Socrates acknowledges the difficulty of his question), *Phileb.* 44a10–b5. This is indeed, on a small scale, a common device of Plato's for enlivening the dialogue and retaining the reader's interest. Since at *Politicus* 296a the Eleatic Stranger does the same sort of thing to 'Young Socrates', it is indeed a device of Plato's, not confined to Socratic interrogations. Such trivia as appear in this list serve to establish a practice, but the ones which to my mind stand out as parallels to the larger-scale bewilderment and explanation of the *Crito* are those of *Smp.* 206b ff. and *Rep.* 375e ff.

At *Rep.* 375e9 Socrates addresses Adeimantus: 'Do you think the man who is to be a fitting guardian needs this too, to be a philosopher by nature in addition to being spirited?' At this point in the *Republic* this question evidently surprises and baffles Adeimantus, as well it might. His reply is 'How [do you mean]? I don't understand.' The Greek for 'I don't understand' here is οὐ γὰρ ἐννοῶ, exactly, word for word, what Crito says at *Crito* 50a5. Socrates in the *Republic* passage then launches into an explanation. That is a case where Socrates puts a question his interlocutor can be virtually guaranteed not to follow.

Then at *Smp.* 206a Diotima hits Socrates, and Plato's readers, with both question and statement. She brings Socrates to the conclusion that *eros*, or desire, is for the good, indeed for the good to belong to oneself always. She then asks, 'Since that is what *eros* is always, whose eagerness and tension would be called *eros*? In what way do they pursue [the good], and in what activity? What is it that they do? Can you say?' The supposedly young and ignorant Socrates, who is replacing the young and ignorant Agathon, replies, very naturally, '[If I could] I wouldn't have admired your wisdom and come to you to learn exactly these things.' Indeed the youthful Socrates of the story, that is to say in effect Agathon, could certainly not have been expected to find the answer Diotima gives: 'I'll tell you: it is procreation in the beautiful both in respect of the body and in respect of the soul.' Socrates' further reply, 'It would take a prophet to divine your meaning, and I don't follow' surely voices the reactions of most, if not all, uninitiated first-time readers of the *Symposium.* Procreation in respect of the *soul*? Diotima (in effect Socrates) has to explain, and does so down to 207a4.

Even these star cases are admittedly not on the scale of the *Crito*-episode. But they suffice to show that Plato's practice in this matter may extend beyond a mere sentence or two. It is the principle which is significant. If Plato can in other places make a questioner cause justified bewilderment and then offer an explanation, then he can do it in the *Crito.* If he can do it in the *Republic* and *Symposium* without making the interlocutor look a fool, then he can do it in the *Crito* without making Crito look a fool. If Plato's Socrates or other questioner can deliberately bring the respondent up short in this way in one dialogue, he or she can do so in another without even being suspect of the kind of hidden agenda which Weiss proposes. Plato's practice suggests very strongly that the argument is not complete when Crito expresses his inability to understand. In view of that practice Weiss' case depends once again on the argument she lends to Socrates being so obvious that Crito 'can reasonably be expected at this point to follow the argument'. But this, here and elsewhere, lands her in a cleft stick: either the argument is indeed obvious, in which case Socrates has only to be for a few sentences as explicit, urbane and patient as he normally is with ordinary people; or it is not, and her case collapses. Escape from this dilemma is easy. One has only to abandon the tenuous link with the *Apology* and to suppose that the Laws subsequently offer on Socrates' behalf the explanations of both the questions Crito finds unintelligible.

Plato's readers often find respondents in a fog of bewilderment lifted by explanations of varying lengths. On at least two counts, however, the *Crito*, if we adopt Weiss' reading of this section, presents a phenomenon unique in Plato's writings. Not so much as once do Plato's readers find Socrates (or his like) bewildering a respondent and then not explaining himself. On Weiss' reading Socrates in the *Crito* loses patience and, rather than explain himself, sails off on quite a different tack. Socrates and his like in Plato never do that. It would take the most overwhelming evidence to make one believe Socrates to be doing it in the *Crito.* Secondly, still on Weiss' interpretation, the Laws of Athens purport, rather clearly, to offer an explanation after all; but it is not, according to Weiss, the true explanation. Where else in Plato do we find puzzlement dispelled by an explanation in which Socrates (or other questioner) does not believe? The answer is simple: nowhere. So whether or not the Laws' explanation counts as an explanation, Weiss' *Crito* is without parallel. Nor, so far as I am aware, are there any examples elsewhere in Plato of Socrates or other questioner ending a complete refutatory argument with something which *for the respondent* stands in need of further explanation.

Only a demonstration that Crito is uniquely foolish would even start to justify Plato in such a unique departure from his normal practice. But, as argued in my main text, Crito is not so foolish as that, and, if he were, he would not be worth arguing with, either for Socrates or for Plato. In the matter of 'those least deserving of harm' in this part (3a) of the argument, Weiss points out that Crito, as an Athenian of normal values, 'would recognize as least deserving of harm…oneself, one's family and one's friends'. Precisely. Crito has pleaded that Socrates by staying to die would be treating himself, family and friends unjustly, betraying them. It is exactly that which gives plausibility to Crito's bewilderment at the question 'Are we, by leaving here without persuading the city, treating badly those we least ought?' That in turn is why Socrates, through the harangue by the Laws, represents not self, family and friends but the city and its laws as 'those whom one ought least to treat badly'.

Weiss' reading of her (3b) fares no better.[309] (3b) suggests, deriving from 50a2–3, that to escape would be to fail to abide by the things we have agreed to, those things being just. Here Weiss believes that 'the things we have agreed to' are separate and distinct from 'the things one agrees to' at 49e6, just four lines earlier in the Oxford text. She buttresses this rather surprising thesis with considerations deserving inspection.

(i) Why, she asks, does her (3b) not follow directly on her (1) and (2), and why would Socrates 'break the flow of the argument' by interposing (3a)?

The answer to this question is simple. It rests on the transparent structure of the whole passage. Socrates has established with Crito, since 49a4, two principles, first that one should not do injustice or wrong to anybody even in return for injustice or wrong, and secondly that one ought to do what one agrees to do provided it is just. He now (at 49e9) turns from the general to the particular: in escaping, first, are we doing wrong to those whom we ought least to do wrong? Secondly, are we abiding by what we have agreed? The parallelism between these two pairs, one general and one particular, should be evident. The particular questions correspond to, and are broached in the same order as, the two general propositions. There is no break whatever in the flow of the argument. 'We', whether that means the escaping Socrates and Crito, or refers just to the escaping Socrates, are examples to be brought under the two general principles they have agreed. That is why Socrates says, before particularizing, 'Look at it on the basis of these things' ('Ἐκ τούτων δὴ ἄθρει, 49e9), by which he means 'on the basis of these principles'. If there is any difference between the things agreed to in the first question about agreement and those in the second, it can only be the difference between the general and the particular. A completely different reference would undermine (L. Brown's word is 'destroy') the passage's structure and its logic. This – and the point is not just incidental – constitutes a further reason for rejecting the interpretation of the first question about agreement as itself particular in reference.

(ii) Weiss next offers two differences between the 'things which one agrees' at 49e6 and the 'things which we agreed' at 50a2–3, differences that prove unconvincing on examination. Obviously the two do differ in that one is general and the other particular. But Weiss says they differ first in that 'the things agreed upon' are in the first case 'things that *one* person agrees to do [emphasis by Weiss]', 'whereas' in the second case 'the things agreed upon are things that "we" – that is two people together – agree upon', and it emerges soon that in her view the two people concerned have agreed things 'with each other'. Now this last point is the crucial one here: Weiss' case depends on the agreement in the second, particular, case being the agreement reached between Socrates and Crito: it depends on 'the things "we" agree upon' being necessarily the things 'we' agree with each other. But this need not be so. It is perfectly possible for each of two people to have made an agreement to the same effect with the same third party. For example, according to the Laws of Athens (51e2–5), all permanently resident citizens of Athens have made an agreement with them. Though Socrates is 'not least' bound by this agreement, it is not confined to him, and presumably, though the Laws do not say so out loud, it binds Crito too, though less strongly. The second difference Weiss draws attention to is that 49e6 concerns itself with 'doing' what is agreed, whereas 50a1–2 speaks of 'abiding by' what is agreed. But she says nothing to show that 'abiding by' what is agreed cannot consist of 'doing' what is agreed. True, ἐμμένειν does not always mean 'doing' that. Since, however, in matters of language one may cite another dialogue to prove a possibility, we may cite *Laws* 840d2–e2 as using 'abide by' (ἐμμένειν) agreements in the sense of 'persist in carrying out', as opposed to remaining in – or of – an opinion. Pl. *Ap.* 30c also uses 'abide by' not of an agreement but of something requested, meaning 'do', or 'carry out', and *Protag.* 353b uses it similarly of 'abiding by' or carrying out a decision. Plato's choice of words in the *Crito* passage might be a mere stylistic variation. So Weiss' second difference remains, like the first, unproved. None of her arguments exhibits sufficient cogency to upset the structure of the passage as a whole, in which structure one should include the verbal repetitions both of the verb 'agree' and of the phrase 'being just' at 49e6 and 50a1–2. These surely mark the parallelism between the two sentences, the one (to repeat) general and the other particular.

This exhausts Weiss' direct case for regarding the argument Socrates deploys in the lead-up to the Laws' appearance as a complete argument in itself, grossly and stupidly misunderstood by Crito. The indirect case, based on the interpretation of the Laws as arguing un-Socratically, has received attention elsewhere in this work. Neither case seems compelling.

NOTES

[1] Frede 1992; Beversluis 2000, 52–4.

[2] The method is not, however, at all closely akin to that of Leo Strauss, though I have found some useful insights in his work. I have not worked with the concept in mind of an esoteric or concealed meaning or reference for what Plato wrote.

[3] Quandt 1989 took me to task in a review of Stokes 1986 on the ground (among others) that my approach is not literary. It would be interesting to know when situation, plot and character in drama ceased to be the literary phenomena they were when I was young – and also to know when literary study started to ignore the content of the work studied.

[4] See esp. Harte 1999; Polansky 1997.

[5] Burnyeat 2003, 24, declares that Plato was more interested in propositions than in people. Talisse 2002, esp. 49–53, argues that Socrates is examining lives, not propositions. The truth lies perhaps somewhere in between. Perhaps Plato examines *groups of propositions* held by certain typical people living typical lives.

[6] In Plato the respondent is always male.

[7] Cohen and Keyt 1992; see especially 173–5 and 195–200.

[8] Cohen and Keyt 1992, 175, their emphasis; I have substituted 'character concerned' for their 'author'.

[9] Waldock 1951, esp. 11–24.

[10] Stokes 1979, esp. 143.

[11] Ausland 1997, 377 n. 16.

[12] Cf. Stokes 1992, 77–9 (=n. 1).

[13] Stokes 1986, 10–12.

[14] Beversluis 2000, esp. 55–8.

[15] Annas 1992, I think, ignores this distinction.

[16] Beversluis 2000, 51.

[17] A list at Beversluis 2000, 37 n. 2.

[18] Gower and Stokes (eds.) 1992, 82–92.

[19] It would be discourteous to take no notice of R. Kraut's views expressed at his 1992, 25–30. One may agree at once that Plato's dialogues are not 'designed merely to give mental exercise to the reader' (Kraut 26); also that Plato did not *in general* deliberately insert fallacies, ambiguities and deficiencies into his works (Kraut 27–8). Kraut (29) insists that 'Our best chance of understanding Plato is therefore to begin with the assumption that in each dialogue he uses his principal speaker to support or oppose certain conclusions by means of certain arguments because he, Plato, supports or opposes those conclusions for those reasons.' Indeed the resemblances between the conclusions Socrates reaches in various dialogues licence the theory that Plato, when they were written, supported those conclusions, positive or negative. But I see no reason at all for believing that the arguments are those by which Plato convinced himself rather than those by which he thought he could refute or confute other [sorts

of] persons holding views in many respects different from his. See further against Kraut's and similar views Corbett 1997.

[20] The early date of the *Crito* is generally assumed by recent scholars who accept an 'early' group at all; but Tarrant (1995, 15 n.22) has argued interestingly on stylistic grounds for a later revision. He pointed out that in the *Crito* verbal adjectives are common, whereas they are rare in Plato before the *Republic*, and rare also in Thucydides, Lysias, Antiphon, Andocides, and the early works of Isocrates. In the *Gorgias* Plato uses them 40 times, and that not in Socrates' conversations with Gorgias and Polus, but only from the point at which the transition to Callicles begins. This is indeed well observed. But verbal adjectives do nevertheless occur in the 'early' dialogues, in clusters: forms in -τέο- in *Ap.* 18e5, 19a1, 19a7 (*bis*), 21e5, 22b6; *Euthphr.* 8d1, 8e1, 9e7–8 (*bis*), 15c11, 15d3; *Crito* 46b4, 47b9–10 (*quater*), 48a5, 48b5, 48b10, 48c8, 49a4–5 (*bis*), 49e6–8 (one *bis*, one different), 51b7–10 (one *bis*, three others). Why these clusters? For the simple reason that in these particular passages of *Ap.*, *Euthphr*, and *Grg.* the subject under discussion is what life one *ought* to lead, or what *ought* to be done. The *Crito* is *par excellence* the dialogue that discusses what ought to be done. Hence its frequent use of these verbal adjectives. The verbal adjective makes an easy stylistic variant for the use of δεῖ, χρή, (ought, should) etc. Parts of δεῖ occur 19 times in the *Crito*, and parts of χρή 7 times; Plato needed a further variant for obvious stylistic reasons.

Also unconvincingly against an early date is McNeal 1992, xi, 30 and esp. 46 ff. Weak arguments for a late date come also from G. Reale, citing G. Turolla *Platone* III (Milan, 1953) which I have not seen. See Reale ap. Montuori 1998 ix–xi and, on a supposed inconsistency with the *Phaedo*, xv–xvi. Reale himself takes an argument from H. Gomperz to the effect that the sequence of events leading up to the *Crito* differs from the frame of the *Phaedo.* Reale complains that in the *Crito* Crito hears of the arrival of the relevant sacred ship, according to Socrates' dream, the day before the eve of Socrates' death, and then comes next day early and alone to persuade Socrates to escape; in the *Phaedo* (59b5 ff.) Crito and his friends hear on the eve of Socrates' death of the ship's arrival, and gather early for a visit to Socrates on his last morning. However, it is not the ship's *arrival* that Crito hears of in the *Crito.* He hears rather of the ship's *impending* arrival, of its visibility from Sunium. Clearly, as Socrates' dream in the Crito forecasts, the ship actually arrived not on the day it became visible from Sunium but on the following day. There is thus no discrepancy.

[21] On the number of arguments see most interestingly Bostock 1990. Annas thought there were none: she writes (1992, 58 n.26) that 'The Laws do not argue with Socrates but simply order him around and tell him without argument that he has to accept some very contentious theses.' My disagreement with this will become apparent below.

[22] Allows: e.g. DeFilippo 1991, 257 ff.; Gallop 1998, 251 ff. Disallows: e.g. Brickhouse and Smith 1989, 137–53 and elsewhere.

[23] Not Socrates' views: most recently Weiss 1998, and Harte 1999, saying the Laws contradict Socrates; no contradiction is found by DeFilippo 1991 or by Penner 2000, 182–9.

[24] Giving in too easily: e.g. Weiss 1998 *passim*; Emlyn-Jones 1999, esp. 4–5; Montuori 1998, *passim*; and Reale ap. Montuori 1998, viii and elsewhere. So also Bostock 1990.

[25] On this question and sub-question see below in the Index of Topics, s.v. *Argument, continuity of.*

[26] R E. Allen 1980, 82.

[27] See Stokes 1986, *passim.*

[28] I use 'unphilosophical' (cf. Reale ap. Montuori 1998, xiii, 'poco filosofo') not as a term for one who does not understand or appreciate Socrates' views so far as he knows them, nor for one who holds different views from Socrates. I use the epithet to indicate Crito's general indifference to Socrates' brand of precise dialectical argument. His indifference is naturally associated with a general feeling that he can ignore Socrates' paradoxical beliefs and reject anything he finds repugnant to his own brand of common sense. Only when drawn willy-nilly into a piece of dialectic in this dialogue does he pay any attention to such logic-chopping. But such indifference to subtle argument and consequent ability to ignore its conclusions do not prevent Crito, once embarked on dialectic, from being able to stand up for himself in a robust and gentlemanly way in general argument. So successful a businessman as he appears to have been (cf. Nails 2002, 114–16) will have done that every day in ordinary commercial life.

[29] So e.g. Weiss 1998; Polansky 1997; Harte 1997.

[30] There are, however, scenes in the *Odyssey*, such as the stories told by Helen, Menelaus, and Nestor in Books 3–4, which dovetail neatly with the *Iliad.*

[31] Kahn 1996.

[32] Congleton 1974, 434–5, followed by Weiss 1998, 52 and Unruh 2000, 25. Fuhrmann's translation, cited by Unruh, 'ich habe mich ein wenig erkenntlich gezeigt' or 'I have shown him a little appreciation', would rule out bribery; but Fuhrmann may have over-translated.

[33] Weiss 1998, 52–3 on *Phaedo* 58c8–9 mentions Echecrates' question, 'Or did the magistrates forbid [Socrates' friends] to be there, and did he die without them?' She treats this as suggesting that the authorities, presumably the φύλακες δεσμωτῶν of [Xen.] *Ath. Pol.* iii 4, sometimes allowed visitors, sometimes not. But the question is no less likely to exhibit Echecrates' ignorance, as a Phleiasian, of Athenian practice. Compare his ignorance at 58a9 of the sacred ship the Athenians sent annually to Delos, alluded to without explanation at *Crito* 43c9 ff., as being familiar to the two Athenians present.

We do not know how long Crito had been there before Socrates awoke, but when Socrates asks the time he says it is 'deep dawn', ὄρθρος βαθύς. Burnet (1924 ad loc.) remarked that this expression denotes part of the night in Socrates' report of Hippocrates' irruption at *Protag.* 310a, but that is perhaps because Socrates was still asleep. Here in the *Crito* it must be light enough for Socrates to recognize Crito before hearing his voice. Crito may thus have arrived either before dawn or as dawn was breaking. In the *Protagoras* Hippocrates arrives early but not too outrageously early for an ordinary friendly household; it appears to be only a few minutes before Socrates can see that Hippocrates is blushing (312a). But it is too early for a more formal call on Protagoras in Callias' house. It is thus understandable that a prison visit at or before daybreak was abnormally early.

[34] See Hunter 1997 and D. Allen 1997. It is conceivable that Socrates was not in his own cell alone, but in a larger room with other inmates; see Hunter 1997, 312–13, 315–16. However that may be, Plato gives his characters no allusion to

others present.

[35] See e.g. Whitlock Blundell 1989, and Gill et al. (eds.) 1998.

[36] The argument is Congleton's 1974, 434.

[37] So Weiss 1998, 52, citing Congleton (my previous note) with approval.

[38] Weiss 1998, 53. Weiss' comparison of the Thessalian aristocrats with our present-day Mafia of Sicily, though supported by Unruh 2000, 171, outruns the evidence for the former.

[39] Xen. *Mem.* I ii 24, cited by Burnet 1924 on *Crito* 53d3.

[40] Below, pp. 33–4.

[41] Not M. Montuori, nor G. Reale. But their arguments are unconvincing.

[42] Rowe 1993 ad loc. For what the point is worth, Dem. XXIV (*Timocrates*) 77 and elsewhere suggests that the power to bail a public *debtor* out of prison, pending payment of the debt, did not exist before Timocrates introduced it in the law Demosthenes is attacking.

[43] Weiss 1998, 53, on this is unconvincing.

[44] Unruh, for example, speaks (2000, 59) of extraordinary agitation ('Unruhe').

[45] See Denniston 1954, 196–7.

[46] Adam 1888 ad. loc. On οὗτος see Kühner-Gerth (repr. 1955) I 645.

[47] Just how far scribal rather than authorial repetitiveness is responsible for the peculiarities of this passage is uncertain; it would not surprise me if the whole clause δῆλον οὖν ἐκ τούτων τῶν ἀγγέλων ὅτι ἥξει τήμερον were scribal in origin. In any case, however, repetition here could be (if genuinely Platonic) a matter of solemn emphasis rather than emotional distraction.

[48] Especially 1954, 379, which discusses this *Crito* passage.

[49] Emlyn-Jones 1999, 81.

[50] 'Elliptical syntax' derives from 'Crito's emotional state' at Emlyn-Jones 1999, 46, on 43b3 ff.; Crito's 'anxious state of mind' is in evidence at p. 48 on 43d3 (and cf. p. 54 on 45a6); 'vehemence' causes Crito to lose his way in the syntax at p. 57 on 45e6–46a1; at p. 59 concerning 45d7–46a3 we read of Crito's 'exasperation verging on real anger'. Somewhat similarly Weiss, 1998, 39, describes Crito as 'distraught to the point of sleeplessness'. But 'distraught' is too specific and needlessly strong for the Greek λύπη (distress) at 43b4.

[51] See below, p. 52.

[52] Weiss 1998, esp. 43–9. Fox 1956, 227, argued for the view that Crito is 'almost completely without philosophical understanding and capacity'. At 238 he cited *Phaedo* 63a for 'Crito is very readily convinced by the first thing he hears from Socrates'; but the *Phaedo* passage does not say this, nor draw any contrast between Crito and Cebes such as Fox envisaged. Note Nails' more recent and neater formulation 'decent but theory-blind' (Nails 1995, 21); and observe the reservations of Harte 2000, 305 f.

[53] Weiss 1998, 48.

[54] For the unwillingness to call it philosophy see Decleva Caizzi 1996, 117 n. 130.

[55] Weiss says (1998, 48) that Crito 'says he gave no thought to his sons' education'; but that is too strong: Crito has looked at possible educations for them and despaired. He has thought, but his thinking has led to no useful action; hence his word 'neglect', ἀμελῆσαι.

[56] Notably Weiss 1998, 48.

[57] See Lloyd-Jones 1971 *passim* and Stokes 1986, 213–26.

[58] So Fox 1956, 238 and Weiss 1998, 42 n. 8. Seeskin 1993, 39 n. 6 thinks that Crito stops putting up a fight at 47a.

[59] R.E. Allen 1980, 67 and n. 2 refers to Hippocrates (?) *Regimen* IV xci–xcii for the white colour as a sign of 'good fortune to come'. Cf. Unruh 2000, 43. Hippocrates writes there about dreams of things belonging to (περί) the dreamer and about dream-visions of the dead. On the whole the evidence of the much later Artemidorus Daldianus (see Pack's *Index Rerum* to his *Artemidori Daldiani* [1963] s.v. λευκόν) bears out Allen's generalization – see e.g. p. 119 ll. 41 ff. P, 119.20 ff., and 267. 15–8. But in Artemidorus dreams in white are a bad omen for the sick (pp. 102–3 and 245), since the dead are dressed in white for their funerals. This could perhaps make one wonder whether Socrates' dream-figure does not by its very colour carry a message of death. And could that be one reason for Crito's immediate reaction?

Strauss at Pangle (ed.) 1983, 55, suggested that the beautiful woman is modelled on the goddess Thetis in her appearance to the waking Achilles to warn him of death impending once he has killed Hector, in *Iliad* XVIII; not perhaps entirely cogent, but attractive.

In saying Λίαν γε, ὡς ἔοικεν, 'Too clear, it seems', at 44b6, Crito appears to agree with Socrates' interpretation. But this need be no more than a sign of unwillingness to argue the matter. His next sentence, turning to the matter of the escape, shows that he does not really agree. Alternatively, Crito may mean that the dream is all too clear to Socrates. Either way, Unruh is too harsh in describing Crito's ignoring of the dream for practical purposes as a self-contradiction.

[60] The expression 'as it seems', ὡς ἔοικεν, occurs in contexts where disappointment is in point, e.g. Soph. *El.* 772.

[61] So Lambinus, cited by Burnet 1924, 178.

[62] Weinrib 1982, 89.

[63] Weinrib 1982, 89.

[64] This is a similar interpretation to Strauss 1983, 55 and 57.

[65] Weinrib 1982, 89, is right in a way that Crito is 'too obsessed with the urgency of his own plea for action to explore the implications of the dream' – but that need not stop Crito from having his own view of it.

[66] White 1996, 101.

[67] Putting friends before money is good popular ethics: see Eur. *Or.* 1155–6, Menander *Dyscolus* 811–12.

[68] So in effect Emlyn-Jones 1999, 7–8, emphasizing Crito's concern, among other things, for his own personal prestige.

[69] Plato *Ap.* 30b is relevant here: see Stokes 1997 ad loc. and 1992,195–6. I am unconvinced by Woolf on 30b in his 1999 review of Stokes 1997. See further Burnyeat 2003b.

[70] Soper 1996, 119 ff., thinks that though supplying no open answer the dialogue as a whole serves to illustrate an answer involving a view of friendship: he believes Socrates will treat the opinions of friends, as of the State, seriously, to the point where 'his actions may well depend, in part, on Crito's opinion, even if that opinion is not justified'. But neither 46b nor 48a says this; Socrates says he wishes to convince Crito, not that he will act differently if he does not. Socrates follows no friend as such, but the best available argument (46b4–6). Soper's solution neither addresses Crito's point nor rests on an exact reading of the text.

[71] Woozley 1979, 7, ignoring the ramifications of 54a5–7, suggests that the reason why Plato had Crito raise this point and Socrates ignore it is 'that it is his way of expressing to the reader the kind of muddleheadedness in argument which he wishes Crito to represent'. He adds, 'It is not even clear that it is being offered as a moral argument.' There is no particular reason in the text why we should suppose it to be offered as a moral argument rather than a worldly one; but it does supply Socrates with an unselfish reason for escaping. Crito's muddleheadedness has been much exaggerated, and Woozley's suggestion was far-fetched.

[72] Ταῦτα μὲν δὴ οὕτως ἐχέτω, 'Let that be so', which Crito says here, is used to indicate acceptance at *Grg.* 476a2, *Rep.* 611a4–5, *Epin.* 991b5.

[73] Achilles in the *Iliad*, Ajax in Sophocles' play, and so on.

[74] See Knox 1964 *passim.*

[75] See on this Weiss 1998, 40 n. 4. She adduces ('perhaps') 48e1–3 in addition; on Crito's repetitiousness or otherwise in the two passages see below.

[76] See Dover 1993 on *Frogs* 1236; the expression 'final appeal' is Dover's.

[77] Pucci 2000, 85, renders simply 'still today'.

[78] Weiss 1998, 40 n. 4, cites also ('perhaps') 46a4–5, '…there is no longer time to take counsel…'; but 'no longer' there needs no hinterland of earlier arguments to explain it: the mere proximity of Socrates' execution suffices. 'No longer' may allude to past possibilities as well as to past actualities.

[79] Woozley 1979, 13, treats Crito's whole argument as potentially moral; but what I have called his 'worldly' case is not nearly so clearly moral as the arguments we are about to consider. H. Brown 1992, 71–2, reads a reference to justice into 44b–c where I cannot find it. R.E. Allen 1980, 82, alludes to the considerations Crito advances as simply 'prudential'. I do not think Young (1996, 49–61, esp. 50–1) is quite fair in reducing the moral element in Crito's argument to a matter merely of emotion and popular opinion.

[80] Harvey 1990, 118, cites, for sycophants seeking the death penalty, Dem. XXV 83, Lys. XXV 26; and see Adam's note 1888, 33, quoted with approval by Emlyn-Jones 1999, 53, on 44e6, describing the phrase 'or something else' as 'euphemistic for death or exile'.

[81] See Todd 1993, 80–1.

[82] See Emlyn-Jones 1998, 57, on 45e2 for the view that the argument is in part a 'direct moral argument'. Commentators do not all speak of this in complimentary terms: Weiss 1998, 55, speaks of Crito as 'appropriating the Socratic virtue idiom' – as if Socrates had a quasi-monopoly of such terms. Woozley 1979, 8, has reservations; R.E. Allen 1980, e.g. 70, remarks fairly that 'Crito is a good and decent man, speaking the language of popular morals', but goes on to voice suspicions. As many have pointed out, there are contradictions in popular morality; but Plato is not here pointing them out, nor playing on them.

[83] See on the meaning of this passage Penner 1997, 153–5.

[84] For more examples, including some outside Plato, see Stokes 1986, 286–7.

[85] See Stokes 1986, 243–4 (with the context).

[86] So most explicitly Woozley 1979, 11–12; also (I think) Emlyn-Jones 1999, 7–8; R.E. Allen 1980, 67–70. Kraut 1984, 79, speaks of the 'many' of 44a4 in connexion with 45d8–46a4, where, as we shall see below, they do not recur. Voigtländer 1980, 109–10, also fails to notice any difference. Neither Burnet 1924 nor Weiss 1998 nor

Unruh 2000, 58–61, is at pains to distinguish the two arguments.

[87] Emlyn-Jones 1999, 58, on 46a3–4 says, 'Crito neatly combines the two main types of appeal he has made in the course of his speech: to self-interest and to morality.' But though Crito rebuts some points he thinks Socrates might make on the theme of his [Crito's] self-interest, he does not advance in this particular speech a single positive argument from self-interest divorced from morality. Not only can κακόν ('bad') be a moral word; after κακία ('badness/cowardice') a few lines earlier it is bound at least to have moral considerations entangled with those of self-interest.

[88] Thus far Emlyn-Jones 1999, 56–7, is right (with many others) on 45d7–8.

[89] Blondell 2002, 70 f.; Burnyeat 2003, 24.

[90] Weiss 1998, 147, says, 'Socrates' preference is to persuade Crito through philosophical argument, but, when it proves impossible to sway Crito by such means, he adopts the means of rhetorical persuasion.' But Socrates in this dialogue *starts off* rhetorically.

[91] Emlyn-Jones' list of rhetorical phenomena in Crito's speech (his 1999, 38–9) overlaps with mine. It is curious that he does not mention Socrates' rhetoric, especially as he mentions Crito's 'rhetorical questions', but ignores Socrates'. See further (on Emlyn Jones' remarks) in my next note.

Meanwhile Gergel 2000, 290, well notes rhetorical devices in Socrates' remarks, such as irony, comparison, *a fortiori* argument (not actually common in the Attic Orators), and mention of the discrepancy between word and actions.

[92] Emlyn-Jones notices this shaping, but seems to treat rhetoric and rhetorical skill as a sign of emotion in Crito. That, in the light of Socrates' rhetoric, will not hold water; or, at least, it will not serve to point a contrast between an emotional Crito and a coolly rational Socrates.

[93] See Stokes 1986, esp. 138 ff., 282–5, 313–23.

[94] Gallop 1998, 253, gives references to modern athetizers of the *Crito*.

[95] Burnet 1924 on 44c7 renders οἱ ἐπιεικέστατοι 'the best men', adding that it is urbane for οἱ βέλτιστοι. This Emlyn-Jones 1999, 51 ad loc., shows to be at best an over-simplification. At 44c the context indicates that the term refers to those with sufficient information, intelligence and fairness to assess properly people's conduct in the matter of Socrates' trial and sentence. Here at 47a the φρόνιμοι, the sensible and intelligent, do not need the knowledge of the facts of Socrates' particular case needed by the ἐπιεικέστατοι of 44c.

[96] Socrates himself observes at *Protag.* 319c7–d7 that the Athenians allow any citizen to speak on state affairs without any inquiry into his qualifications; Protagoras accepts this statement, perhaps unguardedly, at 322d5–323a4, referring to moral questions. There is no reason to suppose the observation new. It is probably better not to invoke here (as Emlyn-Jones 1999, 62, does on 46d2–5) the view of the historical Protagoras on Man as 'the measure of all things': the un-philosophical Crito is not the kind of person to have read, let alone taken on board, Protagoras' work.

[97] See Schwyzer-Debrunner 1959, 25.

[98] Scholars occasionally fudge this point: Weinrib 1982, 95, wrote of 'the expert', which is generic in English as εἷς, 'one', cannot be in Greek. J. Ober 1998, 180, even wrote of 'the knowledgeable *few*' (emphasis mine).

[99] This seems sufficient to rebut Emlyn-Jones' contention, 1999, 64 on 47b8, that Crito's acceptance there of the importance of listening to the expert, not to 'the many',

'blatantly contradicts what he asserted at...44d1–2'.

[100] This strong language reflects the strength of the Greek verbs διώλλυτο (47b7), διαφθερεῖν (47d4) and ἀπώλλυτο (47d5). But Ostenfeld 1991, 6 n. 2, is clearly wrong to take 'destroy' of the soul here as endangering the soul's immortality. If the verbs hereabouts mean literally 'destroy', then the question 'Is life worth living with the body destroyed?' (47e) makes no sense. (It is most unlikely that there is any difference in atmosphere between the two verbs concerned here.)

[101] Should we, and should Crito, pay more attention to disagreement between experts? In this dialogue Plato does not even raise the question. It obviously suits him not to. Plato's Socrates elsewhere tends to discount such agreement, and the fallibility of experts receives little attention. Readers of the *Crito* who happen to know the *Laches* will have noted, if the question occurs to them, that there at 186d Socrates expresses surprise that two men he had believed expert should have offered diametrically opposed opinions. At *Euthd.* 280a7–8 Socrates openly suggests that 'wisdom' or 'expertise' (σοφία) could not make a mistake, but must do rightly and hit the mark; otherwise it would not be σοφία any more. At *Rep.* 304d2 Thrasymachus agrees indeed that we do talk about experts making mistakes, but insists that we do not call anyone an expert when they are making a mistake. A doctor *qua* doctor does not make a mistake, according to him; a mistake is due to deficient knowledge or expertise. The passages suggest Plato had some sympathy for the view that disagreement between 'experts' implies the inexpertness of at least one of them. But the first-time uninitiated reader of the *Crito* could easily follow the dialogue's Socrates in ignoring this whole matter.

[102] Bambrough 1956, 98–115.

[103] So despite Brisson 1997, 193–6. Brisson admits there the Laws' fallibility as the repositories of traditional wisdom, which would rule them out as experts. Nor, *pace* Brisson, does the epithet ἅγιος, 'sacred', make the Laws even nearly divine.

[104] Polansky 1997, 59: 'Where clear experts are lacking...they may have to struggle to gain agreement about what course is most intelligent and best. Yet they are hardly bereft of assistance, for in the coming argument Socrates can introduce the laws as a stand-in for the knower as expert. The law may overall direct deliberation about what is just and unjust in the case of the soul.' For the supporting arguments see Polansky's n. 19. Strauss was perhaps nearer the truth than Polansky when he wrote (1983, 58) that 'the agreements of two take the place of the single expert'; see below.

[105] See Stokes 1997, 26 and 194. I am not here including the *Gorgias* in the earlier dialogues; see 521b4–6, and Stokes 1997, 26–7.

[106] Gallop 1998, 264, tentatively suggests that 'Plato presumably found his own expert "moral trainer" in Socrates'; but that could only be so if Plato believed Socrates to be a moral expert – a hypothesis risky on many counts.

[107] 1996b, 27 n. 23.

[108] Note μόνου 47b2, b4, and note at d2 τοῦ ἑνός...ὅν, not ὅντινα.

[109] Editors, including Nicoll 1995, print 47b5–7 as an assertion. But four questions have preceded this sentence; Socrates is clearly in interrogatory mode; and Οὐκοῦν, which starts this sentence, often introduces a question: see e.g. *Phaedo* 64e4–6, 65c11–d2, 67d4–5, 67d12–e3, 68b8–c1. Ancient readers, lacking punctuation, would certainly have read *Crito* 47b5–7 as a question.

[110] It is not entirely clear how one should punctuate a conclusion to a series of

questions such as this one, and hence whether to put a question mark or a full stop at 47b11. Some such conclusions resist turning into questions because they contain the negative οὐ, which a question mark would risk turning into a a virtual positive (like the English 'Doesn't…?' or 'Isn't…?'). Under certain circumstances such sentences with a negative can be questioning in tone in Greek without becoming positive in effect; but the negative is normally in Attic accompanied by the particles δή or που (Kühner-Gerth [repr. 1955] II, 523–4). However, even if the conclusion is asserted, Socrates may be allowed to draw a conclusion from premisses not his own without necessarily committing himself to it.

[111] See above, pp. 63–4, for detail of this argument.

[112] Spiro Panagiotou kindly reminded me that ὡς ἀληθῶς appears earlier, at 46d4–5; but this is a passing rhetorical flourish for emphasis of a particular point, and of no general significance as a criterion of judgment.

[113] Some might prefer to attribute the presence of the one–many antithesis in the *Crito* to Plato's, or a general Greek, tendency to think in such antitheses; I am not among them. The single knower or expert recurs in the *Laches* and in the *Ion.* In the *Laches*, at 184d–e Socrates speaks to Lysimachus of that man (in the singular) who has been well trained and practised. He is, first, contrasting such a person with the majority vote favoured initially by Lysimachus, and, secondly, looking forward to the immediate sequel. There Laches and Nicias are probed for their training in the subject and consequent expertise – and as the two soldiers have already flatly disagreed they cannot both be right and knowledgeable. Since Socrates is going to adopt his normal stance of ignorance, that leaves a maximum of one expert present. In the *Ion*, 531d11 ff., Ion himself is insisting on the unique authority of Homer, and that uniqueness is essential both to Ion's position and to Socrates' refutation of it. The singularity of the expert is nowhere an arbitrary imposition on the argument; it is rather a necessary part of the dialectic.

[114] Weiss 1998, 61 n. 19, comes nearest to taking this view, but tentatively and without detail.

[115] The point is not of great importance, but perhaps deserves discussion. Clearly Crito is assenting to what Socrates says, and Socrates may be partially praising Crito's assent before going on to object to it. Emlyn-Jones 1999, 67, on 48b1–2 points out that Crito's words Δῆλα δὴ καὶ ταῦτα, 'That too is clear', could by themselves signify assent either to the substantive proposition that 'the many' can kill us or to the proposition that someone might say that. If we keep the MSS reading φαίη γὰρ ἄν, ὦ Σώκρατες , 'He would say [that], Socrates', the latter is much more likely.

In neither case, *pace* Emlyn-Jones, does Crito land himself in any self-contradiction by agreeing both with the judgment that one ought to take no account of 'the many' and with this new proposition. The expression 'can kill us' is factual, is not in dispute at the earlier passage 44d or elsewhere, and cannot contradict Socrates' principles which are not factual. The proposition that someone might draw attention to this power of the many to kill us is equally independent of any Socratic principle.

If, then, we keep φαίη γὰρ ἄν, ὦ Σώκρατες, we are left with the question whether Socrates agrees with Crito's agreement with him, saying Ἀληθῆ λέγεις, 'You speak truth', or whether Crito adds an emphatic third expression of assent to his previous two. Burnet, 1924 ad loc. wrote, subjectively, '…to me the threefold answer rather suggests the eagerness of Crito to catch at any straw', and he could have been right.

If he was, then it is Crito who picks up the cue given in ὁ εἷς καὶ αὐτὴ ἡ ἀλήθεια, 'the one man and the truth' above. This would perhaps help dialectically, in that Crito is then seen to have accepted the relevance of the criterion of the truth as agreed by himself. But no great loss is incurred if it is Socrates who reinforces the notion of 'the truth itself' here, attributing truth to Crito's words.

[116] It has been suggested to me that τῇ ἀληθείᾳ here means 'sincerely'; but in view of the other passages cited here that is open to doubt.

[117] Robinson 1953, 15–17, noted 'the personal character of the elenchus'. Robinson emphasized, rightly discounting *Rep.* 349a, that the victim of Socratic refutation must believe his own primary statement, be convinced of the validity of the subsequent inferences, and accept the introduced premisses, to be refuted properly. I hope it is unnecessary to argue that to believe a proposition is to believe it true. But, as Beversluis has pointed out (2000, 37 ff.), the expression of the requirement of *sincere* assent from the respondent is not ubiquitously expressed and needs to be taken with a grain of salt. Beversluis 2000, 53, has well suggested that that assent need not be 'expressive of antecedently formulated and sincerely held beliefs'. At the same time, however, the respondent shoulders the responsibility for his answers; and Socrates does not allow him to shoulder different degrees of responsibility; the responsibility is absolute so far as he is concerned. See further my Prologue above.

[118] Cf. McNeal 1992, 80, on 45a1–2: 'Crito presumes to know what is just.' Cf. also Talisse 2002, 51, on the elenchus as 'a method of challenging an interlocutor's claim to know'. Neither presumption nor claim need be explicit.

[119] See Lloyd-Jones 1971 *passim*, and Stokes 1986, 219–21.

[120] e.g. 'well-souled', εὔψυχος in Thucydides, means 'courageous' without reference to any other virtue. See, for the development of the concept of 'soul', literature cited by Everson 1991, 220, nos. 44–9 and 53, and add Claus 1981, 69–102.

[121] Weiss 1998, 43 n. 12. Unruh 2000, 72–4, says that there is no need here to explain 'soul' to Crito: Plato is counting on Crito and the public knowing the reference is to the soul. But, if the relation between the soul and morals was so widely recognized and assimilated, why not use 'soul'?

[122] On 48b1–2, Emlyn-Jones 1999, 67.

[123] If this is right, the questions of how to distribute the text between speakers at 48b1–2, and whether the truth to which Socrates or Crito or both assented was the assertion someone might make or the fact that they might make it are much less important than one might think; indeed, the questions' lack of importance may explain why Plato was not specially concerned to avoid ambiguity here.

[124] Gallop 1998, 260–1. Unruh 2000, 112–14, discusses Gallop, bringing against the 'generalizing' type of reasoning arguments I cannot altogether share.

[125] Classical Greek views on exile are collected by McKechnie 1989, 16–33.

[126] Irwin 1995, 361 n. 47 referring to his pp. 46–8. Gergel 2000, 303, also takes on board the point that being a retaliation makes a difference in the eyes of the many to what is unjust. Her position on this passage is the closest I have seen to my own, but is less fully worked out.

[127] Dover 1974, 184.

[128] Review of Weiss 1998, Harte 2000.

[129] Kahn 1989, 34; Bostock 1990, 5–6; Kraut 1984, 25 ff., esp. 26 n. 2 and 45 n. 28; R.E. Allen 1980, 77, with the context and despite his translation (p. 122) 'work

injury'; Irwin 1995, 46–7 with nn., referring to Vlastos. Brickhouse-Smith 1994, 159, say 'Socrates says one ought never to return wrong for wrong nor do evil to any person' – which seems to me ambiguous but may follow Vlastos. Santas 1979, 13 ff., while sticking for much of his exposition to 'harm', often (e.g. on p. 13) inserted '(or evil)' or '(evil)' after it.

[130] For incomprehension and explanation see below pp. 116–17.

[131] Cf. for this important point L. Brown 2002, 19 n. 9.

[132] See Dover (ed.) 1980, 137–8, and Stokes 1986, 146 ff.

[133] 50d1–51c5, analysed below, pp. 132–6.

[134] Harte 1999, 117–47, esp. 120–5.

[135] For detail about 'good faith' see below pp. 135–6.

[136] Panagiotou 1987, 37.

[137] Discussion of this argument below, at pp. 131–6.

[138] Discussion of this point below, at p. 150.

[139] See below, pp. 109–11.

[140] Vlastos 1991, 179–94.

[141] Above, pp. 78–81, below, pp. 95–105.

[142] Weiss (1998, 63 n. 18) insists that Crito is one of the 'many', and would not hold to the views in question. But Crito might like to think himself more just than he actually is. He might indeed in dialectical need, for all we know, be something less than perfectly honest. The important thing for our purposes is that what he agrees to is what he dialectically must agree to. Unruh (2000, 75) on the other hand, thinks the point that to live well is less important than to live well and justly is intelligible only out of Socratic philosophy. This too neglects Crito's earlier remarks and also the hero in Greek literature at large.

[143] On the usage of τροφή and παιδεία in the *Crito* see most recently Neufeld 2003, 122–5.

[144] The reason why the Laws use the noun τροφεύς alone may be that Plato had not yet thought of using the agent-noun παιδευτής , which is not in Plato (according to the usual dating) before the *Republic.* Aristotle apparently distinguishes τροφή from παιδεία at *EN* 1116a16–18.

[145] See for 'external commitment' my Prologue, p. 10 above.

[146] Crito condemns betrayal of oneself and doing as one's enemies would wish by destroying oneself. Socrates, he thinks, is helping his enemies and betraying and presumably harming his friends. Helping enemies and harming friends is thus condemned as unjust. This is not far from the common conception of justice as 'Helping friends and harming enemies', on which see Whitlock Blundell 1989, esp. her chs. I–II. Crito, however, does not directly express that conception; nor does Socrates actually deny or explicitly question such a conception of justice.

[147] See above, pp. 75–7 and below, pp. 99–104.

[148] Balaudé (1997, 245 f.) points out that Plato and his Socrates also fail to define their terms in Socrates' encounter with Gorgias. The *Crito* is not in this respect unique.

[149] Cf. Plato, *Protagoras* 324a6–b5.

[150] See Herman's series of articles, conveniently listed by him at his 2000, 7 n. 2, and in particular his 1993, 1994, and 1995. See for some useful corollaries Schofield 1998, 38–40. That the ideal of leaving vengeance to the courts did not stop feuds

continuing over many years is made clear by Rhodes 1998, but the courts must have been for many the instrument of retaliation against provocation. Against Herman's use of Lysias III in this connexion see Harris 1997.

Gallop (1998, 257) observes also interestingly that 'We may wonder whether [Socrates] could have wounded or killed another, consistently with his stand in the *Crito* against harming others even in self-defence (49c–d).'

[151] Vlastos 1991, 197 n. 58 cites *Rep.* 470a (he presumably meant 471b). The whole passage, 469b5–471c2, repays inspection in the light of the *Crito.* Quarrels with Greek cities are to be pursued to the point where those responsible are forced by the innocent to pay the penalty, and no further. Barbarians, however, are to be treated as Greeks in the real world treat Greeks. Harm may be done, as 'harm' is normally interpreted, and as a Crito would normally interpret it, to barbarians, and even to guilty Greeks. Vlastos says of the ethic in the middle books of the *Republic* that it 'lacks the unqualified universalism of [the principle in the *Crito*] "We should never do evil *to any human being.*"' It lacks more than that. Vlastos' explanation of the difference in attitude between the Socrates of the *Republic* who lets Glaucon agree to this without demur and his version of Socrates in the *Crito* runs as follows: 'Plato's recreation of Socratic thought may limp at this point, possibly because he had not been fully in sympathy with this particular aspect of Socrates' teaching.' What this seems to say is that Plato later rejected this particular paradox, having first publicly attributed it to Socrates without his own full authorial endorsement. One wonders what other Socratic doctrines Plato did not fully endorse, and how Vlastos would have defended his account of Plato's development if he had faced the implications of his theory here.

[152] Vlastos 1991, 213, derives it explicitly from the premiss that to harm another is to treat them unjustly. He did not wonder aloud why a philosophically and dialectically unsophisticated Athenian such as Crito should accept that premiss, unless simply browbeaten by Socrates. The common underestimation of Crito as an opponent also enables most scholars supporting 'harm' as a translation of κακουργεῖν (*kakourgein*) to ignore the injustice this would attribute to every sanction of the Athenian penal code. Only, and characteristically, Vlastos 1991, 196 n. 35 using here the word 'evil', excepts from the prohibition not only self-defence but also punishment, on the grounds that Socrates in the *Gorgias*, 480a–d, 525a–7a, takes punishment to be moral therapy for the wrongdoer and/or retribution and deterrent. That would indeed help Socrates to believe the generalization he puts here to Crito. But Socrates' views, especially on moral therapy, cannot be assumed to be part of Crito's mental furniture or of that of any other normal Athenian gentleman. There are those who think with Weiss (1998, 53–4 and elsewhere), perhaps rightly, that Crito in exhorting Socrates to behave justly relies on the principle 'Help Friends, Harm Enemies'. This interpretation would make Crito's acceptance of 'Harm = Injustice' an implicit contradiction. One doubts, once again, whether a man who will accept instantly not only a unique moral doctrine but also an implied self-contradiction would be worth arguing with at all.

[153] Vlastos 1991, 197.

[154] On Weiss' interpretation of Socrates' argument see Appendix below.

[155] No suggestion that ἀδικεῖν (*adikein*) in the *Crito* actually *means* 'harm' will pass muster. The Laws think it just (51a) to try to destroy Socrates; so there are cases of harm which are not normally describable as unjust, and the two expressions, 'treat

unjustly' and 'harm' are neither synonymous nor coextensive.

[156] See above for Vlastos. Weiss 1998, 67–71, avoids on the whole the word 'harm', rendering κακουργεῖν (***kakourgein***)as 'do bad things'. But she does so (her n. 42) only 'because "harm" may have a technical sense of harm to the soul in several at least of Plato's dialogues'. Her paraphrase on her p. 70 'action whose intention is to affect some human being adversely in body or soul' suggests that she thinks of κακουργεῖν as meaning 'harm' as in common parlance. The clearest rejection of Kahn's 'wrongful harm' paraphrase for κακουργεῖν comes from Harte *AGP* 81, 1999, 123–4.

[157] For references see n. 129 above.

[158] I have derived my data here from the TLG database through 'Pandora'. One cannot thank the boffins enough for this superb tool.

[159] I am grateful to Spiro Panagiotou for having raised this question in discussion some years ago.

[160] Compare the short discussion above, pp. 75–7.

[161] Irwin 1995 as cited above, n. 126.

[162] See pp. 85–6 above for a sketch of the problem and a possible solution.

[163] See pp. 91–4 above.

[164] See outline above, pp. 91–4.

[165] Dover 1974.

[166] For Herman and his critics see n. 150 above.

[167] Whitlock Blundell 1989.

[168] Cf. also Burnett 1998.

[169] Herman at Gill, Postlethwaite, and Seaford (eds.) 1998, 214.

[170] On the *Odyssey*, see Burnett 1998, 34–42, for Odysseus' killing of the suitors in revenge for their slights to his honour as divinely and socially sanctioned. Observe, however, that that does not prevent the suitors' families from wanting revenge for killings they evidently regarded as excessive.

[171] 1989, 55.

[172] Fraenkel on *Agamemnon* 537, cited by West 1978 on *WD* 710–1.

[173] All cited by Whitlock Blundell 1989, 26–59 (her chap. II).

[174] Dover 1974, 184; Gauthier and Jolif (1959/1970) II 372.

[175] 1959/1970, II 360.

[176] See esp. Herman 1993 and 1995, 51 ff., with Harris 1997.

[177] Herman 1995, 56 f.

[178] 1998, 150 n. 25.

[179] E. Schütrumpf's passages from Plato and Aristotle at Eder (ed.) 1995, 65 f., in the discussion of Herman's paper, deserve attention; the *Rhetoric* in particular is largely an Athenian speaker's manual, hardly composed *sub specie aeternitatis.*

[180] See summary above, pp. 85–6.

[181] I see no reason to find with L. Brown 2002, 17, a political reference in βουλή, deliberation, at 49d4. 'Taking counsel' or 'deliberating' is and was an ordinary event in ordinary non-political life.

[182] For a summary of what follows, see pp. 85–6 above.

[183] Brown 2002, 15 f., drawing on Raz.

[184] L. Brown 2002, 15 n. 3 and 17 n. 8 partly anticipates my Appendix, but disclaims any intention of refuting Weiss in detail.

[185] This is easily verifiable by a glance at Brandwood 1976 svv.

[186] Crito's οὐ γὰρ ἐννοῶ here means 'I do not understand', not, as Miller 1991, 125, 'I do not know': see Liddell-Scott-Jones, *Greek Lexicon* s.v. ἐννοῶ, and cf. especially Soph. *OT* 559 and Pl. *Rep.* 376a1. Crito is suffering here not from internal conflict but from bewilderment.

[187] It does not seem necessary to deal separately and *in extenso* with Unruh 2000, 104–5. Unruh also holds that Socrates' argument is complete in itself. He treats Socrates' two questions as concealed assertions. He reasons that if Crito had assented to them Socrates' argument could have stopped here. So it could. But why on earth should Crito or any normal reader assent to such obscure and difficult questions? Unruh rejects Weiss' argument from the *Apology* as unnecessary, on the grounds that what is in the *Crito* suffices. But it does not suffice, and neither does Weiss' argument.

[188] 1979, 22 ff.; and see p. 77 above.

[189] Further arguments of varying cogency appear in Unruh 2000, 96–7.

[190] 1998, 131 n. 104. I have reservations about Weiss' remark that the Laws frequently do not mean, when using Socrates' expressions [assented to by Crito], what Socrates meant.

[191] See the chapter on Socrates' Strategy above, and note L. Brown's statement of this point at her 2002, 19 n. 9.

[192] Diotima in Plato's *Symposium* fulfils a similar urbane function among others. See Stokes 1986, 170–2.

[193] See Stokes 1986 *passim.*

[194] 1995, 46.

[195] Unruh 2000, 115, draws a careful distinction between trying to destroy and destroying. What matters however is Socrates' intention on the one hand and the Laws' intention on the other. The Laws have not yet destroyed Socrates.

[196] e.g. Sobel 1994, 7–8; Gomez-Lobo 1994, 58–9. An exception is Barker 1977.

[197] Cf. the summary above, pp. 73–4.

[198] e.g. Weiss 1998, 86; Gergel 2000, 296. Gergel is right, however, in drawing attention to the oratorical commonplaces that do appear in the Laws' speeches. I have no wish to deny that they contain rhetorical elements.

[199] See Stokes (ed.) 1997, 97–8.

[200] Weiss 1998, 149 with n. 11.

[201] See Weiss 1998, 86 n. 8.

[202] DeFilippo 1991, 255–6, is surely not justified in saying that 'Socrates is *feigning* adherence to the commonly accepted notion that it is simple justice to harm those by whom one has been harmed' [emphasis mine]. Socrates merely asks Crito a question.

[203] If Plato's *Apology* can be trusted, the original jury was divided on the verdict. The mere existence of the Socratic literature suggests that the case of Socrates was much talked about, which suggests further division on its merits. The *Crito* clearly assumes that readers accept Socrates' innocence as at least a working hypothesis.

[204] See above, pp. 73–4 and 79–80.

[205] See summary above, pp. 75–7.

[206] Panagiotou 1987, 37 ff, *contra* Woozley 1979, 64 ff.

[207] See e.g. Mahoney 1998, 2; Irwin 1995, 315 (a cautious formulation); L. Brown 2002, 29 (in passing); Sobel 1994, 6–9 (rather vague on where the argument is to

be found); and for 'the principle of gratitude, the classic formulation of which is in the *Crito*', see Murphy 1999, 321 with n. 10 referring to 50d–51c; note also Neufeld 2003, 116–17, who imports the word 'gratitude' into 50d–e where it makes no appearance in Plato's text; *contra*, rightly in my view, Weiss 1998, 100.

[208] Gallop 1998, 261, points out that Plato's own suggestions in the *Republic* for the procreation and rearing of children 'are very different' from those of the actual laws of Athens or the Personified Laws of the *Crito.* But the hypothetically escaping Socrates, hypothetically answering the Laws, and perhaps accommodating his views to those of Crito, should not be confused with the actual Platonic Socrates, so that the difference need not be significant.

[209] See Sartorius 1999, 144 ff.; Greenawalt 1999, 180–3.

[210] See above, pp. 78–9, and Harte's argument 1999, 120–5. Miller 1996, 131, is much less clear.

[211] One should note Aristotle *EN* VIII ix 3, saying that it is more terrible to strike a father than anyone else.

[212] 2000, 128. Other dissimilarities raised there are less significant.

[213] See Dover 1974, 302 with n. 2.

[214] I render the last phrase 'as is just' in agreement (apparently) with the punctuation of Kral and Goebel in their editions, to which Weiss 1998, 106 n. 39 drew my attention.

[215] DeFilippo 1991, 257.

[216] So Gallop 1998, 257–8; but observe that I do not follow Gallop in believing (his 255) that the Laws' speech(es) are the reflection of Socrates' inner turmoil; Socrates here as elsewhere is quietly and calmly forging a confutation of his opponent, in this case Crito.

[217] So DeFilippo 1991, 257.

[218] It will not do to claim that the Laws are referring to persuasion of the Assembly that the criminal law is wrong; such a reference will not fit the description of the city as 'angry' at the time of the relevant persuasion. See also L. Brown 2002, 20–1.

[219] The argument is thus not one from Parental Authority (Woozley 1979, 70–5), but from paternal status. Examples of a father's authority cited by Dover 1974, 274–5, are therefore not relevant here. But Dover cites examples also which are relevant to paternal status.

[220] Socrates did apparently drink the hemlock, and this might be construed as a positive action. But it is hard to doubt that there was some compulsion in reserve in case any condemned man should refuse to drink. The existence of such compulsion would mean that Socrates is merely suffering his punishment with dignity by swallowing the hemlock wihout being subjected to force.

[221] Weiss 1998, 111.

[222] DeFilippo 1991, 250, points out that the specific conditions which require obedience in Socrates' present situation are clearly not intended to cover all circumstances.

[223] The point I am making here is not simply one of consistency in the characterization of Crito. To assume one's readers to be incapable of raising the question in my text is to write only for the superficial and slipshod reader. If writing only for such readers one would not bother with the elaborate argumentative apparatus of this or indeed of almost any Platonic dialogue.

[224] Weiss 1998, 110 n. 60.

[225] For θωπεύειν in the sense 'behave subserviently' cf. Soph. *El.* 396–7; the related θώπτω probably bears the same sense at [Aesch.] *P.V.* 937, where the Chorus advocate and evince not verbal flattery but subservience. Xenophon's use of θωπεύειν to mean 'caress, pet' (Liddell-Scott-Jones, *Greek Lexicon* s.v.) points also in the direction of soothing *behaviour.* Weiss is right that the Platonic Socrates would have had no truck with flattery; the Laws are suggesting rather that the angry state or father should be placated by subservient behaviour, i.e., in the present context, by knuckling under to the prescribed punishment.

[226] e.g, Woozley 1979, 63–8 ('The Filial Gratitude Argument'); R.E. Allen 1980 ('a claim of debt') 88–9; Vlastos 1974, 520; and as cited with approval by Colson 1989, 32, Irwin 1995, 315 ('obligations to the city in return for what it has given him'); Sobel 1994, 5–9; Bentley 1996, 7; Gray 1996, 134; Mahoney 1998, 2–5 and 13–4; and with some caveats Santas 1979, 24. Have these scholars in mind Aristotle, *EN* 1161a16 ff., where unequal justice and benefits are linked in a context referring to fathers? Disagreement with them comes from Panagiotou 1987, 37 ff. and Weiss 1998, 100–1 with esp. n. 13.

[227] Cf. Stokes (ed.) 1997, 21–30.

[228] Cf. Stokes (ed.) 1997, 26–8; Mahoney 1998, 7.

[229] Bostock 1990, 1–20, esp. 7–9 and 17–18.

[230] Martin 1970, 36.

[231] The Laws have indeed bestowed many admirable things on Socrates, which *could* be regarded as their fulfilment of their side of a bargain. But Plato does not connect these gifts with the making of an agreement. The Laws indeed do not say *they* have agreed to do anything, or that they do anything as a fulfilment of an agreement; and *mutual* agreement is the essence of a contract.

[232] Earliest to my knowledge Colson 1989, 29–31.

[233] 319b–d, 322d–323a.

[234] Cf. p. 137 above.

[235] Weiss 1998, 103 n. 34, follows Kraut 1984, 83 n. 40, in arguing that when the Laws complain that Socrates did not persuade they clearly cannot mean that he did not offer a defence, nor is it likely that the source of their complaint is that his defence was unsuccessful. This, it seems to me, misses the Laws' point. When they attack Socrates on the grounds that he neither persuades nor obeys, they are not attacking him first because he does not persuade and secondly because he does not obey; they attack him because having failed to persuade he does not obey: he neither persuades nor obeys.

[236] One should observe at 51d7–8 the optative of 'remote contingency' used in the conditional clause: 'if we and the city were not to please [him]'. The Laws speak thus in character in not expecting anyone to be displeased by them.

[237] Hardly 'in fact' as Sobel renders it, 1994, 5.

[238] See esp. Woozley 1979, 82–4 and 107.

[239] See *Iliad* XXIII 566–85 (Menelaus complains about Antilochus). Anton Powell kindly reminds me also that cheats detected at the Olympic Games were compelled to set up statues of Zeus.

[240] I think the notion of raising a justifiable expectation undermines two points clearly and forcefully made by L. Brown 2002, 22–4: (a) that for tacit consent there

must be a definite period when expressions of dissent are appropriate; (b) that there is a conflict between the Laws' suggestion that the citizen's agreement was made just after δοκιμασία, enrolment of the young citizen, and their insistence that Socrates has had 70 years in which to express disapproval. Justifiable expectations can be raised over an indefinite period, and can legitimately become stronger the longer the relevant behaviour continues.

241 The crack is forced open especially by L. Brown 2002, 22–4.

242 Bostock 1990, 7–8.

243 Crito's own suggestion earlier in the dialogue that Socrates escape to Thessaly comes with what he evidently hopes at the time is an adequate recommendation, namely (45c) that Socrates will there be valued and safe and not vexed by anybody. Crito, however, and readers who recall that, ought to have realized long before 52a–c, let alone 53b, the insufficiency of that recommendation.

244 The Greek syntax here, in which one has to 'understand' some such addition as 'in that' in the above version, is not very logical either; Burnet 1924 ad loc. was perhaps too cavalierly dismissive of the difficulty. But as Bill Nicoll kindly reminds me, there is a similar main verb with no clear syntax at Plato *Ap.* 36a 1–3.

245 At *Ap.* 37c4 ff., Socrates has just refused to propose any penalty which might harm him because it would do himself an injustice; he has said in effect that he does not fear death because he does not know whether death is bad or good, harmful or beneficial; after rejecting imprisonment too, he says he would have to be very φιλόψυχος 'fond of life' – a common expression for 'cowardly' – to propose exile, and he gives arguments against it. I think this amounts to 'putting on airs' at his equanimity in the face of death. The *Crito* may here be assuming its readers' acquaintance with the general drift of the *Apology*.

246 The word ἀποδιδράσκειν, 'run away', would not be appropriate for the father-son relationship; that constitutes another rhetorical reason for the introduction of the master-slave analogy.

247 For Crito as arbiter of the truth see above pp. 66–7.

248 See the discussion of τὸ σὸν μέρος at pp. 73–4 above.

249 Harrison 1971, 134–5; MacDowell 1978, 242–3. For the mode of 'publication' see M.H. Hansen 1991, 164.

250 The Greek here has μή... μηδὲ...

251 See the Appendix below for discussion of Weiss' view of this matter.

252 See above, pp. 137–9.

253 Vlastos 1994, 92 n. 13.

254 Unruh 2000, 119, suggests that the extreme case of contravening a law fundamental to the city's existence is specially suitable for an example of a general rule enjoining obedience to law. He does not explain why Socrates should want to argue here at all for the general rule.

255 So rightly Santas 1979, 18–19.

256 The case of *Grg.* 519a strikes me as a further possible, though not certain, example of the same linguistic phenomenon.

257 It is disappointing to find Gergel 2000, 298, basing an argument on Woozley's rendering.

258 On this use of γὰρ δή see Denniston 1954, 243–4.

259 To answer one's own question is a trick found in the Orators: so Rehdantz-Blass

1886, 18, s.v. Frage, with examples, e.g. Dem. iv 3.

[260] See notes in Stokes (ed.) 1997, esp. 163–4.

[261] See Bostock 1990, 17–18.

[262] See Harrison 1971, 48 with n. 2, for the jurors' oath, which included a pledge to judge in accordance with law or, failing a relevant law, in accordance with justice.

[263] Compare πλείστη ἀταξία at d3 below, and contrast τοὺς κοσμιωτάτους at c4 with the article.

[264] See Kühner-Gerth (repr. 1955) II 247.

[265] 'Arrant sophistry' was Gallop's expression 1998, 261.

[266] See above, pp. 75–6, 80–1.

[267] On 'nurture and education' see pp. 89–90 above.

[268] Miller 1996, 137 n. 44. Thesleff 1982, 208–10, dating the *Crito c.* 375, holds that it expects the reader to know the *Phaedo* – a wholly unnecessary hypothesis.

[269] Mikalson 1983, 81.

[270] Dover 1974, 263–6.

[271] Dover (ed.) 1993, 251 f.

[272] On the text of this passage see Richardson 1974, 273.

[273] See further the note in Stokes 1997 on Plato, *Ap.* 37a3–38b5.

[274] Bond 1988, 386 f.

[275] See Stokes (ed.) 1997, 26–30.

[276] See Dover 1974, 273–7, esp. 275.

[277] Enigmatic is the word. Is 'the god' a general expression for the gods, or fate, or what is bound to happen? (Cf. the gods [τοῖς θεοῖς] at 43d)? Is it Apollo, Socrates' patron deity according to the *Apology*? Is it Dionysus, à propos of the Corybants, as Unruh suggests at 2000, 102–3? Or is it perhaps Socrates' 'superhuman being' or δαιμόνιον, which has, without Socrates mentioning it, already forbidden him to escape? Of these choices I would prefer the first, but with no confidence at all. Cf. Blondell 2002, 122–4.

[278] See Linforth 1946, 131–72; Weiss 1998, 135–45; Harte 1999, 118–20.

[279] On Miller's attempt to read the 'other' arguments as not being Crito's, see below.

[280] Burnet 1924 ad loc.; Linforth 1946, 136–7.

[281] It is unwarranted also for Unruh 2000, 102 ff., who reads the Corybant-reference as favouring continuity for the dialogue. Unruh suggests that the Corybants purify and restore to reason; but Crito is *not* in the text the person so treated, if anyone is. There is not the slightest hint in the text that Crito hears the Corybants.

[282] Weiss 1998, 136.

[283] Weiss 1998, 137.

[284] Weiss 1998, 138.

[285] Harte 1999, esp. 118–20.

[286] Harte 1999, 119.

[287] Harte 1999, 119.

[288] Harte 1999, 119–20.

[289] Miller 1996, 121–37.

[290] Cf. Weiss 1998, 136 n. 12.

[291] See above, pp. 7–12.

[292] See Prologue above, pp. 12–13.

[293] It is perhaps worth noting here, though it comes from another dialogue, the assertion of Socrates at *Grg.* 473b10 f. that 'the truth is never refuted'.

[294] *Grg.* 457e1 ff.

[295] See Benitez 1996, 29–32.

[296] I draw attention, however, to Harte 2000, 362–5, an admirable critique of Weiss' hypothesis, written from a viewpoint other than mine and deploying different arguments.

[297] Weiss 1998, 59 n. 7.

[298] Weiss 1998, 59 n. 7.

[299] Weiss 1998, 62.

[300] Weiss 1998, 63.

[301] Weiss 1998, 72–81.

[302] Weiss 1998, 80.

[303] See pp. 113–14 above.

[304] I put 'agreement' in quotes here because, as discussed below in my text, there are two senses or types of 'agreement' at large in this passage.

[305] Weiss 1998, 76–7.

[306] Weiss 1998, 77–8.

[307] See Weiss 1998, 74 n. 50. Against Weiss here see the concise and pointed remarks of L. Brown 2002, 18 nn. 7–8.

[308] H. Brown 1992, 69, also draws attention to the commonness of this phenomenon. But in his further analysis he seems to read more into Socrates' questions here than is actually in the text.

[309] Weiss 1998, 78–9.

BIBLIOGRAPHY

Adam, J.
1888 *Platonis Crito*, Cambridge.
Adkins, Arthur W.H., Essays in Honor of,
see Louden, R.B. and Schollmeier, P. (eds.) 1996.
Allen, D.
1997 'Imprisonment in classical Athens', *Classical Quarterly* 47, 121–35.
Allen, R.E.
1980 *Socrates and Legal Obligation*, Minneapolis.
Annas, J.
1992 'Plato the Sceptic', *Oxford Studies in Ancient Philosophy, Supplement*, 43–72.
Ausland, H.W.
1997 'On reading Plato mimetically', *American Journal of Philology* 118, 371–416.
Balaudé J.-F.
1997 'La finalité de l'elenchos d'après les premiers dialogues de Platon', in *Lezione Socratiche* a cura di G. Giannantoni e M. Narcy, Roma (*Elenchos* 26) 237–58.
Bambrough, J.R.
1956 'Plato's political analogies', in Laslett P. (ed.) *Philosophy, Politics and Society*, Oxford, 98–115. Reprinted in R. Bambrough (ed.) *Plato, Popper and Politics*, Cambridge, 1967, and elsewhere.
Barker, A.
1977 'Why did Socrates refuse to escape?', *Phronesis* 22, 13–28.
Benitez, E.
1996 'Deliberation and moral expertise in Plato's *Crito*', *Apeiron* 29 (= Benitez, E. [ed.] *Dialogues with Plato*), 21–47.
Bentley, R.
1996 'Responding to Crito: Socrates and political obligation', *History of Political Thought* 17, 1–20.
Beversluis, J.
2000 *Cross-Examining Socrates: A defense of the interlocutors in Plato's early Dialogues*, Cambridge.
Blondell, R. (formerly Whitlock Blundell, M.)
2002 *The Play of Character in Plato's Dialogues*, Cambridge.
Bond, G.W. (ed.)
1988 *Euripides,* Heracles, Oxford.
Bostock, D.
1990 'The interpretation of Plato's *Crito*', *Phronesis* 35, 1–20.

Bowersock, G., Burkert, W. and Putnam, M.C.J. (eds.)
1979 *Arktouros: Hellenic studies presented to Bernard M.W. Knox*, Berlin and New York.

Brandwood, L.
1976 *A Word Index to Plato*, (*Compendia* vol. 8), Leeds.

Brickhouse, T. and Smith, N.D.
1994 *Plato's Socrates*, Oxford.

Brisson, L.
1997 *Apologie de Socrate, Criton. Introduction…*, Paris.

Brown, H.
1992 'The structure of Plato's *Crito*', *Apeiron* 25, 67–82.

Brown, L.
2002 'Did Socrates agree to obey the laws of Athens?', in G. Clark and T. Rajak (eds.) *Philosophy and Power in the Graeco-Roman World*, Oxford, 13–30.

Burnet, J.
1924 *Plato's Euthyphro, Apology of Socrates, and Crito.* Edited with introduction and notes, Oxford.

Burnett, A. Pippin
1998 *Revenge in Attic and Later Tragedy*, Berkeley.

Burnyeat, M.
2003a 'By the Dog', *London Review of Books* 25 no. 15 (7 Aug. 2003) 23–4.
2003b '*Apology* 30b 2–4: Socrates, money, and the grammar of γίγνεσθαι', *Journal of Hellenic Studies* 123, 1–25.

Cartledge, P., Millett, P. and Von Reden, S. (eds.)
1998 *Kosmos*, Cambridge.

Claus, D.B.
1981 *Toward the Soul*, New Haven.

Cohen, M. and Keyt, D.
1992 'Analysing Plato's arguments – Plato and Platonism', *Oxford Studies in Ancient Philosophy, Supplement*, 173–200.

Colson, D.D.
1989 '*Crito* 51A–C: to what does Socrates owe obedience?', *Phronesis* 34, 27–55.

Congleton, A.
1974 'Two kinds of lawlessness: Plato's *Crito*', *Political Theory* 2, 432–46.

Corbett, J. Angelo
1997 'Interpreting Plato's dialogues', *Classical Quarterly* 47, 423–37.

Decleva Caizzi, F.
1996 *Platone* Eutidemo: *Tradizione e cura di F.D.C.*, Milan.

DeFilippo, J.
1991 'Justice and obedience in Plato's *Crito*', *Ancient Philosophy* 11, 249–63.

Denniston, J.D.
1954 *Greek Particles*, 2nd edn, revised by K.J. Dover, Oxford.

Dover, K.J.
1974 *Greek Popular Morality*, Oxford.

Dover, K.J. (ed.)
1980 *Plato Symposium*, Cambridge.

1993 *Aristophanes Frogs*, Oxford.

Duke, E.A. et al. (eds.)
1995 *Platonis Opera I*, Oxford.

Eder, W. (ed.)
1995 *Die Athenische Demokratie im 4 Jahrhundert v. Chr. Vollendung oder Verfall einer Verfassungsform?* Stuttgart.

Edmundson, W.A. (ed.)
1999 *The Duty to Obey the Law*, Lanham.

Emlyn-Jones, C.
1999 *Plato* Crito, *edited with introduction, commentary and vocabulary*, Bristol.

Everson, S.
1991 *Companions to Ancient Thought 2: Psychology*, Cambridge.

Fox, M.
1956 'The trials of Socrates: an interpretation of the first Tetralogy', *Archiv für Philosophie* 6, 226–61.

Frede, M.
1992 'Plato's arguments and the dialogue form', *Oxford Studies in Ancient Philosophy, Supplement*, 201–19.

Gallop, D.
1998 'Socrates, injustice and the law', *Ancient Philosophy* 18, 251–66.

Gauthier, R.A. and Jolif, J.Y.
1959/1970 *L'Ethique à Nicomaque*, Louvain and Paris.

Gergel, T.
2000 'Rhetoric and reason: the structure of the argument in Plato's *Crito*', *Ancient Philosophy* 20, 289–310.

Gill, C., Postlethwaite, N. and Seaford, R. (eds.)
1998 *Reciprocity in Ancient Greece*, Oxford.

Gomez-Lobo, A.
1994 *The Foundations of Socratic Ethics*, Indianapolis.

Gower, B.S. and Stokes, M. (eds.)
1992 *Socratic Questions*, London.

Gray, C.M.
1996 'Response' to J. Boyd White, in Louden and Schollmeier (eds.) *Essays…* 133–44.

Greenawalt, K.
1999 'Legitimate authority and the duty to obey', in Edmundson (ed.) *The Duty to Obey the Law*, 177–91.

Hansen, M.H.
1991 *The Athenian Democracy in the Age of Demosthenes*, Oxford.

Harris, W.V.
1997 'Lysias III and Athenian beliefs about revenge', *Classical Quarterly* 47, 363–6.

Harrison, A.R.W.
1971 *The Law of Athens: II, Procedure*, Oxford.

Harte, V.
1999 'Conflicting values in Plato's *Crito*', *Archiv für Geschichte der Philosophie* 19, 117–47.

2000 Review of Weiss, *Socrates Dissatisfied*, 1998, *Classical Philology* 95, 362–6.

Harvey, F.D.

1990 'The sykophant and sykophancy: vexatious redefinition?', in P. Cartledge, P. Millett and S. Todd (eds.) *Nomos: Essays in Athenian law, politics and society*, Cambridge, 103–21.

Herman, G.

1993 'Tribal and civic codes of behaviour in Lysias I', *Classical Quarterly* 43, 406–19.

1994 'How violent was Athenian society?', in S. Hornblower and R. Osborne (eds.) *Ritual, Finance, Politics*, Oxford, 99–117.

1995 'Honour, revenge, and the state in fourth-century Athens', in Eder (ed.) *Die Athenische Demokratie*, 43–66.

1998 'Reciprocity, altruism, and the prisoner's dilemma', in Gill, Postlethwaite and Seaford (eds.) *Reciprocity*, 199–226.

2000 'Athenian beliefs about revenge: problems and methods', *Proceedings of the Cambridge Philological Society* 46, 7–27.

Hornblower, S. and Osborne, R. (eds.)

1994 *Ritual, Finance, Politics*, Oxford.

Hunter, V.

1997 'The prison of Athens', *Phoenix* 51, 296–326.

Irwin, T.H.

1995 *Plato's Ethics*, Oxford.

1998 'Common sense and Socratic method', in J. Gentzler (ed.) *Method in Ancient Philosophy*, Oxford.

Kahn, C.H.

1989 'Problems in the argument of Plato's *Crito*', *Apeiron* 22, 29–43.

1996 *Plato and the Socratic Dialogue*, Cambridge.

Knox, B.M.W.

1964 *The Heroic Temper: Studies in Sophoclean Tragedy*, Berkeley.

Kraut, R.

1984 *Socrates and the State*, Princeton.

1992 'Introduction to the study of Plato', in Kraut, R. (ed.) *Cambridge Companion to Plato*, Cambridge, 1–50.

Kühner, R. and Gerth, B.

1898 *Griechische Grammatik* I, II, Leverkusen. Repr. 1955.

Linforth, I.M.

1946 'The Corybantic rites in Plato', *University of California Publications in Classical Philology* 13, no. 5, 131–72.

Lloyd-Jones, H.

1971 *The Justice of Zeus*, Berkeley.

Louden, R.B. and Schollmeyer, P. (eds.)

1996 *Essays in Honor of Arthur W.H. Adkins*, Chicago.

MacDowell, D.M.

1978 *The Law in Classical Athens*, London.

McKechnie, P.

1989 *Outsiders in the Greek Cities*, London.

McNeal, R.
1992 *Law and Rhetoric in the* Crito, Frankfurt-am-Main.
Mahoney, T.A.
1998 'Socrates' loyalty to Athens and his radical critique of the Athenians', *History of Philosophy Quarterly* 15, 1–22.
Mikalson, J.D.
1983 *Athenian Popular Religion*, Chapel Hill.
Miller, M.
1996 'The arguments I seem to hear: argument and irony in the *Crito*', *Phronesis* 41, 121–37.
Montuori, M.
1998 *Per una nuova interpretazione del "Critone" di Platone, Prefazione di Giovanni Reale, 2a edizione*, Milan.
Murphy, M.C.
1999 'Surrender of judgment and the consent theory of political authority', in Edmundson (ed.) *The Duty to Obey the Law*, 319–46.
Nails, D.
1995 *Agora, Academy, and the Conduct of Philosophy*, Dordrecht.
2002 *The People of Plato: A prosopography of Plato and other Socratics*, Minneapolis.
Neufeld, P.
2003 'Socrates and παιδεία in the *Crito*', *Apeiron* 36, 115–40.
Nicoll, W.S.M. (ed.)
1995 ΚΡΙΤΩΝ (*Crito*) in Duke et al.(eds.) *Platonis Opera I.*
Ober, J.
1998 *Political Dissent in Democratic Athens*, Princeton.
Ostenfeld, E.
1991 'The foundations of Socratic morality', *Methexis* 4, 5–19.
Pack, R. (ed.)
1963 *Artemidori Daldiani* Oneirocriticon Libri V, Leipzig.
Panagiotou, S.
1987 'Justified disobedience in the *Crito*?', in Panagiotou (ed.) *Justice…*, 35–50.
Panagiotou, S. (ed.)
1987 *Justice, Law and Method in Plato and Aristotle*, Edmonton.
Penner, T.
1997 'Two notes on the *Crito*', *Classical Quarterly* 47, 133–46.
2000 'Plato's *Apology* and *Crito*', in Rowe and Schofield (eds.) *The Cambridge History of Greek and Roman Political Thought*, 182–9.
Polansky, R.
1997 'The unity of Plato's *Crito*', *Scholia* 6, 49–67.
Pucci, P.
2000 *Xenophon's Defense of Socrates*, Amsterdam.
Quandt, K.
1982 'Socratic consolation; rhetoric and philosophy in Plato's *Crito*', *Philosophy and Rhetoric* 15, 238–56.
1989 Review of Stokes, *Plato's Socratic Conversations* (1986), *Classical Philology*

84, 60–4.

Reale, G.

1998 See Montuori (1998).

Rehdantz, C. and Blass, F. (eds.)

1886 *Demosthenes Neun Philippische Reden*, Heft II, Abt. II, Leipzig.

Rhodes, P.J.

1998 'Enmity in fourth-century Athens', in Cartledge et al. (eds.) *Kosmos*, 144–61.

Richardson, N. (ed.)

1974 *Homeric Hymn to Demeter*, Oxford.

Robinson, R.

1953 *Plato's Earlier Dialectic*, 2nd edn, Oxford.

Rowe, C.J. (ed.)

1993 *Plato's* Phaedo, Cambridge.

Rowe, C.J. and Schofield, M. (eds.)

2000 *The Cambridge History of Greek and Roman Political Thought*, Cambridge.

Santas, G.

1979 *Socrates*, London.

Sartorius, R.

1999 'Political authority and political obligation', in Edmundson (ed.) *The Duty to Obey the Law*, 143–57.

Schofield, M.

1998 'Political friendship and the ideology of reciprocity', in Cartledge et al. (eds.) *Kosmos*, 37–51.

Schwyzer, E. and Debrunner, A.

1959 *Griechische Grammatik* II (Syntax und syntaktische Stilistik), Munich.

Seeskin, K.

1993 'Vlastos on elenchus and mathematics', *Ancient Philosophy* 13, 37–54.

Sobel, J.H.

1994 'Plato's *Crito*: a question of agreement', *Theoria* 60, 1–26.

Soper, P.

1996 'Another look at the *Crito*', *American Journal of Jurisprudence* 41, 103–32.

Stokes, M.

1979 ' Sophocles, *Electra* 1087; text and context', in Bowersock et al. (eds.) *Arktouros*, 134–43.

1986 *Plato's Socratic Conversations; Drama and dialectic in three Dialogues*, London and Baltimore.

1992 'Socrates' Mission', in Gower and Stokes (eds.) *Socratic Questions*, 26–81.

1996 Review of S.R. Slings, (revised from papers of E. de Strycker), *Plato's Apology of Socrates*, Leiden, 1994, *Archiv für Geschichte der Philosophie* 16, 192–8.

Stokes, M. (ed.)

1997 *Plato's* Apology of Socrates, Warminster.

Strauss, L.

1983 *Platonic Political Philosophy*, Chicago.
Talisse, R.B.
2002 'Misunderstanding Socrates', *Arion* 9 (3), 46–56.
Tarrant, H.
1995 'Plato's *Euthydemus* and the two faces of Socrates', *Prudentia* 47, 4–17.
Thesleff, H.
1982 *Studies in Platonic Chronology*, Helsinki.
Todd, S.
1993 *The Shape of Athenian Law*, Oxford.
Unruh, P.
2000 *Sokrates und die Pflicht zum Rechtsgehorsam*, Baden-Baden.
Vlastos, G.
1974 'Socrates on obedience and disobedience', *Yale Review* 63 no. 5 (summer), 517–34.
1991 *Socrates, Ironist and Philosopher*, Cambridge.
1994 *Socratic Studies*, Cambridge.
Voigtländer, H.D.
1980 *Der Philosoph und die Vielen*, Wiesbaden.
Waldock, A.J.A.
1951 *Sophocles the Dramatist*, Cambridge.
Weinrib, E.
1982 'Obedience to the law in Plato's *Crito*', *American Journal of Jurisprudence* 27, 85–108.
Weiss, R.
1998 *Socrates Dissatisfied*, Oxford.
West, M.L. (ed.)
1978 *Hesiod, Works and Days*, Oxford.
White, J. Boyd
1996 'Plato's *Crito*: the authority of law and philosophy', in Louden and Schollmeier (eds.) *Essays…*, 97–133.
Whitlock Blundell, M.
1989 *Helping Friends and Harming Enemies*, Cambridge.
Woolf, R.
1999 Review of Stokes (ed.) *Plato's* Apology of Socrates (1997), *Archiv für Geschichte der Philosophie* 85, 330–4.
Woozley, A.D.
1979 *Law and Obedience*, London.
Young, P.
1996 'Intellectualism and moral habituation in Plato's earlier dialogues', *Apeiron* 29, 49–61.

INDEX OF PROPER NAMES

INDEX OF GREEK WORDS AND PHRASES

INDEX OF TOPICS